1001 THINGS TO DO WITH YOUR PERSONAL COMPUTER

Acknowledgments

The author would like to thank the following people for suggesting ideas and improvements or providing material: Steve Witham (author of MUSE program), Larry Hughes, Jack Atwater, George Gross, Dr. E.P. Miles and his associates, Janis Qualls, Dr. and Mrs. Robert Sawusch, Bob Johnson, Ed Manning, and Louis Brasovan.

The following firms also provided illustrative material for the book: AMI Corp., Bally Manufacturing, Colorado Video, Inc., Compucolor Corp., Computer Portraits, Inc., Video Brain Corp., ECD Corp., Interstate Electronics Corp., RCA, Magnavox, and Apple Computer Corp.

No. 1160
$13.95

1001 THINGS TO DO WITH YOUR PERSONAL COMPUTER
BY MARK SAWUSCH

TAB BOOKS Inc.
BLUE RIDGE SUMMIT, PA. 17214

FIRST EDITION

NINTH PRINTING

Printed in the United States of America

Library of Congress Cataloging in Publication Data

Sawusch, Mark.
    1001 things to do with your personal computer.

    Includes index.
    1. Microcomputers.   2. Electronic data processing.
I. Title.
QA76.5S219   001.6′4′04   79-25795
ISBN 0-8306-9963-5
ISBN 0-8306-1160-6 pbk.

Contents

Introduction

This book is unique. It offers a catalog of potential applications for your personal computer; it's not just a "how-to-do-it" book, but a "what-to-do" book. Over 1000 ideas are presented and explained herein on the premise that one idea leads to another.

Several thousand microcomputers are now dedicated to the personal service of the owner. Often consumers have purchased a small computer almost on impulse, amazed at the interesting demonstration games or video graphics. But, within weeks, the interest in "hi-lo" and other related computer games usually dwindles. Many of the fantastic applications mentioned by the computer salesmen are not available for sale as software or additional computer peripherals are required to implement them (computer terms such as "software" and "peripherals" are explained in the glossary). Thus, the owner is often left with a very-expensive, seldom-used maze of wires (such owners are usually novices at programming and would like to attempt simple programming problems which are more practical and interesting than those found in "how-to-program" books).

Other computer hobbyists have a definite, practical application in mind when they empty their checking account for a microcomputer. However, they often fail to recognize other important applications to cost-justify their computer to a greater extent.

Another group of hobbyists use their computers in versatile ways, developing assorted software for personal use or to sell/distribute to other computer owners. This group often includes the computer "professionals" who recognize practical applications and write good software to fill a need. These hobbyists are searching for good ideas.

You may not fit in one of the groups just discussed, but whether or not, this book was written for you—the person interested in or owning a microcomputer. The purpose of *1001 Things To Do With Your Personal Computer* is to provide a compendium of applications of interest to the microcomputer owner, to discuss briefly or illustrate how to create the software for the applications, and to spawn ideas for other personal computer applications for the reader.

It has been stated by the media that there are about 20,000 computer applications yet to be discovered, although the number of applications is actually almost infinite. To ask what can be done with a computer is essentially the same as asking what can be done with mathematics; mathematics is present in virtually every aspect of our environment. The important question is whether a given application will be practical to computerize. Take, for instance, the suggestion that a home computer be used to recognize anyone who comes to your doorstep (using such factors as weight, height, and width) and announce the visitor vocally. It would probably be less expensive to hire a butler to accomplish the same task (if such a complicated application was possible). Simple computations which need only be done once or twice should not be computerized; it would be a waste of time to write a program for such an application. But, on the other hand, such a program could be useful for others to use (the author could write an article describing it for a personal computer magazine).

Your computer is an extension of your mind, a mind appliance. Use it to do complex calculations you would not have previously done manually (e.g. the amateur/professional photographer may calculate more precise values for camera settings to achieve a certain effect). Examples of simple formulas are presented herein and are intended to be part of a larger, more complex program to be written for the reader's personal application. In most cases, due to space restrictions, the reader is left to find the information necessary to write a program based on an idea given; all information should be readily available at a local library. In certain cases the formulas or methods necessary to write the program (or the program itself) are provided to illustrate an idea and set you on the right track. Analyze the programs within; learn to write an applied program.

Program ideas are intended not only for microcomputers, but for programmable calculators as well. Although anyone who has programmed a calculator will realize the tremendous advantages of a microcomputer system, the programmable calculator does have its place. For those applications where portability is important (i.e. marine navigation), the calculator comes in handy.

Some applications are intended for use with special computer peripherals (i.e. plotters, floppy disks, high density video displays, printers, etc.). Although the prices for these devices often exceed the cost of the computer itself, prices are falling and should be reasonable soon.

There has been much debate as to whether the control of household devices is a practical application. Of course, it would be ridiculous to interface a $1000 computer system to an air conditioner to switch it on and off since a $10 thermostat can accomplish the same task; the object is to find control applications which cannot be done with simple, inexpensive mechanical devices. A specially-designed "household maintenance" computer could control many devices, play games, and manage your finances simultaneously. One must realize that virtually any electromechanical device may be emulated with a computer, an analog/digital (A/D) converter, and proper mechanics. Because of the many important applications which make use of an A/D converter, a simple A/D converter peripheral circuit is contained herein and may be constructed for less than $30.

One of the author's intentions is that the reader will be better able to recognize applications for his personal computer and write good software. Thus, applications of restricted interest have been included as examples of specialized uses.

Some readers may question the inclusion of a game section; game playing is often thought to be a wasteful application for an expensive personal computer (the popular video game units are often more fun and less expensive). Computer games do have their good points. Games are often the best learning-to-program challenges for the beginner, yet the "professional" programmer may also find himself defeated in attempting to write a complicated game program (i.e. chess). They encourage imaginative and constructive programming or responses. Games develop abilities to react creatively, solve problems logically and make decisions, but most of all games are fun!

The author doubts that anyone interested in computers will fail to discover several new applications for a personal computer within these pages. But, if nothing else, use this book to quickly satisfy those who ask the naive question, "What are you going to do with a computer?"

Mark Sawusch

Chapter 1
Applications for Everyone

Applications For Everyone

This chapter will cover many ways in which a computer can be used to help us in our daily lives. With the many complexities of everyday life, the computer is an excellent means of organizing and tabulating the numerous tiny details. From phone calls to recipes, the personal computer can handle them all.

PERSONAL REFERENCE SOURCE

Useful reference information, which is often referred to, but too complex to memorize, could be stored for instant retrieval. Possible reference charts/information to store include:

1. Calories and Nutritional content of selected foods
2. Appointment itinerary
3. Important articles (magazine name and date)
4. Sports statistics, amateur or professional
5. Product sources and prices from various suppliers
6. Addresses and phone numbers
7. Stock market data
8. Recipes and shopping lists
9. Postal and shipping rates, requirements, and regulations
10. Metric conversions and information
11. Time differences and phone rates between cities
12. Words commonly misspelled

13. Ham Radio log
14. Collection inventory
15. Private pilot flight planning data
16. Household inventory
17. Astronomical and astrological data

PROGRAM—ELECTRONIC MEMORANDUM

This program should be useful to everyone; think of it as a memory extension. The program allows one to store any type of information (household, business, charts, finances, etc.) under a "keyword" for instant retrieval at a later date. For instance, if you had an appointment on a certain date, the pertinent information could be stored under the keyword "9/11/79;" on that date you would simply type "9/11/79" to receive a print-out of all appointments/reminders stored under that keyword. Likewise, a reminder for an occasion each year could be entered under a keyword specifying only the month and day. Telephone numbers, business contacts, or sources could all be stored without worry of forgetting. Additionally, information could be stored under more than one keyword to insure the ability to retrieve it.

This program is designed for use with floppy disks. A conversion to cassette use could be accomplished, but would be undesireable due to the amount of time necessary to access the information.

```
00010  REM ELECTRONIC MEMORANDUM
00020  CLEAR 3000
00030  CLS 'CLEAR SCREEN
00040  PRINT "SELECT AN OPTION:"
00050  PRINT "COMMAND", "FUNCTION"
00060  PRINT "INPUT", "INPUT A NEW ITEM"
00070  PRINT "CAT", "GENERATE A CATALOG OF
       COMMON ENTRIES"
00080  PRINT "FIND", "FIND A PREVIOUSLY STORED
       ITEM"
00090  PRINT "REDO", "EDIT A PREVIOUSLY
       STORED ITEM"
00100  PRINT "DEL", "DELETE A PREVIOUSLY
       STORED ITEM"
00110  PRINT "END", "END THE PROGRAM"
```

```
00120    INPUT A$
00130    IF A$ = "INPUT" THEN 1000
00140    IF A$ = "CAT" THEN 3000
00150    IF A$ = "FIND" THEN 4000
00160    IF A$ = "REDO" THEN 2000
00170    IF A$ = "DEL" THEN 5000
00180    IF A$ = "END" THEN CLOSE: END
00190    PRINT "ILLEGAL COMMAND- PLEASE ENTER
         ONE OF THE FOLLOWING-"
00200    GOTO 50
01000    INPUT "ENTER AN ID. CODE (MAY BE UP TO
         20 LETTERS LONG)"; B$
01010    IF LEN (B$) >20 THEN 1000
01015    PRINT "IS THIS CORRECT (1 = YES, 2 = NO): ";
         B$
01017    INPUT D
01018    IF D > < 1 THEN 1000
01020    INPUT "ENTER THE DATA FOR THE ID CODE
         (MAY BE UP TO 105 LETTERS LONG)"; C$
01030    IF LEN (C$) > 105 THEN 1020
01040    D$ = LEFT $ (B$, 1) + "*"
01050    CLOSE
01060    OPEN"R",1,D$:Z=1
01070    FIELD #1, 3 AS E$, 20 AS F$, 105 AS G$
01080    GET #1, Z
01090    IF E$="999" THEN Z=Z+1:IFZ=LOF(1)+1THEN
         1200 ELSE 1080
01200    LSET F$ = B$
01210    LSET G$ = C$
01220    LSET E$ = "999"
01230    PUT #1, Z
01240    CLOSE
01250    GOTO 30
02000    INPUT "ENTER THE ID CODE FOR THE DATA
         TO BE EDITED"; B$
02010    D$ = LEFT$ (B$, 1) + "*"
02020    CLOSE: Z = 1
02030    OPEN"R",1,D$:IF LOF(1)=0 THEN PRINT"FILE
         END":CLOSE:GOTO 40
02040    FIELD #1, 3 AS E$, 20 AS F$, 105 AS G$
02050    IF Z = LOF(1)+1 THEN PRINT"FILE END":
         CLOSE: GOTO 40
```

```
02060    GET #1, Z
02070    IFE$ < > "999" THEN Z=Z+1:GOTO 2040
02080    IF LEFT $ (F$,LEN (B$)) > < B$ THEN
         Z = Z + 1: GOTO 2040
02090    CLS 'CLEAR SCREEN
02100    PRINT "MEMORANDUM:"
02110    PRINT G$: PRINT
02120    INPUT "DO YOU WISH TO EDIT THIS ITEM (1 =
         YES, 2 = NO) "; Y
02130    IF Y = 2 THEN Z = Z + 1: GOTO 2040
02140    CLS 'CLEAR SCREEN
02150    INPUT "RE-ENTER ALL DATA:"; C$
02160    IF LEN (C$) > 105 THEN PRINT "DATA >105
         CHARS. LONG- REENTER.": GOTO 2150
02170    LSET G$ = C$:LSETF$=B$:LSETE$="999"
02180    PUT #1, Z
02190    Z = Z + 1: GOTO 2040
03000    PRINT "SELECT: 1) LIST A CATALOG OF ALL
         ITEMS ON FILE"
03005    INPUT "           2) LIST ALL ITEMS WHOSE
         ID'S HAVE A SPECIFIED CODE"; Y
03010    ON Y GOTO 3300, 3020
03020    INPUT "ENTER THE ID CODE"; H$
03030    D$ = LEFT $ (H$, 1) + "*"
03040    CLOSE: Z = 1: PRINT: PRINT "SECTOR", "ID"
03050    OPEN "R",1,D$:IF LOF(1)=0 THEN PRINT"FILE
         END":CLOSE:GOTO 40
03060    FIELD #1, 3 AS E$, 20 AS F$, 105 AS G$
03070    GET #1, Z
03080    IF Z = LOF (1) THEN PRINT "-----------------":
         PRINT: CLOSE: GOTO 40
03090    IF E$ < > "999" THEN Z=Z+1:GOTO 3060
03110    PRINT Z, F$
03120    Z = Z + 1
03130    GOTO 3060
03300    CLS 'CLEAR SCREEN
03305    PRINT "SECTOR", "ID"
03310    FOR X = 65 TO 90
03320    J$ = CHR$ (X)
03330    D$ = J$ + "*"
03340    Z = 1
03350    CLOSE
```

```
03360    OPEN "R",1,D$:IF LOF(1)=0 THEN NEXT
         X:CLOSE:GOTO 40
03370    FIELD #1, 3 AS E$, 20 AS F$, 105 AS G$
03380    IF Z=LOF(1)+1 THEN NEXT X:CLOSE:GOTO 40
03390    GET #1, Z
03400    IF E$ < > "999" THEN Z=Z+1:GOTO 3370
03410    PRINT Z, F$
03420    Z = Z + 1
03430    GOTO 3370
04000    CLS ' CLEAR SCREEN
04010    INPUT "ENTER ID CODE"; B$
04020    D$ = LEFT$ (B$, 1) + "*"
04030    CLOSE: Z = 1
04040    OPEN"R",1,D$:IF LOF(1)=0THEN PRINT"FILE
         END":CLOSE:GOTO 40
04050    IF Z =LOF(1)+1THEN PRINT "FILE END":
         CLOSE: GOTO 40
04060    FIELD #1, 3 AS E$, 20 AS F$, 105 AS G$
04070    GET #1, Z
04080    IF LEFT$ (F$, LEN (B$)) = B$ THEN 4130
04090    IF E$ < > "999" THEN Z=Z+1: GOTO 4050
04100    Z = Z + 1
04110    GOTO 4050
04130    PRINT "ID:", "F$;" SECTOR:";Z
04140    PRINT G$
04150    PRINT
04160    Z = Z + 1
04170    GOTO 4050
05000    CLS 'CLEAR SCREEN
05010    INPUT "ENTER THE ID CODE,SECTOR";B$,Z
05020    D$ = LEFT$ (B$, 1) + "*"
05030    CLOSE
05040    OPEN "R", #1, D$
05050    FIELD #1, 3 AS E$, 20 AS F$, 105 AS G$
05060    GET #1, Z
05070    IF LEFT$(F$, LEN (B$)) > < B$ THEN PRINT
         "ID AND SECTOR DON'T MATCH": CLOSE:
         GOTO 40
05080    CLS 'CLEAR SCREEN
05090    PRINT "ID"; F$
05100    PRINT G$
```

```
05110   PRINT
05120   INPUT "IF YOU WANT TO DELETE THIS RE-
        CORD TYPE '1'"; Y
05130   IF Y > < 1 THEN CLOSE: GOTO 40
05140   FIELD #1, 3 AS E$, 20 AS F$, 105 AS G$
05150   LSET E$ = " "
05160   LSET G$ = " "
05170   LSET F$ = " "
05180   PUT #1, Z
05190   CLOSE
05200   GOTO 40
```

INDEX TO YOUR LIBRARY

A cross-referenced index to all your books and periodicals could be quite useful. For example, you could prepare an index to software published in computer magazines.

This type of program would store information regarding each item on file as a continuous "string" of data. Individual pieces of data within the string are called "fields." An example string, describing a magazine article, could be:

The Stock Market, Business Today, 5, 6/78, I, S, 1, Smith

name of magazine/book   date category #2 author
name of article/book   volume no. category #1 storage location

If data is formatted in a manner similar to the above example, a computer can "randomly" search all files to pick out items you specify. For instance, you could request that the computer make a search of your library for all items published after 1977 concerning the stock market. The computer would search both the category and date fields for data meeting the above requirements. A listing of all the information for each item would be outputted at the conclusion of the search. Again, floppy disks are best suited for this application.

LETTER WRITING

A specialized text editor, designed to edit and format your letters, could expedite the process considerably. For example, if writing a business letter, the address of the recipient could be stored when typed at the beginning of the letter and later recalled to print the envelope. If you are writing the same letter to several people, the body could be stored in the computer. Thus, one need type only the addresses and other personalized information, and this would be integrated with the text to print out a complete letter. Additionally, while typing the body, if a mistake is encountered, it may easily be corrected on a video display rather than on paper.

```
10   REM SPECIALIZED WORD PROCESSOR- WRITES
     LETTERS
20   CLEAR 5000
30   DIM A$ (500)
40   INPUT "ENTER THE DATE"; D$
50   INPUT "ENTER RECIPIENTS NAME"; D1$
60   INPUT "ENTER COMPANY NAME OR TITLE
     (TYPE ENTER IF NONE)"; C$
70   INPUT "ENTER STREET ADDRESS"; N1$
80   INPUT "ENTER TOWN STATE ZIP AS ONE
     STRING"; T1$
90   INPUT "ENTER NAME FOR LETTER ADDRESS
     (EG. DEAR ----)"; A1$
400  PRINT "ENTER SUCCESSIVE LINES FOR THE
     BODY. IF YOU MAKE AN ERROR ON"
410  PRINT "A LINE AND WOULD LIKE TO CORRECT
     IT ENTER '#' AND THE NUMBER"
420  PRINT "OF THE LINE (EG. # 5) AS ANY OTHER
     LINE."
430  PRINT "TYPE 'END' TO PRINT OUT A COPY"
440  FOR X = 1 TO 500
445  PRINT "#"; X
447  INPUT A$ (X)
450  IF LEFT$ (A$(X), 1) = "#" THEN 800
460  IF A$ (X) = "END" THEN 480
470  NEXT X
480  PRINT: PRINT "READY THE PRINTER TO OUT-
     PUT LETTER"
485  REM CHANGE ALL 'PRINT' STATEMENTS TO
     'LPRINT' OR OTHER COMMAND
490  PRINT: PRINT: PRINT: PRINT
500  PRINT TAB (55); D$
510  READ N$, A$, T$, A2$
520  PRINT TAB (55); T2$
```

```
530   PRINT TAB (55); A2$
540   PRINT:PRINT
550   PRINT TAB (5); D1$
560   IF C$ < >"" THEN PRINT TAB (5); C$
570   PRINT TAB (5); N1$
580   PRINT TAB (5); T1$
590   PRINT:PRINT
600   PRINT TAB (5); "DEAR " ; A1$; ":"
610   PRINT
620   FOR B = 1 TO X − 1
630   PRINT TAB (5); A$(X)
640   NEXT B
650   C = 23 + B
660   PRINT
670   PRINT
680   PRINT TAB (55); "CORDIALLY,"
690   PRINT
700   PRINT
710   PRINT TAB (55); N$
720   IF A$ > < "X" THEN PRINT TAB (55); A$
721   PRINT: PRINT: PRINT: PRINT: PRINT: GOTO 10
730   REM ENTER YOUR ADDRESS HERE
740   DATA JOHN DOE
750   DATA CITIZEN 'IF NO TITLE PUT 'X' HERE
760   DATA 321 ANYSTREET WEST
770   DATA NEW YORK, NY 10036
800   REM EDIT ROUTINE
810   Y = VAL (RIGHT$ (A$(X), LEN (A$ (X)) −1))
820   INPUT "SELECT: 1) RE-ENTER ENTIRE LINE 2)
      EDIT"; A
830   ON A GOTO 840, 860
840   INPUT A$ (Y)
850   X = X − 1: GOTO 470
860   C = 0
870   FOR Q = 1 TO 10000
880   Q$ = INKEY$ 'STROBE KEYBOARD
885   REM USE SPACE BAR TO SEARCH THROUGH LINE
886   REM USE 'D' TO DELETE A CHARACTER
887   REM USE 'I' TO INSERT CHARACTERS
888   REM USE 'L' TO LIST A LINE
889   REM USE 'B' TO BACKSPACE AND 'ENTER' TO
      END
890   IF Q$ = " " THEN C = C + 1: PRINT CHR$ (29); :
```

```
      PRINT LEFT$ (A$ (Y), C); : GOTO 880
900 IF Q$ = "L" THEN PRINT: PRINT A$ (Y): GOTO 880
910 IF Q$ = "I" THEN INPUT J$: A$(Y) = LEFT$(A$(Y),
    C) + J$ + RIGHT$(A$(Y), LEN (A$(Y))– C):
    C = C+LEN (J$): PRINT LEFT $ (A$(Y), C);
920 IF Q$= "D" THEN A$(Y)=LEFT$ (A$(Y), C) + RIGHT
    $ (A$(Y),
    LEN (A$ (Y))– C–1): GOTO 880
930 IF  Q$ = "B"  THEN  C=C–1: PRINT CHR$(8); :
    PRINT CHR$ (29);:
    PRINT LEFT$ (A$(Y),C); : GOTO 880
940 IF Q$ = CHR$(13) THEN PRINT: PRINT CHR$ (29); .
    PRINT A$ (Y):
    GOTO 470
950 NEXT Q
```

PROGRAM—CATEGORIZER

The purpose of this program is to categorize information
which has been stored on cassettes (the program could be
easily modified for use with disks). As each piece of information is stored on cassette, a "keyword" of one or more letters
is placed at the front of the information string. Thus, if you
wanted to have a print-out of all information stored under the
same keyword, the keyword would be entered and the computer would search for all strings with that keyword at the
beginning.

Businessmen, writers, and other individuals who must
categorize much information will find this program helpful in
writing reports, manuscripts, etc. (the program was used in
the preparation of this book).

```
10 REM CATEGORIZER PROGRAM
20 CLEAR 5000 ' ADJUST ACCORDINGLY
30 DIM A$ (1000)
40 INPUT "SELECT: 1) ENTER STRINGS, 2)
   CATEGORIZE, 3) END"; A
50 ON A GOTO 60, 200, 300
60 PRINT "ENTER STRINGS WITH KEYWORD
   AT THE BEGINNING"
65 INPUT A$
70 IF A$= "END" THEN 40
80 PRINT # –1, A$: 'STORES DATA TO CAS-
   SETTE
```

```
90    GOTO 65
200   GOTO "ENTER KEYWORD"?B$
210   INPUT "ENTER NUMBER OF FILES TO BE
      SEARCHED";Z
220   INPUT "REWIND TAPE TO STARTING POSI-
      TION"; A
230   FOR C = 1 TO Z
240   INPUT # – 1, A$ ' INPUTS DATA FROM CAS-
      SETTE
250   IF B$ = LEFT$(A$,LEN(B$))THEN PRINT A$
260   NEXT C
270   PRINT: PRINT
280   GOTO 40
300   END
```

RECIPE INDEX/CALCULATOR

A collection of your favorite recipes can be stored on your computer for easy and selective retrieval. A list of characteristics for each recipe would be included (for example, time for preparation, hot or cold, number served, for dinner/lunch/breakfast, expense, and calories). With these characteristics, the computer could index recipes and print lists of recipes with a selected characteristic for a special occasion.

A recipe calculator could change the amounts of each ingredient such that the proper amount of the recipe will be made for a given number of people.

If the costs for various ingredients were stored in your computer, the cost of a given recipe could be instantaneously computed; allowance would also be made for the number of persons to be served.

A sample field of information concerning one recipe (item) is below:

MEATLOAF, 6, 1.5 lb. gr. beef* 1 cup milk *.5 cup onion* 1 egg,

name of item   no.
            servings.
                                   abbreviated ingredients

350,   1.5 hr.,   Bill's favorite

oven temp.   bake time   comments

```
00010   REM RECIPE CALCULATOR
00020   REM COULD BE IMPROVED TO CONVERT
        UNITS OF MEASUREMENT (EG. PINTS TO
```

23

```
          QUARTS)
00030   INPUT "HOW MANY SERVINGS IS THE ORIGI-
          NAL RECIPE INTENDED FOR"; S1
00040   INPUT "HOW MANY SERVINGS ARE TO BE
          PREPARED"; S2
00050   R = S2/S1
00060   N = 1
00070   PRINT
00080   PRINT "ENTER THE NAME OF EACH INGRE-
          DIENT, THE AMOUNT (EG. MILK, 1, PINT)."
00090   PRINT "ENTER 'END, 1, 1' WHEN FINISHED"
00100   INPUT A$ (N), B (N), C$ (N)
00110   IF A$ (N) = "END" THEN 130
00120   N = N + 1: GOTO 100
00130   FOR X = 1 TO N
00140   PRINT A$ (N), R*B (N), C$ (N)
00150   NEXT X
00160   PRINT
00170   END
```

ITINERARY ASSISTANT

A list of appointments, deadlines, and various tasks could be stored in a computer and outputted in a specified format to assist you with your itinerary. One format could be that of a calendar; each day-block would be filled with things to do. Is there something you must do periodically, but often forget? Program the computer to automatically remind you each time.

PHONE TIMER

When making long distance phone calls, keeping track of the elapsed time can save you a considerable amount of money. Usually, up to the first three minutes is charged a flat rate, but for the remainder of the call the charges are updated by the minute. A countdown timer (making use of a "timing loop"—eg. FOR X = 1 to 500: NEXT X may require approximately 1 second) display on your video screen could indicate to you the amount of time remaining until the next charge. Also, a record could be kept of the number called and the cost for the call, for use with income-tax deductions or comparison to the telephone bill.

```
10 REM LONG DISTANCE TELEPHONE CALL TALLY
20 INPUT "NEED TELEPHONE TIPS", A$
```

```
30 IF A$ = "YES" THEN 300
40 PRINT "TELEPHONE COST TALLY"
50 INPUT "IS THIS AN OPERATOR ASSISTED CALL",
   A$
60 IF A$ = "YES" THEN O = 1 ELSE O=0
70 INPUT "ENTER INITIAL FLAT RATE"; B
80 INPUT "ENTER ADDITIONAL CHARGE PER MI-
   NUTE"; C
90 INPUT"ENTER DISCOUNT AS A PERCENTAGE#";D
100 D = D*. 01: IF D = 0 THEN D = 1
110 PRINT "TO BEGIN TIMING TYPE 'ENTER'"
120 PRINT "TO END TIMING TYPE 'BREAK'"
130 INPUT A$
135 CLS' CLEARS SCREEN
140 PRINT@ 512, "ELAPSED MIN", "CURRENT COST",
    "SECONDS TO ADD CHARGE";
150 S = 60: B = B * D
160 PRINT @ 576, T, B, S;
165 REM LINE 170 ACTS AS A TIMING LOOP; ADJUST
    TO YOUR BASIC
170 FOR X = 1 TO 300: NEXT X
180 S = S−1
190 IF S = 0 THEN T = T + 1: S = 60: ELSE 160
200 IF (O = 1) AND (T<3) THEN 160
210 B = B + C * D
220 GOTO160
300 PRINT "THE FLAT RATE FOR OPERATOR AS-
    SISTED CALLS IS FOR THE FIRST"
310 FIX "3 MIN AND FOR THE FIRST MIN. ON
    DIRECT-DIAL CALLS"
320 PRINT "DISCOUNT TIMES FOR CALLING ARE:"
330 PRINT "65%- 8AM-5PM SUNDAY/ 8AM-11PM
    SATURDAY / 11PM-8AM NIGHTLY"
340 PRINT "35%- 8AM-11PM ON HOLIDAYS/5PM-11PM
    SUNDAY-FRIDAY"
350 PRINT: GOTO40
```

TELEPHONE FILE

Listings of emergency telephone numbers, as well as those commonly referred to, could be stored if the list is sufficiently long to warrant computer search capabilities. Additionally, telephone messages could be stored and later retrieved by the recipient.

The data strings used to store this information could be formatted as follows:

HOSPITAL, AMBULANCE, 643-1998 * 643-1997

| identifier | additional related identifier (to cross-reference) | tel. numbers |

GREETING CARD LIST

A mailing-list program could be used to address your Christmas greeting cards. If your list is large enough, the computer could sort zip codes, allowing you to send your cards under the bulk mail rate (this would probably only be practical for businesses with large customer files). Additionally, the computer could print a short "Hello" note on the back of each card. The same idea could be applied to producing an invitation list for a party or meeting.

PERSONAL TIME MANAGEMENT SYSTEM

A personal time managing system would assist you in planning the most effective schedule necessary to complete a list of tasks. Input could include the description of each goal, the priority of that goal (eg. A, B, C . . .), and the deadline date. The program could use PERT ("Program Review and Evaluation Technique") analysis to plan and output a schedule most evenly distributing the work load. Many people have found that they can accomplish much more if they make schedules and deadlines for themselves; PERT analysis will make that all the more simpler.

DECISION MAKER

Complex decision making may be facilitated with the computer. The computer first questions you to obtain a list of the factors involved in making a decision. Next, you are asked to rate the relative personal importance of each of these factors on a scale of ten. Finally, for each possible outcome to the decision, you are asked to rate the favorability of each factor on a scale of ten. This data is then analyzed, and the outcome with the most favorability for the most important factors is the one chosen as the final decision.

The most favorable item will have the highest score, computed by summing the rate of favorability multiplied by the relative importance for each factor.

For example, if you had several locations in mind for building a home and could not come to a decision due to its complexity, you could form the following chart of factors for making the decision; these factors would be inputted to the decision-making program.

Shopping—Are there adequate facilities nearby?

Churches—Are they available and convenient?

Community—Is the community well planned?

Neighbors—Are they likely to be compatible with your lifestyle?

Police and Fire protection—Are they adequate for the area?

Schools—Are the schools your children will attend nearby?

Hospital—Is there a medical center nearby?

Hazards—Are there hazards such as oil tanks or streams that might overflow?

Recreation—Are there suitable facilities within walking distance?

Traffic—Are the streets busy or quiet?

Transportation—Is public transportation available?

Lay of land and landscaping—Is the land well-drained and not subject to erosion?

Water—Is there an adequate pressure and is it drinkable?

Nuisances—Are there nearby sources of excessive noise, smoke, soot, dust, or odors that will degrade your environment?

If this process is still too complex, try this program:

```
5 PRINT "THE DECISION IS:"
10 X = RND (0): IF X <.5 PRINT "NEGATIVE" ELSE PRINT "AFFIRMATIVE"
```

HEALTH

Your personal computer can even help you maintain your health. A listing of the caloric or nutrient content of various foods could be stored and subsequently referenced for determination of the nutritive value of the food you eat. Additionally, data on the sugar or salt content of foods could be stored for the diabetic or person on a salt-free diet. Of course, such a program lends itself well to diet planning.

A diet-planning program, based strictly upon reducing your caloric intake, could compute the number of calories you use per day (on the basis of weight, sex, height, and activities). Presumably, the exact amount of weight you could lose would be mathematically calculated in this manner by either reducing intake or reducing activities. The following data should be helpful in writing a program to help one lose weight or maintain health through exercise.

One gram of Carbohydrate = 4 calories
One gram of Fat   = 9 calories
One gram of Protein   = 4 calories

Intensity of Exercise	Heart Beats/ Minute	Respiration (Breaths/ Minute)	Energy Consumption Calories/ Hour
maximum	200	50	1440
very heavy	150	30	1008
heavy	140	25	864
fairly heavy	130	20	720
moderate	120	18	576
light	110	16	432
very light	100	14	288
resting	70	10	100

One hobbyist uses a computer to determine his pulse rate and lead him through an exercise session, acting as the coach and timer. Along similar lines, another hobbyist computes the aerobic points he earns in bicycling.

```
00010 REM CALCULATION OF PULSE RATE
      (BEATS/MIN)
00020 PRINT"HIT ANY KEY FOR EACH BEAT":X =
      1: N = 0
00030 A$ = INKEY$: IF X = 2000 THEN 60 'CHANGE
      VALUE FOR YOUR COMPUTER'S SPEED
00040 IF A$ = "" THEN X = X + 1: GOTO 30
00050 N = N + 1: GOTO 30
00060 PRINT "THE NUMBER OF BEATS/MIN ="; N *
      2
00070 TRAINING PULSE=INT (.6)* (220-YOUR AGE)
```

SHORTHAND TRANSLATOR

You could develop a shorthand system which your computer could be programmed to understand and translate. The system could be similar to that used by court reporters, in which a single key represents a word or part of a word. In this manner, you could quickly commit your thoughts to paper, and the computer could analyze the shorthand and print the English equivalent.

In likewise manner, a machine language program could translate a single keystroke into a full command. For instance, such a program could translate a CONTROL P or shifted P to the word PRINT, thereby facilitating the input of a program.

KITCHEN INVENTORY

A file of all food items on hand (pantry inventory) could be useful in determining whether a given recipe can be prepared. As each item is added or subtracted, a computer entry of the transaction would be made. If a desired level of inventory is specified, the computer could automatically print out a shopping list of items which are below desired quantity levels. An inventory program of this type would be best suited for the gourmet cook who must have a wide variety of seasonings and other ingredients on hand. The inventory of a wine collection or food in the deep freezer may also be maintained.

RATING CALCULATIONS

An equation to determine a rating for a particular stock, car, horse, or home could be computerized if it is referred to often or is complex. For example, the horse racing fan could use the following equation to determine an objective rating for a particular horse:

$$Rating = (W + P/3 + S/6) \times 100/R + E/850$$

where W = the number of wins
  P = the number of places
  S = the number of shows
  R = the number of races
  E = the amount of earnings in dollars

INVENTORY OF POSSESSIONS

A file of your personal property could be stored in computer format for insurance purposes or determining your net worth. The advantage is that items may be easily added, deleted, or categorized, and a cassette or floppy disk copy of the inventory may be stored in a safe-deposit box. If you own a business, use this type of program for your business equipment.

REFERENCE SOURCE TO IMPORTANT LITERATURE

Your favorite lines of literature or passages from the Bible can also be stored. The lines are categorized, indexed, and cross-referenced for easier retrieval.

An example string describing one item could be as follows:

BUSINESS, EMPLOYEES,
general subject specific subject

DEALING WITH EMPLOYEE PROBLEMS,
title of article

MOD. BUS., 9/20/78
magazine name issue date of magazine.

If all items were inputted in this manner, you could simply select a subject (general or specific) for the computer to search for among the items in memory.

DAY OF THE WEEK CALCULATION:

Calculation of the day of the week corresponding to a given date is not only useful for the businessman, but those interested in history as well. Some research has been done as to the day on which U.S. Presidents were born and other events in history. Occasionally, amazing congruencies are found.

To calculate the day of the week for a specific date in the 20th century, use the following formula:

$$N = D + M + Y + [(0.8(2M+1)] + [Y/4]$$

where D= Day of the month

M= Month, where March is considered the first month, April the second, . . . and February the twelfth

Y= Last two digits of the year

][= The integer part of the result

Next, divide the sum N by 7. The remainder from the division gives the day of the week. Count 0 as Sunday, 1 as Monday, etc.

10   REM CALCULATION OF THE DAY OF THE WEEK CORRESPONDING TO A GIVEN DATE

```
20    REM APPLICABLE TO ANY DATE IN THE 20TH
      CENTURY
25    DEFINT A
30    INPUT"ENTER THE MONTH, DAY, YEAR
      (MM,DD,YY)";M,D,Y
40    IF M > 2 THEN M=M-2 ELSE M=10+M:Y=Y-1
50    N=D+M+Y+INT(.8*(2*(M+1))+INT(Y/4)
60    A=(N/7-INT(N/7))*7.1
70    FOR X=0 TO 6
80    READ A$(X)
90    NEXT X
100   PRINT"THE DAY IS ";A$(A)
110   END
120   DATA SUNDAY, MONDAY, TUESDAY, WEDNES-
      DAY, THURSDAY, FRIDAY, SATURDAY
```

FOOD STORE SHOPPING AID

Your programmable calculator can sum and categorize prices and types of items as they are removed from the shelf at the supermarket. Provisions should be made for categorizing items into meat, groceries, produce, and taxable subdivisions. Plus, provisions for multiple entries, unit price calculations and comparison, error correction, and a warning if a preset cash limit has been exceeded. Outputs could include: total cost, tax, item count, and subtotals of each category.

COUPON FILE

For those who have the money-saving habit of collecting food coupons, a computerized list of your coupons could be helpful. Enter each coupon by its amount, brand name, product name, and filed location. Next, enter your shopping list. A computer search between your list and the available coupon list should yield a roster of coupons that may be used and the filed location of each.

IDEA FILE AND CATEGORIZER

Anyone who does any writing should appreciate a computer program designed to store and categorize various ideas which will later be used to prepare a manuscript. Such a program could recognize a "keyword" at the beginning of each idea the author inputs (eg. a sample entry could be "introduction—discuss the purpose of the manuscript," with " introduction" being the keyword). All ideas sharing a common keyword would be grouped together and later printed in the form of a specified outline.

HOME PLANNING

An interesting program could be written to help a family design a house to fit their needs; the expense of a house certainly justifies an in-depth analysis of the design before building. Video graphic capability could be provided to draw and transform basic house-plan drawings (preferably with a light pen).

Square footage could be calculated with the following guidelines in mind: minimum square footage should equal number family members • 200, desirable square footage equals number family members • 300. An activity list such as the one below could be included to insure that the family's activities will not conflict and that there will be provisions for all activities. A program could question which activities are to be done in each room and the times involved; conflicts could thus be analyzed such that one could alter the plans accordingly.

Group Activities
1. Lounging—indoors and outdoors
2. Television watching
3. Listening to stereo, tapes, etc.
4. Playing a musical instrument
5. Meals
6. Children's play areas

Social Activities
1. Holding a meeting in the home
2. Children's/adult's games
3. Viewing movies/slides
4. Visiting with guests

Work Activities
1. Meal preparation and clean-up
2. Household business
3. Food preparation
4. Laundry
5. Ironing, sewing or drying clothes
6. Workshop area

Private Areas
1. Study or reading areas
2. Grooming or dressing facilities

Traffic patterns could also be analyzed as well as storage requirements.

Storage requirements:

Bedrooms —minimum of 4' × 6' × 24" closet space/person

Utility areas —about 36" wide and 16" deep

Kitchen —approximately 10 linear feet of base and wall cabinets

PRIVATE INFORMATION STOREHOUSE

Almost everyone has some private information/numbers/diaries that they would like to keep more private than in a filing cabinet. A program could be written to store this information in coded form which can only be retrieved by someone with a proper password. Copies of such data could be stored in a safe-deposit box.

GENERAL PURPOSE CLOCK/TIMER

If your computer is equipped with a real time clock, it could be used as an electronic timer/time controller for scientific research or sporting events. Without a real time clock though, the computer can still keep track of elapsed time for long distance telephone calls or act as a simple timer for applications where accuracy is not a major factor. When not using their computer for more practical tasks, some hobbyists have transformed them into very expensive clocks, with a graphic display of hour and minute hands, digital displays, simulated sundials or even sand timers. Digital watch circuits may be interfaced to facilitate time keeping.

BLOOD ALCOHOL CONTENT

It would be a good idea to calculate your blood alcohol content after a few drinks, before attempting to drive. The formula used to calculate the percentage alcohol content in the blood is:

$$C = \frac{OZ \cdot p \cdot 0.037}{W}$$

where C = blood alcohol content
OZ = ounces of drink consumed
p = proof
W = body weight (lbs)

00010   REM BLOOD ALCOHOL CONTENT CALCULATOR

```
00020  INPUT "ENTER THE NUMBER OF OZ. CON-
       SUMED, THE PROOF OF THE DRINK"; OZ, P
00030  INPUT "ENTER YOUR WEIGHT IN POUNDS";
       W
00040  C = (OZ * P * .037)/W
00050  PRINT "YOUR ESTIMATED BLOOD AL-
       CHOHOL CONTENT ="; C
00060  PRINT: PRINT
00070  END
```

CARPENTER AND MECHANIC'S HELPER

Your computer can serve as a replacement for the carpenter's square or mechanic's data charts by storing information commonly referred to and performing unit conversions.

Some useful formulas include:

A.) Wall Paper Estimator

$$N = \frac{8640}{W \cdot (H + R)} \qquad P = \frac{S}{W \cdot N}$$

where N = the number of strips in one roll
     W = the width of the paper
     H = the height of the wall
     R = the repeat length of the pattern
     P = the number of double rolls needed
     S = the width of the wall to be covered

B.) Concrete Block Estimator
     $N = H \cdot L \cdot 1.125$
where N = the number of blocks
     H = the height of the wall
     L = the length of the wall

C.) Concrete Yardage Estimator
$$Y = \frac{L \cdot W \cdot T}{324}$$
where Y = the volume of concrete in cubic yards
     L = the length (ft)
     W = the width (ft.)
     T = the thickness (in.)

CAR MAINTENANCE

Other than calculating your car's miles per gallon, the computer could keep track of mileage statistics and signal you when a periodic check-up, overhaul, or oil change is necessary. For people having the priviledge of deducting automotive expenses, the computer could keep tabs on amounts spent.

RAFFLE TICKET PRODUCER AND DRAWER

If your organization is sponsoring a raffle drawing, your computer could print out serialized raffle tickets and then draw the winning ticket based on a random number generator.

PROGRAM—LIFE EXPECTANCY CALCULATOR

Here's another program of interest to guests. Your life expectancy in years is calculated on the basis of life insurance studies. This program is interesting to run with data supplied for your present condition, and then run with data about yourself if you had kept your New Year's Resolutions (stop smoking, lose weight, etc.). The difference in years is often surprising.

```
10   REM LIFE EXPECTANCY CALCULATOR
20   REM ESTIMATES HOW LONG YOU WILL LIVE-
30   REM PROGRAM IS BASED ON SCIENTIFIC DATA
40   PRINT "LIFE EXPECTANCY CALCULATION FOR
     ADULTS 20-65 YRS. OF AGE"
50   PRINT "TYPE "1" FOR YES, "2" FOR NO TO ANS-
     WER QUESTIONS"
60   A = 72
70   INPUT "ARE YOU MALE"; B
80   IF B = 1 THEN A = A −3 ELSE A = A + 4
90   INPUT "DO YOU LIVE IN AN URBAN AREA-
     POPULATION > 2 MILLION"; B
100  IF B = 1 THEN A = A−2 ELSE INPUT "DO YOU
     LIVE IN A TOWN-POPULATION < 10,000 "; B:IF B
     = 1 THEN A = A + 2
110  PRINT "IF YOU WORK BEHIND A DESK TYPE '1'"
120  INPUT "IF YOUR JOB REQUIRES REGULAR,
     HEAVY PHYSICAL LABOR TYPE '2'; B
130  IF B = 1 THEN A = A−3 ELSE IF B = 2 THEN A = A
     + 3
```

```
140   PRINT "IF YOU EXERCISE STRENUOUSLY
      MORE THAN 5 ½HR. SESSIONS/WK"
150   INPUT "TYPE '1'. IF YOU DO 2-3 TIMES/WK.
      TYPE '2'"; B
160   IF B = 1 THEN A = A + 4 ELSE IF B = 2 THEN A =
      A + 2
170   INPUT "DO YOU LIVE WITH A SPOUSE OR
      FRIEND"; B
180   IF B = 1 THEN A = A + 5 ELSE INPUT "HOW
      MANY DECADES HAVE YOU LIVED WITHOUT
      OTHERS SINCE 25 YRS. OLD"; B: A = A – B
190   INPUT "DO YOU SLEEP MORE THAN TEN HRS.
      PER NIGHT"; B
200   IF B = 1 THEN A = A –4
210   PRINT "IF YOU ARE INTENSE, AGGRESSIVE,
      EASILY ANGERED TYPE '1'"
220   INPUT "IF YOU ARE EASY-GOING, RELAXED,
      FOLLOWER TYPE '2'"; B
230   IF B = 1 THEN A = A – 3 ELSE IF B = 2 THEN A =
      A + 3
240   INPUT "IF YOU'RE HAPPY TYPE '1'; UNHAPPY
      TYPE '2'"; B
250   IF B = 1 THEN A = A + 1 ELSE IF B = 2 THEN A =
      A – 2
260   INPUT "HAVE YOU HAD A SPEEDING TICKET
      WITHIN THE LAST YEAR"; B
270   IF B = 1 THEN A = A – 1
280   INPUT "DO YOU EARN MORE THAN $50,000/
      YR."; B
290   IF B = 1 THEN A = A – 2
300   INPUT "IF YOU'VE FINISHED COLLEGE TYPE '1';
      GRAD SCHOOL TYPE '2'"; B
310   IF B = 1 THEN A = A + 1 ELSE IF B = 1 THEN A =
      A + 2
320   INPUT "IF YOU'RE 65 OR OVER AND STILL
      WORKING TYPE '1'"; B
330   IF B = 1 THEN A = A + 3
340   INPUT "IF ANY OF YOUR GRANDPARENTS HAVE
      LIVED TO 85 TYPE '1'"; B
350   IF B = 1 THEN A = A + 2: INPUT "DID ALL 4 LIVE
      TO BE 80"; B: IF B = 1 THEN A = A + 6
360   INPUT "DID EITHER OF YOUR PARENTS DIE OF
      STROKE/HEART ATTACK BEFORE 50"; B
```

```
370    IF B = 1 THEN A = A – 4
380    PRINT "HAVE ANY OF YOUR PARENTS OR
       BROTHERS/SISTERS UNDER 50 HAD A"
390    INPUT "HEART CONDITION, CANCER, OR
       CHILDHOOD DIABETES"; B
400    IF B = 1 THEN A = A – 3
410    PRINT "IF YOU SMOKE: > 2 PACKS/DAY TYPE
       '1', 1-2 PACKS/DAY TYPE '2' "
420    INPUT "½-1 PACK/DAY TYPE '3'"; B
430    IF B = 1 THEN A = A – 8 ELSE IF B = 2 THEN A =
       A – 6 ELSE IF B = 3 THEN A = A – 3
440    INPUT "DO YOU DRINK THE EQUIVALENT OF ¼
       BOTTLE LIQUOR/DAY"; B
450    IF B = 1 THEN A = A – 1
460    PRINT "IF YOU ARE OVERWEIGHT BY > 50 LBS.
       TYPE '1', 30-50 LBS. TYPE '2'"
470    INPUT "10-30 LBS. TYPE '3'"; B
480    IF B = 1 THEN A = A – 8 ELSE IF B = 2 THEN A =
       A – 4 ELSE IF B = 3 THEN A = A –2
490    PRINT "IF YOU'RE MALE AND HAVE AN AN-
       NUAL CHECK-UP TYPE '1' AND IF"
500    INPUT "FEMALE TYPE '1' IF YOU SEE A
       GYNECOLOGIST ANNUALLY"; B
510    IF B = 1 THEN A = A + 2
520    PRINT "IF YOU'RE BETWEEN 30-40 TYPE '1',
       40-50 TYPE '2', 50-60 TYPE"
530    INPUT "'3', >70 TYPE '4'"; B
540    IF B = 1 THEN A = A + 2 ELSE IF B = 2 THEN A =
       A + 3 ELSE IF B = 3 THEN A = A + 4 ELSE IF B = 4
       THEN A = A + 5
550    PRINT ""
560    PRINT "YOUR LIFE EXPECTANCY IS ";A;"
       YEARS."
```

PROGRAM—DATA BASE DEMONSTRATION

Many of the program ideas described in this chapter can
be implemented with a general purpose "data base" computer
program. This type of program should be able to store information pertaining to many items on a cassette tape or floppy
disk and retrieve selected information.

The usual method of storing data on a cassette or disk
involves the use of one string of information containing sev-

eral "fields" of separate data. For example, a string containing five fields could be as follows:

Boolean Algebra* Byte Magazine * 25* Schwartz *Feb 1978

The first field signifies the title of the item (in this case a magazine article); all of the strings to be stored would be formatted in the same way, with the title of the item in the first field. Also, a limit is usually set on the length of any field (so that the data will fit neatly on a cassette or disk). If the information in one field does not contain enough characters to fill the allocated space, extra spaces are added.

Continuing with the example above, the second field contains the name of the source of the item; the third, fourth, and fifth fields contain the page number, author and issue date respectively. An adequate data base program should be able to search through many such strings and output those which contain items you want. For example, you can store an index to your library on a data base system and subsequently obtain a listing of all the references pertaining to the stock market written after some date. One would simply instruct the computer to search for all items containing "stock market" in some field and require that they also have a date in another field later than the date specified. Since the position of each field in all strings is fixed, the computer can search through a string (using the "MID$" command, for example) to the beginning of the proper field; specific information can easily be accessed in this manner.

Data base programs are perhaps the most useful personal computer programs due to their wide application. Yet, more comprehensive versions need to be written.

```
10   REM DATA BASE DEMONSTRATION PROGRAM
20   REM MAY BE USED TO MAINTAIN MAILING
     LISTS, COLLECTIONS
30   REM INVENTORY, ETC.
40   REM THE COMMAND 'HELP' PROVIDES IN-
     STRUCTIONS
50   CLS 'CLEARS SCREEN
70   REM INITIALIZED FOR UP TO 200 RECORDS
     WITH 30 FIELDS EACH
80   CLEAR 6000
90   REM ALTER THESE DIM STATEMENTS TO
     ALLOW FOR MORE RECORDS
```

```
100   DIM R$(200), D$(200)
110   DIM N$(30), B$(20), B(20)
120   INPUT"SELECT: 1) BEGIN ANEW, 2) LOAD OLD
      DATA FILE" ; WM%
140   CLS' CLEARS SCREEN
160   IF WM%=2 THEN 1890
180   B1$ = "        ":B$="":N$(0)="BUFFER EMPTY"
190   PRINT:PRINT
200   PRINT "INPUT FIELD NAME, FIELD TYPE
      (A=ALPHA, N=NUMERIC)"
210   REM
220   FOR I=1 TO 30
250   PRINT I; ") "
270   T$= "": INPUT T$, T1$
280   IF T$= "" THEN GOTO 420
290   IF (T1$ < > "A") AND (T1$ < > "N") THEN 330
      ELSE 340
330   PRINT "INCORRECT SYNTAX, PLEASE RE-
      ENTER":GOTO 270
340   T$=LEFT$(T$+B1$,4)+" "+ T1$
380   GOSUB 2470 'ROUTINE TO THROW-OUT EX-
      TRANEOUS SPACES
390   N$(I)=T$
400   NEXT I
410   GOTO 430
420   N$(I)="END"
430   PRINT:PRINT"THE RECORDS AND FIELDS EN-
      TERED WERE:"
460   FOR I=1 TO 10
470   IF LEFT$(N$(I),4)="END" THEN GOTO 500
480   PRINT I; ": ";N$(I)
490   NEXT I
500   PRINT: GOTO 540
530   PRINT "INCORRECT SYNTAX, PLEASE RE-
      ENTER YOUR COMMAND"
540   INPUT "COMMAND";T$
550   N1=0:PRINT
560   RESTORE
580   READ Z$, T
590   IF Z$="##" THEN 530
600   IF LEFT$(Z$,3)< >LEFT$(T$,3)THEN 580
610   ON T GOSUB 750, 1120, 1120, 1120, 2090, 3340,
      1310, 1220, 3180, 1120, 3340
```

```
620   GOTO 540
630   DATA ADD, 1, LIST,2, CHANGE, 3, LABELS, 4,
      HELP, 5, END, 6, SEARCH, 7
640   DATA SUM, 8, SAVE, 9, RUBOUT, 10, SORT, 11,
      ##, −1
750   REM ADD RECORD ROUTINE
755    PRINT "BEGIN ADDING RECORDS. TYPE
      'END'WHEN FINISHED."
760   N=N+1: N1=N1+1: T$ = ""
790    PRINT N; ") ";
810    FOR I = 1 TO 30
820   IF LEFT $ (N $ (I), 4) = "END" THEN GOTO 980
830   PRINTTAB (7) N$ (I); ": ";
840   T1$= " ": INPUT T1$
850   REM
860   IF T1$=""THEN T1$=" " 'ADD A SPACE
870   IF T1$= "END" " THEN 1060
880   IF MID $ (N$(I), 6, 1) < > "N" THEN 920
890   IF ASC (T1$) > 43 AND ASC (T1$) < 58 THEN 920
900   PRINT "THIS IS A NUMERIC FIELD-ENTER
      NUMBERS ONLY": GOTO 830
920   REM
950   IF LEN (T$) + LEN (T1$) > 245 GOTO 1010 ELSE
      T$=T$+CHR$(126)+T1$
970   NEXT I
980   N$ = STR$(N)
990   T$=N$ + T $ + CHR$ (126)
1000  GOTO 1030
1010  PRINT "YOU HAVE EXCEEDED THE ALLOWED
      RECORD LENGTH, PLEASE RE-ENTER": GOTO
      790
1030  R$ (N)=T$
1040  PRINT
1050  GOTO 760
1060  REM END OF ADDITION TO RECORDS
1070  N=N−1: N1=N1−1
1090  PRINT "YOU ADDED"; N1; "RECORDS"
1100  RETURN
1110  REM ROUTINE TO LIST RECORDS
1120   GOSUB 2170: REM DETERMINE RECORD
      RANGE TO LIST
1125  IF T=10 THEN 1465
1130  IF T< > 4 THEN 1360
```

40

```
1135   INPUT "WOULD YOU LIKE TO TEST LABEL
       ALIGNMENT"; Z$
1137   IF Z$="NO" THEN 1360
1140   FOR I=1 TO 2
1150   INPUT "ALIGN PRINTOUT AND HIT ' ENTER'
       WHEN READY"; W9%
1160   FOR J=1 TO 5
1170   PRINT "XXXXXXXXXXXXXXXXXXXXXXXXXX"
1180   NEXT J
1190   PRINT: NEXT I
1210   GOTO 1360
1220   REM ROUTINE TO SEARCH RECORDS AND
       PERFORM SUMMATIONS
1230   INPUT "ENTER THE NUMBER OF THE FIELD
       TO BE SUMMED"; SM%
1240   IF MID$(N$(SM%), 6, 1) = "N" THEN 1270
1250   PRINT "INCORRECT TYPE OF FIELD , PLEASE
       RE-ENTER"
1260   GOTO 1230
1270   INPUT "DO YOU WANT TO SUM OVER ALL RE-
       CORDS ? (Y/N)"; S1$
1280   IF S1$ < > "Y" THEN 1310 ELSE S%= 0: GOTO
       1330
1310   INPUT  "ENTER THE FIELD NUMBER AND
       EXPRESSION TO BE COMPARED"; S%, S$
1330   T1=1: SM=0: T2=N
1360   FOR I=T1 TO T2
1370   T1$ = R$ (I)
1410   T$=LEFT$(T1$,5)
1420   T3=VAL (T$)
1430   T$=T1$
1440   T1$=CHR$ (126)
1450   GOSUB 3050 'ROUTINE TO PARSE STRING
1460   GOTO 1490
1463   REM RUBOUT COMMAND ROUTINE
1465   FD=T2-T1+1
1470   FOR I=T2+1 TO N+1
1475   R$(I-FD)=R$(I)
1480   NEXT I
1484   N=N-FD
1488   RETURN
1490   IF T<=4 THEN 1570
```

```
1500   IF S%=0 THEN 1520 ' 'SUM THE RECORDS
1510   IF B$(S%) <>S$ THEN 1850 ' 'GOTO SEARCH
       ROUTINE
1520   IF T= 7 THEN 1650
1530   PRINT "(";I;")";
1540   T3=VAL (B$(SM%))
1550   SM=SM+T3
1560   GOTO 1850
1570   ON T-1 GOTO 1650, 1650, 1580
1580   REM ROUTINE TO PRINT LABELS
1590   FOR J=1 TO 5
1600   PRINT B$(J)
1610   NEXT J
1620   PRINT
1630   GOTO 1850
1640   REM
1645   PRINT "YOU HAVE EXCEEDED THE ALLOWED
       RECORD LENGTH, PLEASE RE-ENTER"
1650   PRINT I;") "
1670   FOR J= 1 TO 10
1680   IF LEFT$ (N$(J), 4)= "END" THEN GOTO 1760
1690   PRINT N$(J); ": "; B$(J)
1700   IF T<>3THEN 1740
1710   INPUT T1$
1720   IF T1$="-"THEN GOTO 1740
1730   B$(J)=T1$
1740   NEXT J
1750   REM
1760   IF T< > 3 THEN 1850
1770   N$=B$(0) ' ROUTINE TO ADD A CHANGED RE-
       CORD
1780   PRINT N$
1790   T$=N$+CHR$(126)
1800   FOR J=1 TO 10
1805   IF LEN (T$)+LEN (B$(J))> 245 GOTO 1645
1810   T$=T$+B$(J)+CHR$(126)
1820   IF N$(J)="END" THEN 1840
1830   NEXT J
1840   R$ (I) =T$
1850   NEXT I
1860   IF T< > 8 THEN 1880
```

```
1870    PRINT "THE SUM OF RECORD"; N$(SM%);" =";
        SM
1880    RETURN
1890    REM ROUTINE TO LOAD DATA FROM CAS-
        SETTE
1900    REM
1910    INPUT "ENTER FILE NAME";F$
1914    INPUT#-1, T$
1918    IF T$=F$ THEN GOTO 1935
1922    PRINT "FILE ";T$;" HAS BEEN FOUND"
1923    INPUT"WOULD YOU LIKE TO CONTINUE THE
        SEARCH (Y/N)";T$
1930    IF T$="N" THEN 540
1935    INPUT#-1,N
1940    J=0
1945    J=J+1
1950    INPUT#-1,N$(J)
1955    IF N$(J)="END" THEN 1965
1960    GOTO 1945
1965    FOR X=1 TO N
1970    INPUT#-1, R$(X)
1975    NEXT X
1980    GOTO 540
1990    REM
2000    REM
2010    GOSUB 3040
2020    FOR I=0 TO 10
2030    N$(I)=B$(I)
2040    IF LEFT$(N$(I),4)="END" THEN 2060
2050    NEXT I
2055    I=I-1
2060    N=VAL (B$(I+1))
2070    GOTO 540
2090    REM HELP SEQUENCE
2100    PRINT "COMMANDS AVAILABLE:"
2150    PRINT "ADD: ADDS RECORDS TO THE
        FILE":PRINT "CHANGE: CHANGES RECORDS
        IN FILE"
2155    PRINT "RUBOUT: DELETES A RECORD FROM
        THE FILE":PRINT"LIST:LISTS ALL OR CER-
```

TAIN RECORDS"
2156 PRINT "LABELS: LINE PRINTS CONTENTS OF THE FILE": PRINT "SAVE: LOADS DATA TO CASSETTE"
2157 PRINT "SORT: SORTS RECORDS INTO ALPHANUMERIC ORDER BY A SPECIFIED FIELD":PRINT "SUM: SUMS A SPECIFIED FIELD OVER A GROUP OF RECORDS"
2158 PRINT "SEARCH: FINDS A RECORD CONTAIN-ING A SPECIFIED FIELD"
2159 PRINT "HELP: BRINGS YOU HERE":PRINT "END: ENDS THE PROGRAM"
2160 RETURN
2170 REM DETERMINE THE RANGE
2180 IF N=0 THEN PRINT "EMPTY FILE"
2190 IF N= 0 THEN 540
2200 PRINT "ENTER MODE: A(ALL), O(ONE), R(RANGE)"
2210 INPUT T$
2220 IF T$<> "A" THEN 2260
2230 T2=N: T1=1
2250 GOTO 2430
2260 IF T$< > "O" THEN 2310
2270 INPUT "ENTER NUMBER OF RECORD"; T1
2280 IF T1>NTHEN 2440
2290 T2=T1
2300 GOTO 2430
2310 IF T$="R" THEN 2340
2320 PRINT "IMPROPER SYNTAX, PLEASE RE-ENTER"
2330 GOTO 2200
2340 PRINT "INPUT THE LOWER BOUND"
2350 INPUT T1
2360 IF T1<1THENT1=1
2370 IF T1>N THEN GOSUB 2440
2380 INPUT "INPUT THE UPPER BOUND"; T2
2390 IF T2>N THEN 2440
2430 RETURN
2440 PRINT "THERE ARE ONLY"; N; "RECORDS IN THIS FILE"

```
2450   GOTO 2200
2460   REM
2470   REM ELIMINATE EXTRANEOUS SPACES FROM
       STRINGS
2480   T1=LEN (T$):B$=" ": IF T1=0 THEN 2600
2510   FOR T2=2 TO T1
2520   IF MID$(T$, T2-1, 1) < > B$ THEN 2550
2530   T$=MID$(T$,2,T1-1)
2540   NEXT T2
2550   T1 = LEN (T$)
2560   IF T1 = 0 THEN 2600
2570   IF RIGHT $ (T$, 1) < > B$ THEN 2600
2580   T$ = LEFT $ (T$, T1 -1)
2590   GOTO 2570
2600   RETURN
2610   PRINT "PLEASE RE-ENTER DATA"
2620   INPUT "INPUT THE FIELD NUMBER TO BE
       SORTED"; S%
2630   PRINT "THE FIELD NAME IS:";N$(S%)
2660   T2=N:T1=1
2670   T2=N
2690   FOR I=T1 TO T2
2700   T$=R$(I)
2710   T1$=CHR$(126)
2720   GOSUB 3040
2730   D$(I) = B$(S%)
2740   NEXT I
2750   IF MID$(N$(S%),6,1)< > "A" THEN 2780
2760   SR%=1
2770   GOTO 2820
2780   IF MID$(N$(S%), 6,1)= "N" THEN 2810
2790   PRINT "ERROR: THE WRONG FIELD TYPE WAS
       INPUTTED"
2800   GOTO 540
2810   SR%=2
2820   REM SORT ROUTINE
2830   M=N
2840   M=INT (M/2)
2850   IF M=0 THEN 3020
2860   J=1
2870   K=N-M
2880   I=J
```

45

```
2890    L=I+M
2900    IF SR%=2 THEN 2930
2910    IF D$(I) < D$(L) THEN 2990
2920    GOTO 2940
2930    IF VAL (D$(I))<VAL (D$(L)) THEN 2990
2940    T$=D$(I)
2942    D$(I)=D$(L)
2944    D$(L)=T$
2950    T$=R$(I)
2952    R$(I)=R$(L)
2954    R$(L)=T$
2960    I=I-M
2970    IF I<1 THEN 2990
2980    GOTO 2890
2990    J=J+1
3000    IF J>K THEN 2840
3010    GOTO 2880
3020    GOTO 540
3040    REM
3050    REM STRING PARSING ROUTINE
3060    K=-1
3070    FORJ2=1TOLEN (T$)
3080    IF T1$=MID$(T$, J2, 1) THEN 3110
3090    NEXT J2
3180    RETURN
3110    M%=J2-1
3120    K=K+1
3140    B$(K)=MID$(T$, 1, M%)
3150    T$=MID$(T$, J2, 1)
3160    J2=0
3170    GOTO 3070
3180    REM ROUTINE TO SAVE DATA
3190    INPUT "INPUT A NAME FOR FILE BEING
        SAVED";F$
3200    PRINT#-1,F$
3210    PRINT#-1,N
3220    FOR X=1 TO 10
3230    PRINT#-1,N$(X)
3240    IF N$(X)="END" THEN 3260
3250    NEXT X
3260    FOR X=1 TO N
```

```
3270    PRINT#-1, R$(X)
3280    NEXT X
3290    RETURN
3340    END
```

Chapter 2
Business and
Financial Applications

Business And Financial Applications

In the world of business and finance, the home computer can be used to solved many of the complex financial formulas. With high interest rates, it is advantageous to be able to analyze loans and other financial dealings. In addition to these types of business problems, the computer can be used to set up bookkeeping systems, or even analyze a real estate investment.

FINANCES AND INVESTMENTS

A cost-justifying application for your personal computer is the area of investments and other personal finances. Ways that your computer can be useful in the stockmarket include:

1. Given the purchase data of your stock, the number of shares, the average or current dividend rate, dates, and price per share, the following stock analysis factors may be computed: dividends paid per year, dividends paid during holdings, gain/loss since purchase—with and without dividends, profit/loss per year, growth rate, percentage appreciation/depreciation, stock price index per unit of time, and intrinsic valve per share.

For instance, calculation of the intrinsic value of a stock is calculated with this formula:

$$I = \frac{TC \cdot AMT}{CS}$$

Where I = intrinsic value
       TC = total corporation capital
     AMT = price per share
        CS = amount in dollars of capital stock

If several stocks are being analyzed simultaneously, these analysis factors may be computed for the entire portfolio: sum of cost prices, sum of current value, sum and percentage difference between cost and current price, percentage return on a cost basis, and percentage return on the current value.

2. Earnings per share estimation may be accomplished using a historical balance sheet and income data to estimate future earnings for a given stock; future estimations may be made with trend-line analysis.

3. A stock valuation program could find current and future values of a stock before and after tax rate of return. Commissions would be considered in all calculations.

4. Brokerage commissions on standard and odd lots, as well as for stocks selling below one-dollar per share, could be calculated.

5. Mathematical Analysis of the stock market is another useful application. The save stastical computations of the stock market performed by professional investment companies may be accomplished easily on your computer. Any investor should learn to use statistics in analyzing the market. There are four major statistical computations in stock market analysis: arithmetic average, standard deviation, coefficient of correlation, and trendline analysis.

The arithmetic average, also called the mean, is simply the sum of the values used divided by the number of values. In mathematical symbolism, this is represented as:

$$\mu = \frac{\sum\limits_{i=1}^{n} X_i}{n}$$

where μ = the mean
     n = the number of scores

However, the arithmetic average can be misleading—(1,100) and (49,51) have the same average although the two sets of data are quite different.

51

The standard deviation of a set of data is computed to indicate characteristics of the data which cannot be determined with the arithmetic mean. Standard deviation indicates how much the values differ from the average and the probability of a certain value occuring. It is computed using this formula:

$$S = \sqrt{\frac{1}{n-1} \sum_{i=1}^{n} (X_i - \mu)^2}$$

where n = the number of scores
X_i = the individual scores
μ = the mean
s = standard deviation

Many phenomena can be described graphically with a curve called normal distribution (the curve is described by the formula)

$$\frac{1}{S \sqrt{2\pi}} \; e^{-(\frac{1}{2})((x-\mu)/S)^2}$$

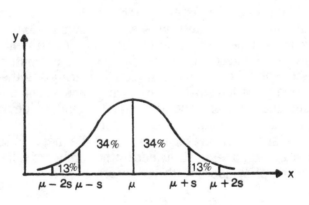

This distance from μ to μ + s or to μ − s is called 1 deviation; to μ + 2s or μ − 2s is 2 deviations. The percentage values inside the curve indicate the percentage of values under the curve between the two adjacent lines. Thus, one could state that the probability for a data point being within one deviation of the arithmetic average is about 68 percent.

The coefficient of correlation is a measure of the similarity between two sets of data. If the data is directly or inversely similar, each value in one set will have a corresponding value in the other set which may be determined mathematically. The formula to compute the coefficient of correlation is as follows:

$$R = \frac{\dfrac{1}{n-1} \displaystyle\sum_{i=1}^{n} (X_i - \mu_x)(Y_i - \mu_y)}{\sqrt{\dfrac{1}{n-1} \displaystyle\sum_{i=1}^{n} (X_i - \mu_x)^2} \; \sqrt{\dfrac{1}{n-1} \displaystyle\sum_{i=1}^{n} (Y_i - \mu_y)^2}}$$

where R = the coefficient of correlation

n = the number of scores

X_1, Y_i = individual x and y values respectively

$\mu_x \, \mu_y$ = the means for the x and y values respectively

R will always fall between − 1 and 1. If the absolute value of R is greater than .81 the probability of a correlation existing is greater than 50 percent. If R is positive, then x moves proportionally to y; if R is negative, then x moves inversely proportionally to y.

The coefficient of determination is used to determine how well the data relationship can be described by a linear formula. It is computed by squaring the coefficient of correlation.

Trend analysis is the final major statistical computation. Trend-line analysis is accomplished using a method called "least squares." Suppose you obtained a set of data listing the value of one stock over a period of time. If these values were plotted vs the Dow Jones Index the result could appear as:

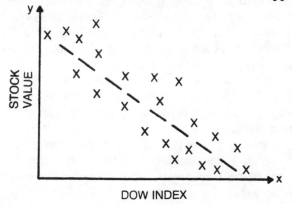

STOCK VALUE

DOW INDEX

The various points form a "scatter gram." The purpose of trend-line analysis is to compute the equation for the line which best describes the data. All lines may be described by the equation: $y = mx + b$

where m = the slope
   b = the y intercept
   x, y = corresponding values in the two sets of data

The least squares equation for computing the slope (m) is:

$$M = \frac{\frac{1}{n-1} \sum_{i=1}^{n} (X_i - \mu_x)(Y_i - \mu_y)}{\frac{1}{n-1} \sum_{i=1}^{n} (X_i - \mu_x)^2}$$

To find the value for b, simply plug in sample values for x and y, the computed slope, and solve for b; the following equation may also be used

$$b = \left(\sum_{i=1}^{n} Y_i - m \sum_{i=1}^{n} X_i \right) / n$$

Once this linear equation is determined, it may be used to forecast future events (assuming that events will continue as they have in the past). For example, if you computed a trend line for a particular stock vs the Dow index and the index was expected to rise to some value, you could determine the cooresponding value for that stock.

These four statistical parameters can be used effectively in investment analysis. The standard deviation indicates the probability that the value of a stock at any point in time will be within one or more deviations from the mean (based upon past performance). Although this prediction will not necessarily be true, use of the standard deviation is the best method for mathematical analysis. The data obtained should be used to determine the probability that one will make money with a particular stock (considering brokerage costs).

The correlation coefficient analysis can be applied to a variety of factors to determine the possible relationships between financial indicators and the performance of a stock or the stock market in general. The most probable correlation will be between the Dow index and the performance of a bluechip stock. If one obtained "evidence" that the Dow index was to rise to a certain level, he could predict a corresponding rise in the value of such a stock.

Trend-line analysis could be used to find consistencies in the stock market and financial world. Of course, if such consistencies are found they may be used to predict future values. Several financial indicators could enter the analysis: Dow Jones Industrial Average, specific industrial indicators, Gross National Product, employment statistics, disposable personal income statistics, indexes of industrial production, bank deposits, Federal Reserve amounts, inventory levels, accounts receivable/payable, paperboard production, and railroad freight usage. Several of these factors would probably have to be combined to determine a general consistency.

Additional statistical parameters that can be computed include confidence intervals, exponential equations and smoothing, alpha and beta, expected return, standard deviation of returns, variance, mean average deviation, and the probable error.

Obviously, the power of your computer can be effectively utilized to determine these and other statistics for a variety of stocks, storing stock data for future reference, and finding the most profitable stock market strategy. One can develop and test a theory without countless manual calculations.

PROGRAM—OPTIONS ANALYSIS

The purpose of this program is to assist the investor in planning the most profitable stock-option buy and sell strategy. The strategy used by the program involves the selling of options against stock bought; this is usually considered the least risky and often most profitable strategy. For example, one could buy 100 shares of stock to use as collateral for each call option sold. A call option, which is sold at a premium, allows the purchaser the right to buy the stock at a certain price (called the strike point), no matter what the true stock price becomes. However, the option is valid for a certain length of time only, known as the life of the option. This computer program will request information pertaining to the stock and will calculate the value of the stock and return on investment (ROI) over a range of 40% to 160 % of the current value. Using this data, the investor should be able to decide the probability that a certain buy and sell strategy will be profitable. In the final analysis, the program uses a set of financial formulas to recommend a specific buy-sell strategy and then prints an itemized listing of all costs, brokerage fees, proceeds and returns. To make the best use of this program, it is suggested that the user study books concerning stock-option strategies.

```
10   REM STOCK OPTION ANALYSIS PROGRAM
20   REM
30   DIM D (12), A$ (20), B (10), F (12),K$(12)
40   FOR D4 = 1 TO 12
50   READ D (D4): F (D4) = D4:READ K$(D4)
60   NEXT D4
70   INPUT "ENTER THE NUMERICAL MONTH, DAY,
     YEAR"; M1, D9, Y1
80   INPUT "IS THE STOCK TO BE BOUGHT ON MAR-
     GIN (1 = YES, 2 = NO)"; M
90   INPUT "ENTER THE % MARGIN RATE"; M2
100  IF M = 1 THEN D5 = .5 ELSE D5 = 1
110  INPUT "ENTER THE NAME OF THE STOCK OR
     ID, THE DIVIDEND IN $'S PER SHARE PER
     QUARTER"; D6$, D7
120  INPUT "ENTER THE NUMBER OF SHARES TO
     BE PURCHASED (MULTIPLE OF 100 SHARES)";
     D8
130  INPUT "ENTER THE PRICE PER SHARE"; P9
140  INPUT "SELECT MARKET 1) NYSE, 2) OTC"; E
150  INPUT "ENTER THE EXPIRATION MONTH (EG. 1
     = JANUARY, 2 = FEBRUARY. . .)"; E2
160  INPUT "ENTER THE STRIKE PRICE"; E3
170  INPUT "ENTER THE COST PER OPTION (MUL-
     TIPLY PRICE BY 100)"; E4
180  E5 = D8/100
190  INPUT "ENTER THE JANUARY, APRIL, JULY,
     OCTOBER, PREMIUMS";B (1), B (4), B (7), B (10)
195  C4 = 100: C3 = 100
200  FOR C8 = 1 TO 10 STEP 3
210  IF B (C8) = 0 THEN 590
220  C9 = B (C8)
230  A4 = C8 * 30. 4225
240  A8 = A4 + A7 − ((M1 − 1) * 30. 4225) − D9
250  C = P9*C3
260  FOR A9 = 1 TO 2
```

```
270   C4 = A9*C4
280   D = C4*C9
290   B4 = D*. 034 + . 017*C
300   B5 = B4 + C - D
310   B6 = B5*. 085*A8/365
320   D1 = B6 + B5
330   PRINT "MONTH OF CALL"; C8
340   PRINT "INITIAL INVESTMENT"; B5
350   PRINT "TOTAL INVESTMENT"; D1
360   PRINT "EFFECTIVE WRITING RATIO"; A9
370   PRINT
380   PRINT "STOCK PRICE  RETURN  ROI  ROI/YR"
390   FOR D2 = -4 TO 6
400   A1 = (1 - (.1*D2))*C
410   IF A1/C3 > (. 25 + E3 ) THEN 460
420   B9 = 0
430   B7 = A1 - D1
440   GOTO 480
450   D1 = (1 - A9)*A1 + D1
460   B7 = C3*E3 - D1 - 100* (A9 - 1)*E3
470   B9 = (((A1/C3 + 1) - (1. 068*C9))*100)/(1. 068*C9)
480   B8 = B7/D1*100
490   C2 = A1/C3
500   D3 = B8/(A8/365)
510   PRINT C2, B7, B8, D3
520   NEXT D2
530   NEXT A9
590   NEXT C8
600   IF A8 > 180 THEN PRINT "LONG TERM"
610   PRINT
620   E6 = INT (E5*E3*100)
630   E7 = INT (E4*E5)
640   E8 = Y1*365
650   E9 = D9 + D (M1) + E8
660   F = E8 + 20 + D (E2)
670   F1 = F - E9: IF F1 < 0 THEN F1 = F1 + 365
680   F2 = INT ((F1/90) +. 5)
685   F3 = INT (F2*D7*D8)
690   F4 = F3 + E7 +E6
700   F5 = INT (P9*D8)
710   F6 = INT (D5*F5)
720   F7=F5- F6:F8=E:F9=F5:G=D8/100
```

```
770   GOSUB 1150
780   G1=G2:F9=E6:G=D8/100:GOSUB1150
820   G3=G2:F9=E7:G=E5:F8=3
860   GOSUB 1150
870   G4 = G2
880   G5 = F7 - E7 - F3 + G3 + G4 + G1
900   IF D5 = 1 THEN G6 = 0 ELSE G6 = INT((((M2/
      100)*G5)*F1/365)
910   G7 = G6 + G3 + F7 + G4 + G1 + F6
920   G8 = F4 - G7
930   G9 = F6 - F3 - E7 + G6 + G3 + G1 + G4
940   H = INT((G8*1000)/G9)/10
950   H2 = INT ( ( ( G7 - F3 - E7)*100)/D8)/100
960   H1 = INT (3650*H/F1)/10
970   INPUT "TYPE ENTER TO CONTINUE"; A$:
      PRINT
980   PRINT "COVERED WRITE:"; D6$" DATE
      (MM DD YY):"; M1; D9; Y1
990   PRINT "HEDGE STRATEGY:"
1000  PRINT "BUY"; D8; "SHARES.(PRICE = $"; P9;")"
1010  PRINT "SELL"; E5; " "; K $(E2); E3; " 'S
      ($"; E4; "APIECE)"
1029  INPUT "TYPE ENTER TO CONTINUE"; A$
1030  CLS:PRINT"EXPENSES:"
1040  PRINT"   IMMEDIATE        $";F6
1045  PRINT"   LOAN (50%)       $";F7
1050  PRINT"   BROKER'S FEES $"
1055  PRINT"        OPTION      $";G4
1060  PRINT"        IN          $";G1
1065  PRINT"        OUT         $";G3
1070  PRINT"   MARGIN COST   $";G6
1080  PRINT"TOTAL             $";G7
1100  PRINT"INCOME:":PRINT" STOCK $";E6
1105  PRINT"   OPTION      $";E7
1110  PRINT"   DIVIDENDS $";F3
1120  PRINT"TOTAL          $";F4
1125  PRINT:PRINT"THE RETURN ON YOUR MONEY
      IS";H;"% ($";G8;" ON $";INT(G9);")"
1130  PRINT"FOR";F1;" DAYS,";H1;"% ANNUALLY."
1140  PRINT"THE BREAK-EVEN POINT IS A PRICE
      OF $"; (INT(H2*10))/10:END
```

```
1150   G2 = ( (. 009*F9) + 22) + (6*G)
1160   ON F8 GOTO 1180, 1190, 1200
1170   IF G2 < 25 THEN G2 = 25
1175   RETURN
1180   G2 = INT (. 7*G2) : RETURN
1190   G2 = 21*G: RETURN
1200   G2 = INT (. 82*G2): RETURN
1300   DATA 0, JANUARY, 31, FEBRUARY, 59, MARCH,
       90, APRIL, 120, MAY, 151, JUNE, 182, JULY, 212,
       AUGUST, 243, SEPTEMBER, 272, OCTOBER,
       304, NOVEMBER, 334, DECEMBER
```

6. Analysis of Annual Reports. Often, some of the most important indicators of a companies' financial position are left out of annual reports. Over the years, security analysts, brokers, and investors have found that financial statements become more meaningful when ratios are computed between some items in the income and balance sheets. These ratios are important to an in-depth analysis of a company before purchasing stock. A simple computer program could request the necessary input values for the following ratios and output the results, perhaps providing an over-all rating of the company as well. Useful ratios include:

Operating profit margin—The basic indicator of the efficiency of operations is profit (before interest and taxes) expressed as a percentage of sales. Profits usually fluctuate more than sales since certain overhead costs (interest, rent, property taxes, etc.) are steady and do not change with sales volume.

Current/Working capital ratio—The current ratio is simply the ratio of current assets to current liabilities; a two to one ratio is generally accepted as standard. Improvements in financial strength are often reflected by a gradual increase in this ratio. However, a ratio of more than four or five to one is considered excessive and could indicate increasing inventories, under-utilization of cash for expansion, or a contraction in the business.

Liquidity ratio—This ratio is a comparison between "quick assets" such as cash and marketable securities to total current liabilities and has been called the "acid-test" ratio.

This ratio should be used in conjunction with the current ratio to insure that a company can meet current obligations or pay larger dividends. During periods of expansion and rising prices, the liquidity ratio often declines. If the decline continues it may become necessary for the company to raise additional capital. However, one should not be concerned unless this ratio drops considerably.

- $\dfrac{\text{Current assets}}{\text{Current liabilities}}$

- $\dfrac{\text{Liquid assets}}{\text{Liquid liabilities}}$

- $\dfrac{\text{Cash and marketable securities}}{\text{Current Liabilities}}$

Capitalization ratios—Capitalization ratios are the percentages of total investment capital represented by long-term debt, preferred stock, common stock, and surplus. Industrial companies usually have less proportion of debt than relatively stable industries such as utilities. The higher the ratio of common stock and surplus the less prior claims ahead of stockholders.

Sales to fixed assets—This ratio is determined by dividing annual sales by the value of plant and equipment. It indicates whether funds have been properly invested in fixed assets; if an expansion in facilities does not result in increased sales volume there could be a problem in marketing strategy.

Sales to inventories—"Inventory turnover" is another name for this ratio which approximates the number of times inventory is turned over in one year. Thus, this ratio is particularly important to the retail industry analysis in which a high ratio indicates well selected and priced merchandise.

Net income to net worth—This ratio is indicative of the companies' earning on the investment of shareholders. A high or increasing value is favorable although a very high value may indicate intense competition. Additionally, temporary inventory profits may be the result of increasing commodity prices. A high value could also be due to general prosperity or a declining position.

Interest coverage—This ratio is computed by dividing the earnings before taxes by the annual interest charges. A manufacturing company should cover interest more than four times and public utilities should cover interest about three times.

Combined coverage—Combined coverage is computed by dividing annual interest and debt costs plus preferred dividends into the adjusted operating profit after taxes and before interest. A combined coverage of four is considered acceptable for an industrial company; a coverage of three times the combined requirements would make a utility stock high-grade.

Dividend payout—The dividend payout is the percentage of earnings on common stock that are paid out as dividends. Industrial companies average about 55%, utilities 70%, and growth companies less than 55%.

Book value per share—The book value per share is determined by adding the stated or par value of the common stock to the additional paid-in capital and retained earnings accounts and dividing by the number of common shares. The book value would be lower for companies in which preferred stock is entitled to share in additional paid-in capital. The book value is not as important an indicator as earnings and prospects for industrial companies. However, the book value of stock for financial institutions and utilities is important in analysis.

7. An options valuation program, using the Black-Scholes or other economic model, could determine the optimum hedge ratio and spread of any option. When selling partially covered called, or when selling puts and shortening stock, an options writing program could be used to find the maximum profit and upper and lower break-even points.

8. The following program may be used to calculate company growth rates using historical financial data:

```
00100   REM CALCULATION OF THE GROWTH RATE
00110   A=0
00120   INPUT "ENTER THE NUMBER OF DATA
        POINTS";Z(0)
00130   PRINT "ENTER DATA POINTS SUCCES-
        SIVELY"
00140   FOR B=1 TO Z(0)
00150   INPUT Z(B)
```

```
00160   NEXT B
00170   FOR B=1 TO Z(0)
00180   IF Z(B)=<0 THEN PRINT "DATA LESS THAN
        ZERO NOT ALLOWED": GOTO 110
00190   A=A+LOG(Z(B) )
00200   NEXT B
00210   A= (1/Z (0)) *A
00220   Z6=0: Z7=0
00230   FOR B=1 TO Z(0)
00240   Z6=Z6+(LOG(Z(B))-A)*(B-(Z(0)/2))
00250   Z7=Z7+((B-(Z(0)/2))↑2)
00260   NEXT B
00270   V=Z6/Z7
00280   PRINT "THE GROWTH RATE IS"; INT
        ((100*V)+.5); " %"
00290   PRINT
00300   END
```

PERSONAL ACCOUNTS RECEIVABLE/PAYABLE:

A personal AP/AR program similar to a business AP/AR program could manage a large portion of your financial affairs. The program could include these features:

1. Checking/savings account management to enable one to maintain the current balance of checking/savings accounts. Interest credits could be calculated and added. A file of each check (with its number, purpose, notes, amount, and payee) could be stored for later income tax preparation. Specialized reports could be generated from this check file including: a check register for a specified time period, the distribution of expenditures, and statements of selected accounts. The ideal program would prompt all information concerning each check written, store this information, and print the check itself.

2. A budgeting program to keep one up to date on expenditures in various areas, such that income can be allocated appropriately. A plan for family spending could take the following format:

> Set-asides
> >   Emergencies and future goals   --------------
> >   Seasonal expenses   --------------
> Debt payments   --------------
> Regular monthly expenses   --------------

Rent or mortgage payment	-------------
Utilities	-------------
Installment payments	-------------
Other	-------------
Total	-------------
Day to day expenses	
Food and beverages	-------------
Household maintenance	-------------
Furnishings, equipment	-------------
Clothing	-------------
Personal	-------------
Transportation	-------------
Medical care	-------------
Recreation, education	-------------
Gifts, contributions	-------------
Total	-------------
Total of all expenses	-------------

3. A financial behaviorism determination program to analyze your expenditures and summarize your spending in various areas (the categories of the budget above), useful in preparing a budget plan.

4. A file of unfullfilled contracts, mail orders, etc. for which you have sent checks, yet have received no reply. As replys are received, the appropriate account is removed from the file; keep track of your expenditures.

Simple interest—A program could be written to calculate the exact number of days between two dates, the simple interest amount between these two dates, and the number of months, days, and years in the interest period; leap years would be accounted for.

$$i = \frac{cpd}{100 \cdot 360}$$

Where i=interest on the capital
   c = capital, invested or borrowed
   p = rate of interest
   d = no. of days

Compound Interest—Knowing any three of the four following variables in a compound interest problem,

FV = future value
PV = present value
i = interest rate per period in percent
n = number of periods

A simple computer program could compute the remaining value:

$$FV = PV(1 + i)^n$$

$$PV = \frac{FV}{(1+i)^n}$$

$$n = \frac{\log FV/PV}{\log(1+i)}$$

$$i = 100((FV/PV)^{1/n} - 1)$$

The compound amount situation refers to an amount of principal that has been placed into an account and compounded periodically, with no further deposits. An additional variable is added to be above equation in this calculation such that the values for any variable given the remaining four may be determined using these equations:

I = the amount of interest accrued

$$n = \frac{\ln(FV/PV)}{\ln(1 + i)}$$

$$i = \left(\frac{(FV)}{PV}\right)^{1/n} - 1$$

$$PV = FV\,(1 + i)^{-n}$$

$$FV = PV\,(1 + i)^n$$

$$I = PV\left[(1 + i)^n - 1\right]$$

True interest rate—The true interest rate, often used by businessmen, is calculated as follows:

$$R = \frac{24F_c}{m\,I_m\,(m + 1)}$$

where R = the true interest rate
F_c = finance charge
m = number of months
I_m = monthly installment

```
10    REM TRUE ANNUAL INTEREST RATE COMPU-
      TATION
20    REM FOR USE WITH INSTALLMENT LOANS
25    CLS ' CLEAR SCREEN
30    INPUT "ENTER THE AMOUNT OF THE LOAN
      (WITHOUT INTEREST)";B
40    INPUT "ENTER THE AMOUNT OF EACH PAY-
      MENT"; A
50    INPUT "ENTER THE TOTAL NUMBER OF PAY-
      MENTS";C
60    INPUT "ENTER THE NUMBER OF PAYMENTS
      PER YEAR"; D
70    PRINT:PRINT
80    IF C=1 THEN 680
90    IF C *A > = B THEN 150
100   PRINT:PRINT
110   PRINT "THE PAYMENTS SUM TO LESS THAN THE
      AMOUNT OWED";
130   PRINT
135   INPUT"TYPE ENTER WHEN READY";A$
140   GOTO 10
150   E=0:F=100
160    GOSUB 260
170   IF A=G THEN 360
180   IF A>G THEN 220 ELSE E=E−F: GOTO 230
220   E = E + F
230   F = F/2
240   IF F<. 0001 THEN 360
250   GOTO 160
260   H =E/(100*D)
270   J=H+1
280   IF C*J< =75 THEN 310
290   G=B*H
300   RETURN
310   IF G>1 THEN G=B*J[ C*H/(J]C-1) ELSE G=B/C
320   RETURN
360   E= .01*INT(.05 + 100*E)
370   IF E<199.5 THEN 430
380   PRINT
390   PRINT "THE INTEREST RATE IS TOO HIGH,
      RE-ENTER";
420   GOTO 10
```

```
430    PRINT: PRINT "TRUE ANNUAL INTEREST RATE
       =";E; "%"
440    PRINT:PRINT
450    INPUT "TYPE ENTER WHEN READY";A$
460    GOTO 10
680    E=(A/B−1)*D
690    E=100*E
700    GOTO 360
```

Mortages

It may be worth your while to analyze a mortgage agreement on your computer *before* signing any contracts.

Mortgage loan analysis—A yearly amortization program could calculate a schedule of payments, annual debt service, mortgage constant, remaining balance, payment to principal, payment to interest, accumulated principle, and accumulated interest for each year. A general amortization program could solve for these additional factors: the number of payments, the number of payments to reach a certain balance, payment amount, annual percentage rate, and principal amount.

Special programs could calculate the above values for wraparound mortgages and determine the price and yield of discounted mortgages.

```
00100    REM MORTGAGE SCHEDULE CALCULATION
00110    REM BASED ON MONTHLY PAYMENT
00120    DIM A(3), B(3)
00130    B$="##      $#####.##        $#####.##
         $#####.##    $#####.##"
00140    INPUT "ENTER THE NUMBER OF YEARS OF
         THE MORTGAGE";X
00150    INPUT "ENTER THE YEARLY INTEREST
         RATE"; X1
00160    INPUT "ENTER THE AMOUNT OF THE MORT/
         GAGE";B
00170    B1=12*X
00180    X1=X1/1200
00190    B2=B*X1/(1−(1/(1+X1))⬆B1)
00200    T=0
00210    B(2) =0: B(1) =0: B3=B2*B1−B: A(2)=0:
         A(3)=B: A(1)=0
```

```
00220    PRINT USING "MONTHLY PAYMENT IS
         ###.##";B2
00230    PRINT
00240    PRINT "YEAR  PRINCIPAL PAID  PRINCIPAL
         LEFT  INTEREST PAID   TOTAL PAID"
00250    FOR I=1 TO X
00260    FOR J=1 TO 12
00270    T=T+B2
00280    B(1)=A(3)*X1
00290    A(1)=B2-B(1)
00300    A(2)=A (2) + A(1)
00310    A(3)=A(3)-A(1)
00320    B(2)=B(2)+B(1)
00330    B(3)=B(3)-B(1)
00340    NEXT J
00350    PRINT USING B$; I, A(2), A(3), B(2), T
00360    NEXT I
00370    PRINT
00380    END
```

A loan program amortization schedule as well as time required for loan payment may be calculated by the following program:

LOAN AMORTIZATION SCHEDULE

PRINCIPAL= $4800.00
# OF PERIODS= 12
INTEREST RATE= 5.6%

PAYMENT NUMBER	REMAINING PRINCIPAL	MONTHLY PAYMENT	PRINCIPAL PAYMENT	INTEREST PAYMENT
1	4410.16	412.24	389.84	22.40
2	4018.51	412.24	391.66	20.58
3	3625.02	412.24	393.48	18.75
4	3229.70	412.24	395.32	16.92
5	2832.54	412.24	397.16	15.07
6	2433.52	412.24	399.02	13.22
7	2032.64	412.24	400.88	11.36
8	1629.89	412.24	402.75	9.49
9	1225.26	412.24	404.63	7.61
10	818.74	412.24	406.52	5.72
11	410.32	412.24	408.42	3.82
12	0.00	412.24	410.32	1.91
OVERALL TOTALS		$4946.84	$4800.00	$146.84

```
10    REM LOAN AMORTIZATION CALCULATOR
20    CLS ' CLEAR SCREEN
30    PRINT"LOANS" :PRINT
40    PRINT "SELECT: 1) PAYMENT AMOUNT CALCU-
      LATION"
50    INPUT" 2) TIME OF PAYMENT CALCULATION"; A
60    ON A GOTO 70,2000
65    GOTO 40
70    INPUT "ENTER THE AMOUNT OF THE LOAN";
      AM
80    INPUT "ENTER THE NUMBER OF PAYMENTS
      (YRS. * 12 USUALLY)";N
90    INPUT "ENTER THE ANNUAL INTEREST RATE";I
100   B=I/1200
110   C=N
120   INPUT "ENTER THE MONTH OF THE FIRST
      PAYMENT (1-12)";M
130   INPUT "ENTER THE YEAR OF THE FIRST PAY-
      MENT";Y
140   D=1: FOR X=1 TO C
150   D=(1 + B)* D
160   NEXT X
170   D=1/D: F=B/(1−D)*AM
180   G=F:   GOSUB 5000
190   F=G
200   H = Y: J = 1: L = AM: K = M − 1: E = 0: P = 0
210   CLS ' CLEAR SCREEN
220   PRINT "AMORTIZATION TABLE"
230   PRINT "MONTHLY PAYMENT: $";F
240   PRINT "AMOUNT OF LOAN: $"; TAB(14); AM;
      TAB(24); "INTEREST RATE="; I;
260   IF S=0 THEN PRINT: GOTO 280
270    PRINT "TERM+"; TAB(51); N; TAB (55);
      "MONTHS"
280   PRINT "NO.";
290   PRINTTAB (8); "DATE"; TAB (19); "INTEREST";
      TAB(33); "PRINCIPAL"; TAB(50) "BALANCE"
300   FOR X=J TO J+9
310   K=K+1
320   IF K=13 THEN K=1: H=H+1
330   A2=L*B: G=A2
340   GOSUB 5000
350   A2=G: S=F−A2: G=S
```

```
360   GOSUB 5000
370   S=G
380   L=L−S: G= L
390   GOSUB 5000
400   L=G: P=A2+P: E=S+E
410   PRINT J; TAB (6); K; "−"; H; TAB (19); A2; TAB
      (33); S; TAB (49); L
420   IF J=C−1 THEN 600
430   J=J+ 1
440   NEXT X
450   G=P
460   GOSUB 5000
470   P=G
480   PRINT "TOTAL INTEREST TO DATE $"; P;"
      TOTAL PRINCIPAL TO DATE $";E
490   INPUT "TYPE ENTER TO SEE NEXT PAGE"; A1
500   GOTO 210
600   A2=B*L
610   G=A2: GOSUB 5000
620   A2=G: S=L: A3=F: F=S+A2: K=K+ 1
630   IF K=12 THEN K= 1: H=H+1
640   L=L−S: J=J+1: E=S+E: P=P+A2
650   PRINT J; TAB (6); K; "-"; TAB(19); A2; TAB (33); S;
      TAB(49);L
660   PRINT "TOTAL INTEREST TO DATE= $";P
670   PRINT "TOTAL PRINCIPAL TO DATE = $"; E
680   PRINT "FINAL PAYMENT= $";F
690   G=F: GOSUB 5000
700   F=G: F=A3
710   INPUT "TYPE ENTER WHEN READY"; A4
720   GOTO 30
2000  CLS ' clear screen
2010  INPUT "ENTER THE AMOUNT BORROWED";
      B1
2020  INPUT "ENTER THE INTEREST RATE/YR.";B2
2030  INPUT "ENTER THE MONTHLY PAYMENT";E
2040  INPUT "ENTER THE MONTH PAYMENTS
      BEGIN (1-12)";M
2050  INPUT "ENTER THE YEAR OF THE BEGINNING
      PAYMENT";Y
2060  B3=B1*B2/1200−E
2070  IF B3<=0 THEN 2130
```

```
2080    PRINT: PRINT: PRINT: PRINT
2090     PRINT " THE MINIMUM PAYMENT  =  $";
         B1*B2/1200
2100    GOTO 2010
2130    B=1-B2/1200*B1/E
2140    X=B: GOSUB 4000
2150    B=R
2160    F=1+B2/1200
2170    X=F: GOSUB 4000
2180    F=R
2190    J=-(B/F)
2200    PRINT
2210    IF B3=0 THEN PRINT "PAYMENTS COVER IN-
         TEREST ONLY": GOTO 2230
2220    PRINT "NO. OF MONTHS FOR PAYMENTS =";J
2230    H=INT (J/12): N=J-H*12
2240    IF N>1 THEN N=N+ 1
2250    N=INT (N): C=12*H+N
2260    IF N>11 THEN H=H+ 1: N=N-12
2270    IF B3=0 THEN S=0: GOTO 2290
2280    PRINT "="; H; "YEARS +  ";N; "MONTHS TO PAY
         LOAN"
2290    PRINT: PRINT: PRINT
2300    INPUT "TYPE ENTER TO CONTINUE"; A$
2310    J=N:  B=B2/1200:  F=E:  N=N+12*H:  AM=B1:
         R=B2
2320    F=F/B3
2325    F=E: I=B2
2330    GOTO 180
4000    AM=(X-1)/(X+1)
4010    C=AM*AM*AM
4020    R=2*(AM+1/3*C+1/5*AM*AM*C+1/7*C*C*AM
         +1/9*C*C*C+1/11*C*C*C*AM*AM)
4030    RETURN
5000    G=INT ( (G-INT (G) )*100+.50001)/100+INT (G)
5010    RETURN
```

Loans

Installment loans—Given the amount borrowed, add-on interest rate, payment amount for each period, service charge, and insurance, if any, a program could calculate the finance charge, the amount financed, the contract term, and APR.

Direct reduction loan—The payment, present value, or number of time periods for a direct reduction loan may be calculated given two of the three and the interest rate:

$$PMT = PV \frac{i}{1 - (1 + i)^{-n}}$$

$$PV = PMT \frac{1 - (1 + i)^{-n}}{i}$$

$$N = \frac{\ln (1 - iPV/PMT)}{\ln (1 + i)}$$

where n= number of payment periods
PV=the present value or principal
PMT=the payment
i=the periodic interest rate expressed in decimal form

Depreciation Calculations

Standard, composite, and excess depreciations may be calculated with the following methods:

Straight line depreciation
$$D = PV/n$$
$$B_k = PV - kD$$

Sum-of-the-years-digits depreciation

$$B_k = \frac{S + (n-k)D_k}{2} \qquad D_k = \frac{2(n - k + 1)PV}{n(n + 1)}$$

Variable rate declining balance depreciation

$$D_k = PV \frac{R}{n} (1 - R/n)^{k-1}$$
$$B_k = PV (1 - R/n)^k$$

In each of the above depreciation formulas,
PV=original value of asset (less salvage value)
n=lifetime number of periods of asset
B_k=book value at time period K
D=each year's depreciation
k=the number of the time period (eg. 1, 2, 3...n)
S=salvage value
R=depreciation rate
D_k=depreciation at time period k

71

```
10   REM DEPRECIATION METHOD COMPARISON
20   INPUT"ENTER PURCHASE COST";C
30   INPUT"ENTER LIFE IN YEARS";L
40   INPUT"ENTER SCRAP VALUE";S
50   A$="  ##        $#####. ##       $#####. ##
          $#####. ##"
60   B=C-S:D1=B/L:M=((L+1)/2)*L:F=L
65   PRINT"YEAR NO.","STRAIGHT LINE", "DOUBLE
     DECL.","SUM OF DIGITS"
70   FORX=1 TO L:D2=B*(F/M):F=F-1
80   D3=2*C/L:C=C-D3
90   PRINTUSINGA$;X,D1,D3,D2:NEXT X
```

SAMPLE RUN:
ENTER PURCHASE COST? 5500
ENTER LIFE IN YEARS? 4
ENTER SCRAP VALUE? 500

YEAR NO.	STRAIGHT LINE	DOUBLE DECL.	SUM OF DIGITS
1	$ 1250.00	$ 2750.00	$ 2000.00
2	$ 1250.00	$ 1375.00	$ 1500.00
3	$ 1250.00	$ 687.50	$ 1000.00
4	$ 1250.00	$ 343.75	$ 500.00

Annuities

Given the required variables as input data, an annuity program could calculate the remaining variable in any of the following situations:

Sinking fund—A sinking fund is an annuity where a future value is accumulated by equal payments at equal intervals at a certain interest rate. The equation below answers questions such as "If I wish to accumulate a future value of $200,000 in a bank account which pays 6.5% interest, and I will make payments for forty years, what will the monthly payments be?"

$$FV = PMT * \frac{(1 + n)^n - 1}{i}$$

Annuity due—Calculate the future or present value. Use to answer a question such as "If I borrow $40,000 at 9.5% interest with monthly payments for thirty years, what will the payments be with an annuity due loan?"

Ordinary annuity—May or may not include a balloon payment. Use to answer questions such as "If I borrow $20,000 from a bank for twenty-five years at 9.75% interest with monthly payments, what will those payments be each month;" answer is $178.23 computed with the second formula below.

$$PV = PMT * \frac{1-(1-i)^{-n}}{i}$$

$$PMT = PV * \frac{i}{1-(1+i)^{-n}}$$

$$n = \frac{\ln(1-PV(i/PMT))}{\ln(1+i)}$$

In the above annuity equations,
   PV=present value
PMT=payment per period
   n=number of periods
   i=periodic interest rate (expressed as decimal)
FV=future value

Curve fit—A program to fit such data as land prices or construction cost per square foot, to a curve may be used to make more accurate forecasts, bids, and estimates.

Internal rate of return and cash flows—One purpose of an internal rate of return and cash flow program would be to calculate the net present value of a series of cash flows. In general, an investment, V_0, is made in some enterprise which is expected to bring periodic cash flows C_1, C_2...C_n. Given a discount rate, i, the program will compute for each cash flow the net present value at period k, NPV_k. A negative value for NPV_k indicates that the enterprise has not been profitable. A positive value for NPV_k indicates that the enterprise has been profitable to the extent that a rate of return, i, on the original investment has been exceeded.

$$NPV_k = -V_0 + \sum_{j=1}^{k} \frac{C_j}{(1+i)^j}$$

Portfolio selection and bookkeeping—Using Sharpe's or some other method, the proportion of funds that should be allocated to each security in a portfolio to maximize returns. Calculations would be based on historical stock indicators and an acceptable level or risk. A portfolio bookkeeping program could evaluate the historical profitability of a given portfolio, as well as realized gains for income tax purposes.

Bond and warrant valuations—A useful, simple program could be written to determine the value of both short and long term warrants. Given present value, coupon interest, yield to maturity, maturity value, or number of periods (three values out of the four), the remaining term may be found by a computer program. Taxes, commissions, and current yield could also be determined. The formula used to calculate the present value (cost) of a bond with annual coupons is as follows:

$$\text{Price} = \left[\frac{1 - (1 + i/c)^{-n}}{i/c} \ _{(1000 \ Cr/2)} \right]$$
$$+ [(1+i/c)^{-n}(1000)]$$

where i=discount rate as %
    n = no. of years to maturity multiplied by 2
   Cr = coupon rate of bond
    c = no. compounding periods per year

The formula used to calculate the bond yield of an annual coupon is as follows:

$$j = \frac{\dfrac{Fg - (B.V.)_1 - (B.V.)_n}{n}}{\dfrac{(B.V.)_1 + (B.V.)_n}{2}}$$

where j = nominal yield rate
  (B.V.)_1 = original bond value
  (B.V.)_n = bond value at n years
     F = face value
     g = nominal dividend rate
     n = no. years

Capital accumulation planning—The present and future net worth of an individual or business based on current or historic worth, rate of investment, and rate of investment return may be calculated.

Residential purchase analysis—A useful program could calculate the total monthly payment, the income tax deductions, and the equity buildup resulting from the purchase of a given home.

Convertable security analysis—Given a securities' price, coupon/discount rate, common stock price, common dividend and common shares per convertable, a handy program could compute the indicated convertable price, anticipated stock price, conversion premium percentage, current convertable yield, and incremental payout return.

Savings and checking account bookkeeping—A checking account reconciliation program could keep track of all checks written, including such information as the amount paid, purpose, number, amount, category, and other remarks. An itemized listing could be outputted for tax review purposes or for checking open accounts.

```
00050  REM DAILY INTEREST PASSBOOK SAVINGS
       COMPUTATION
00110  REM ENTER DEPOSITS AS POSITIVE NUM-
       BERS, DEDUCTIONS AS NEGATIVE NOS.
00120  REM ENTER 0 AT THE FINAL DATE TO COM-
       PUTE THE INTEREST
00130  CLS 'CLEAR SCREEN
00140  INPUT "ENTER THE ANNUAL INTEREST IN
       PERCENT"; F
00150  E = F/36000
00160  INPUT "SELECT: 1) USE ACTUAL DAYS IN
       MONTH 2) USE 30 DAYS FOR MONTH"; D
00170  G = 0
00180  INPUT "ENTER THE STARTING DATE NUM-
       ERICALLY AS MONTH, DAY"; A, B
00190  INPUT "ENTER THE STARTING BALANCE"; C
00200  IF D = 1 THEN INPUT "IS THIS A LEAP YEAR (1
       = YES, 2 = NO)"; H: GOSUB 1000: ELSE GOSUB
       500
00210  J = K: PRINT
00220  PRINT "#    DATE   WITHDRAWAL DEPOSIT
       BALANCE      INTEREST"
```

```
00230    PRINT K; A; ","; B; TAB (32); C
00240    INPUT "ENTER MONTH, DAY, AMOUNT:"; A,
         B, L
00250    IF D = 2 THEN GOSUB 500 ELSE GOSUB 1000
00260    GOTO 700
00500    M = B
00510    IF (A = 2) OR (A = 4) OR (A = 6) OR (A = 9) OR (A
         = 11) THEN 520 ELSE 600
00520    IF A = 2 THEN IF B = 28 INPUT "IS THIS A LEAP
         YEAR (1 = YES, 2 = NO)"; N: IF N = 1 THEN
         RETURN: ELSE 590
00530    IF B > 27 THEN B = 31
00590    IF B = 30 THEN B = 31
00600    K = B + (A − 1)*30
00610    RETURN
00700    O = K
00710    IF J = K THEN 750
00720    FOR P = J TO K − 1
00730    G = G + G*E + C*E
00740    NEXT P
00750    C = C + L
00760    G = (INT ( (G − INT (G) )*100 + .5001) )/100 +
         INT (G)
00770    PRINT K; A; ","; M;
00780    IF L < 0 THEN PRINT TAB (13); L;: GOTO 00790
00785    PRINT TAB (24); L;
00790    PRINT TAB (24); C;
00800    PRINT TAB (44); G
00810    J = O
00820    GOTO 240
01000    ON A GOTO 1010, 1020, 1030, 1040, 1050, 1060,
         1070, 1080, 1090, 1110, 1120, 1130
01010    K = B: GOTO 1140
01020    K = B + 31: GOTO 1140
01030    K = B + N + 59: GOTO 1140
01040    K = B + N + 90: GOTO 1140
01050    K = B + N + 120: GOTO 1140
01060    K = B + N + 151: GOTO 1140
01070    K = B + N + 181: GOTO 1140
01080    K = B + N + 212: GOTO 1140
01090    K = B + N + 243: GOTO 1140
01110    K = B + N + 273: GOTO 1140
```

```
01120  K = B + N + 304: GOTO 1140
01130  K = B + N + 334: GOTO 1140
01140  M = B: RETURN
```

MONEY-MAKING APPLICATIONS

Many applications exist for making money from small computers; you might consider starting a side-line or full-time business based on one of the following ideas.

Stock Market

One "hobbyist" is making a substantial amount of money from his stock prediction newsletter which is composed of market predictions determined with "twelve confidential indicators" on his home computer. The hobbyist who discovers a consistent method of predicting the stock market fluctuations stands to earn a substantial amount of money. Using statistical techniques, it should be possible to input to the computer various financial indicators in an attempt to discover trends or equations that may be used to predict future outcomes.

An oversimplified, but often useful method of forecasting the effect of a given inflation rate on the stock market is as follows. First, the assumption is made that the cost of money is constant at three percent. Added to this value will be a one-percent constant which will be assumed to be the risk factor for owning stocks instead of bonds. To this sum add the current inflation rate. Divide this final sum into 100, the result being the average stock market multiple of earnings. Now, multiply this result by the sum of the estimated yearly earnings of the thirty Dow Jones Industrial stocks. If the sum of the estimated earnings is not known, a simple computer program could determine earnings for the industrial stocks from the newspaper listings of price and price/earnings ratios (earnings=price/price-earnings ratio); a method of determining future earnings growth would have to be employed. The final product calculated is a projected Dow Jones industrial stock average.

The calculations would be as follows, assuming an inflation rate of five percent and estimated Dow industrial stock earnings of $110:

$$\frac{100}{(3\% + 1\% + 5\%)} \cdot 110. = 1222.$$

Evaluation of the options market is an excellent personal computer application. Calculation of return on an investment, cash flow, and total impact for each transaction is useful. Using the strategy of selling options against stocks bought, the computer can advise the most profitable buy and sell times; a chart of all possibilities could also be generated.

Services

Mailing lists—A mailing list of people in your area could be used by local firms with direct mail campaigns. The mailing list could be compiled from area phone books, association directories, etc. and inputted for permanent storage on your computer. The list may be printed on adhesive labels and sold to local businesses. The advantage of being a local business serves to eliminate competition from large mailing list brokers in other cities.

Resumes—All metropolitan areas can use a resume preparation service to write, type, and mail resumes to potential employers. A computer word-processing system could automate this business almost entirely.

Typesetting, indexing, editing—All businesses and organizations can use a printing preparation enterprise for typesetting and editing promotional material. Small computers interfaced to IBM composer or executive typewriters, DIABLO proportional printers, or laser printers can produce excellent justified and "camera-ready" material for printing. The cost savings of using a computer will allow the entrepreneur to offer lower prices for such services. Additionally, an indexing service using a simple computer program to create book or magazine indexes could find employment by small publishing firms.

Home swap and rental locator services—The practice of "swapping" one's home with other people during vacation time is becoming popular. A service to categorize homes available and homes wanted with the use of the computer could profit from publishing a newsletter of listings. A rental locator service categorizes homes and apartments for rent from classified newspaper ads or other sources. In metropolitan areas, where finding a home to rent is a difficult task, a service to match people with the right living conditions at the right price would do well monetarily. In a similar manner, a service company could match people with cars for sale by the owners.

Finder's fees—A "finder's fee" is a sum of money paid to someone who finds something wanted by another person who is willing to offer an award for it. Usually, finder's fees are expressed as a percentage of the amount of money involved in purchasing the item to be found. A few organizations publish newsletters listing finder's fee opportunities. A hobbyist could computerize hundreds of listings for future reference.

Telephone answering message service and newspaper clipping service—Telephone answering services of sufficient size can use a small computer to increase efficiency and lower costs. A newspaper clipping service, which clips articles of interest to paying clients, could use a computer to keep track of the varied categories to search for.

Computer dating service—Popular a few years ago, computer dating services could make a return appearance, especially in metropolitan areas.

Sports predictions—An enterprising hobbyist uses his computer to predict college football scores. The information produced is sold as "CLYDE the computer" sports forecasts to television stations for use on local news broadcasts. Other entrepeneurs have used computer predictions of sporting events to publish flyers which are sold at dog and horse races.

Employment agency—The computer could be useful to an employment agency in matching the right people with the right jobs. The use of the computer may also serve to increase business.

Business analysis and bookkeeping—A hobbyist who developed a business accounting system with software at a reasonable price has made a substantial amount of money. Similarly, accounting services done on one's own computer may be sold to small businesses. Other services include: PERT analysis (used to create complicated schedules), analysis of placement modules (used to optimize productivity), and linear programming services.

Collection service—A word-processing computer system could output personalized collection letters automatically. Thus, a low-cost collection service charging a flat rate or percentage of the money collected would be an excellent side-line business for the computer hobbyist.

Word Processing—A word-processing service is employed by businesses to prepare typewritten, personalized sales letters. Such a business would be almost totally automated by a small computer.

Bowling league bookkeeping—A few hobbyists have side-line businesses to calculate bowling league scores and handicaps for ten to thirty cents per player per week. This cost is usually less than present costs for hiring a person to do the bookkeeping.

Personalized Books

Children's books containing a child's name, address, and other personalized information can be printed by a small computer economically. Studies show that children prefer reading personalized books over any other type of book, and there is a considerable demand for them. An enterprising hobbyist could develop a large-scale business along these lines. Perhaps a humorous personalized book could be sold for adults as well.

Educational Programs

One enterprise that has a definite potential is a service to distribute educational computer materials to schools and other institutions. The hobbyist market for educational computer program is also growing. Popular tutorials could be developed concerning electronics, higher mathematics, business and investments, and computers.

Computer Cash Register and Bookkeeping System

Small stores are in the market for a small computerized "cash-register" (actually a video terminal) system. Using such a system, each item number would be entered as the item is purchased. The price and total cumulative purchase would be automatically calculated and displayed. An inventory listing would be updated simultaneously.

REAL ESTATE

Possible applications for personal computers in real estate include the following:

Residential purchase analysis—A useful program could calculate the total monthly payment, income tax deductions, and equity build-up resulting from the purchase of a home.

Replacement value of a home—The worth of a home for a given year may be calculated based on the date built and the purchase price.

Multi-family land use evaluation—Inputs to this program are local zoning restrictions, land dimensions or size, and estimated cost per square foot. Outputs could include the number of family dwelling units allowed, parking space requirements, percentage land coverage by building, total land coverage, and total estimated building cost.

General real estate investment analysis—With such factors as inflation, interest rates, mortgages, cash flow in percent growth return, taxable income (tax shelter), and financial feasibility may be calculated. Income property and closing statements may also be generated.

PROGRAM—REAL ESTATE EVALUATION

The following program is designed for use by a potential investor in evaluting a piece of real estate, preferably an apartment building. The program estimates the total monthly income, annual rate of return, and tax-deductions based on such input data as cost, down payment on mortgage, estimated overhead costs and income.

Sample run:

ENTER THE PURCHASE PRICE OF THE REAL ESTATE? 75000
ENTER THE MORTGAGE INTEREST (%) ? 9.75
ENTER THE MORTGAGE DOWN PAYMENT AS A % OF PURCHASE COST? 10
ENTER THE NUMBER OF YEARS IN THE LOAN TERM? 25
ENTER THE CLOSING COST (% OF PURCHASE PRICE)? 2
ENTER MISCELLANEOUS INITIAL EXPENSES AS ONE SUM? 100
ENTER THE ESTIMATED INCOME PER MONTH FROM THE PROPERTY? 1125
ENTER THE REAL ESTATE TAX FOR ONE YEAR? 1300
ENTER THE ESTIMATED OVERHEAD COSTS (MAINT., UTILITIES, INSUR., ETC.)? 525

FOR TAX DEDUCTION PURPOSES, ENTER THE EST.
    PROPERTY VALUE? 15000
ENTER YOUR TAX BRACKET AS A % OF YOUR IN-
    COME? 40
IS THE BUILDING ON THE PROPERTY NEW OR USED
    ("N" OR "U")? N

TAX AND CASH FLOW ANALYSIS:

MONTHLY EXPENSES $525.00
MONTHLY TAXES $108.33
MONTHLY MORTGAGE $601.52
MONTHLY INCOME $1125.00

MONTHLY CASH FLOW $109.85–

TAX HEDGE:

EXPENSES (YR. #1) $7650.00
DEPRECIATION (YR. #1) $6000.00
DEDUCTABLE INTEREST $6581.25
REAL ESTATE TAX (YEARLY) $1300.00

TOTAL: (YR. #) $21531.30
TOTAL INCOME (YR. #1) $13500.00
NET DEDUCTION (YR. #) $8031.25
TAX ADVANTAGE (YR. #1) $3212.50

RETURN ON INVESTMENT   18%

```
10   REM REAL ESTATE PURCHASE EVALUATION
     PROGRAM
20   REM DETERMINES TAX ADVANTAGE AND CASH
     FLOW OF
30   REM A PROSPECTIVE PURCHASE
40   INPUT "ENTER THE PURCHASE PRICE OF THE
     REAL ESTATE"; A
50   INPUT "ENTER MORTGAGE INTEREST (%)"; B
55   INPUT "ENTER MORTGAGE DOWN PAYMENT AS
     A % OF PURCHASE COST"; C
60   B = B/100: C = C/100
70   INPUT "ENTER NUMBER OF YEARS IN THE LOAN
     TERM"; D
```

```
80   INPUT "ENTER THE CLOSING COST (% OF
     PURCHASE PRICE)"; E
90   E = E/100
100  INPUT "ENTER MISCELLANEOUS INITIAL EX-
     PENSES AS ONE SUM"; G
110  INPUT "ENTER THE ESTIMATED INCOME PER
     MONTH FROM THE PROPERTY"; J
120  INPUT "ENTER THE REAL ESTATE TAX FOR
     ONE YEAR"; K
130  INPUT "ENTER THE EST. OVERHEAD COSTS
     (MAINT., UTILITIES, INSUR., ETC.)"; L
132  INPUT "FOR TAX DEDUCTION PURPOSES,
     ENTER THE EST. PROPERTY VALUE"; M
134  INPUT "ENTER YOUR TAX BRACKET AS A % OF
     YOUR INCOME"; R7
136  C$ = " **$##,###.##—"
138  INPUT "IS THE BUILDING ON THE PROPERTY
     NEW OR USED ("N" OR "U")"; B$
140  X = B/12 + 1
150  Y = X↑(12*D)*(X − 1)/(X↑(12*D) − 1)*(A − C*A)
160  N = L + K/12 + Y
170  P = (A − C*A)*B
180  IF B$ = "N" THEN Q = 2 ELSE Q = 1.25
190  R = L + E*(A − C*A)/12
200  R1 = (A − M)/20*Q
210  R2 = K + R1 + P + 12*R − 12*J
220  R3 = R7/100*R2
230  R4 = G + E*A + C*A − 12*(J − N)
240  R5 = INT (100*( (J − N)*12 + R3)/R4)
260  PRINT "TAX AND CASH FLOW ANALYSIS:"
270  PRINT "MONTHLY EXPENSES    ";
280  PRINTUSING C$; L
290  PRINT "MONTHLY TAXES    ";
300  PRINTUSING C$; K/12
310  PRINT "MONTHLY MORTGAGE    ";
320  PRINTUSING C$; Y
330  PRINT "MONTHLY INCOME    ";
340  PRINTUSING C$; J
350  PRINT "MONTHLY CASH FLOW    ";
360  PRINTUSING C$; J-N
370  PRINT: PRINT
380  PRINT "TAX HEDGE:"
```

```
390    PRINT "EXPENSES (YR. #1)   ";
400    PRINTUSING C$; 12*R
410    PRINT "DEPRECIATION (YR. #1)   ";
420    PRINTUSING C$; R1
430    PRINT "DEDUCTABLE INTEREST (YR. #1)   ";
440    PRINTUSING C$; P
450    PRINT "REAL ESTATE TAX (YEARLY)   ";
460    PRINTUSING C$; K
470    PRINT: PRINT "TOTAL: (YR. # 1)   ";
480    PRINTUSING C$; K + P + R1 + R*12
490    PRINT "TOTAL INCOME (YR. #1)   ";
500    PRINTUSING C$; J*12
510    PRINT "NET DEDUCTION (YR. #1)   ";
520    PRINTUSING C$; R2
530    PRINT "TAX ADVANTAGE (YR. #1)   ";
540    PRINTUSING C$; R3
550    PRINT: PRINT "RETURN ON INVESTMENT";
560    PRINT R5; "%"
570    PRINT: PRINT: END
```

BUSINESS DECISION MAKING

Long and short term financing requirements—A long term financing requirement calculation program could compute the cost of capital for various forms of funding common stocks, preferred stocks, bonds, etc.), select the cheapest form, and determine the amount needed to support operating plans. A short-term financing requirement calculation program could compute the amount and timing of short term financing based on sales forecasts, inventory purchases, collection, and payment policies.

Planning and budgeting computations in the following areas could be applied to monthly, quarterly, or annual operating projections:

Breakeven analysis—Compute breakeven points for projects or products based on fixed and variable costs and selling prices; learning curves may also be applied.

Economic reordering and production runs—Compute economic reorder or production quantities by minimizing the sum of ordering, production, and carrying costs; resource projection could also be incorporated in such a program.

Reorder timing—Compute the reorder point based on inventory carrying costs, stockout costs, and demand variation.

Facility scheduling—Compute job shop performance (average turn-around time, percent late, etc.) based on a variety of scheduling rules (first in-first out, most over-due items first, etc.) and on job processing times.

Demand forecasting—Compute a forecast of future demand by exponentially smoothing past demand.

Queing theory computations—(facility capacity determination).

Market and media research—(including questionnaire analysis)

Job cost estimation—(for service and contracting companies)

Purchasing—a program to analyze vendors (order-filling speed, previous complaints, etc.) to select the best over-all would be quite useful.

Modeling—a mathematical model of a companies' earnings, sales, etc. should incorporate the following features for analysis on a computer:

- Data analysis—The ability to input historical data and manipulate it into a forecast suitable for analysis by the model.
- Parametric analysis—The ability to vary a set of input values systematically and observe the effect on the outcomes.
- Sensitivity analysis—The ability to determine the relative effect of changes in the input variables on the outcomes.
- Breakeven analysis—The ability to find the value of an input variable that yields a desired outcome.
- Risk analysis—The ability to determine the effect on outcomes of randomness in the input variables.
- Optimization—The ability to find particular values for the input variables to yield the best outcomes.

GENERAL BUSINESS
CALCULATIONS AND BUSINESS SYSTEMS

Accounts receivable—Prepare aged trial balances, monthly statements, follow-up sales and collection letters, and provide on-line account status inquiry handling.

Order processing—Allow for order editing, freight cost computation, credit checks, stock availability checks, and order status checks. A billing/invoicing calculation program could provide the following information: net total, total tax, total tax plus freight, total profit, percent of net profit, total value of back-ordered items, total discount amount, total gross amount, and total cost amount.

Sales—Prepare a breakdown of sales volume and profitability by product, customer, or salesman.

General accounting—General accounting functions include: cost record keeping, budgeting, daily exception record, and profit and loss statements.

Mailing list up-keeping—Names may be selected for special promotions.

Payroll—A complete payroll calculation program would include the following features: time-card hours computation, check writing, and provisions for commissions, bonuses, piecework salaries, incentives. W-2 forms and payroll summaries could also be outputted.

Inventory—A complete inventory management program should be able to output the following reports: detailed inventory, inventory status, on-order, order exception, analysis by cost, list for use in physical inventory, period to data, year to data, minimum quantity search, inventory projections. The following file update functions should also be provided: place an order, cancel an order, add a new inventory item, delete an existing inventory item, initial a new period or year.

Contract preparation—A word-processing system could print personalized contract forms, and cost estimation could be done as well.

General business calculations—The following mathematical calculations for business uses are best done by a small computer: selling price from cost and gross profit prorating, unit price comparisons, order quantity for optimum price break, moving average, seasonal average, cyclical analysis, auto covariance, cross covariance, exponential smoothing, histogram generation, probability calculations, worse-case analysis, universal rate of return, summation of ledger columns, target return calculations, optimum mark-up/mark-down, net present value, choice between debt and equity, lease vs. buy determinations, funds statement preparation, capital structure determination, perpetual sales quantity, gross sales revenue, bid preparation.

economic order quantity $= \sqrt{\dfrac{2\,RS}{C}}$

> where R = annual no. units required
> S = set up costs per order
> C = inventory cost to carry 1 unit 1 year

INCOME TAX

Preparation of income tax forms is a task that lends itself well to computers. Tax preparation programs range from simple arithmatic calculation to a complete personal accountant program. In the most popular approach, the computer requests answers to such questions as, "What are your federal withholding taxes?". One proceeds to answer all the possible questions necessary to prepare a 1040 tax form (approximately 50), but unfortunately one must do considerable calculation to answer some of the questions. The program completes the simple arithmetic for filling in the 1040 form and prints the proper values in the boxes on the form.

A more complex approach would involve the periodic storage of all elements of your finances on cassette or floppy disk (e.g. each week store the names, addresses, purposes, numbers, and amounts of all checks written or cashed). At years end, the computer would search and group all relevant data and do all of the necessary calculations. In this latter approach, a complete summary of all deductions, income, etc. could be printed categorically. References could be included to the filed location of the original checks, bills, etc. for proof of the transactions. A warning could also be issued in the event that your deductions exceed ten percent of your income (a tax audit would be likely). Provisions could be made to calculate the comparative taxes to be payed if filling jointly with your spouse or singly.

SALES DEVICE

The small computer may be used as a sales device in several ways. Now that telephone dialing interfaces are available, one may use the computer to call every possible telephone number in an exchange and deliver a tape-recorded sales message to anyone who answers. At expositions, or in retail sales outlets, a computer with video display can continually list sales information. Question answering capabilities could also be provided.

Use of the computer as a customer advisor can increase sales traffic as well. For example, a garden supply shop could provide customers with access to a computer programmed to answer questions about specific plants (e.g. growing season and nutrient requirements), amount and type of fertilizer for a certain size lawn and type of grass, and possibly output a complete garden plan. A wine shop computer could advise the type wine to accompany a given meal, the glass and temperature to use, and comparitive prices of wines. The make-up department of a store could use the computer to suggest brand-name make-up to use in achieving a certain complexion.

A swimming pool maintenance company advertises that it offers a free computer analysis of anyone's swimming pool water. From water samples the computer analyzes the type and amount of chemicals necessary to maintain a specific pool; these chemicals are then sold to the pool owner.

MAINTENANCE OF ORGANIZATION RECORDS

Clubs and other organizations may find it worthwhile to purchase or use a member's small computer to ease paperwork. Anyone who develops software for this application may be able to sell it to local organizations or charge for computing services done on his own computer.

TABULATOR

A simple program could transform your computer into a tabulator, adding machine, or simple calculator for bookkeeping purposes (e.g. the decimal place may be set and calculations are done in the same manner). The advantage of using a computer in this application is that the output of figures may be formatted in any desired manner, and all information may be stored for future reference on cassette or floppy disk. Perhaps an entire bookkeeping form could be filled out by the computer printer. Additionally, special calculations not available on adding machines may be performed automatically (e.g. delta percentages and interest calculations).

CALCULATE REFERENCE TABLES

Any mathematical function may be expressed as a table of values corresponding to the factors in the equation. Businessmen who need to calculate the value of a particular function could produce a table listing values at specified intervals, for easy reference. For example, a portion of a chart used in converting British pounds to American dollars is reproduced here:

						CENTS				
		.00	.10	.20	.30	.40	.50	.60	.70	.80	.90
DOLLARS	1	1.90	2.09	2.28	2.47	2.66	2.85	3.04	3.23	3.42	3.61
	2	3.80	3.99	4.18	4.37	4.56	4.75	4.94	5.13	5.32	5.51
	3	5.70	5.89	6.08	6.27	6.46	6.65	6.84	7.03	7.22	7.41
	4	7.60	7.79	7.98	8.17	8.36	8.55	8.74	8.99	9.12	9.31

The conversion rate for this chart is 1.9 dollars per pound. As an example, the number of dollars equivalent to 4.90 pounds is 9.31. The BASIC program used to print the chart is listed here:

```
 5   A$ = "# #.# #"
10   A = 1.9
15   PRINT ".00 .10 .20 .30 .40 .50 .60 .70 .80 .90"
20   FOR X = 1 TO 10
25   PRINT X;
30   FOR B = 0 TO 1 STEP .1
35   PRINT USING A$; A*(X + B);
40   NEXT B
50   PRINT
60   NEXT X
70   END
```

Your computer can save much time by computing and outputting such tables as:

- stock commissions
- values of an investment or savings account at certain periods of time
- unit prices after certain quantity purchases
- break-even values for various prices and sales of a product
- UPS/USPS postal rates to various cities for various weights

CALCULATION OF THE NUMBER
OF DAYS BETWEEN TWO DATES

Businessmen often need to know how much time (usually in terms of days) there is between two given dates. A program which stores the number of days in each month could serve to calculate this value. Additionally, time conversions between seconds, minutes, hours, days, weeks, months, and years may be performed.

```
00010    REM DAYS BETWEEN TWO DATES CALCU-
         LATION (IN SAME YEAR)
00020    DIM M (12)
00030    FOR X = 1 TO 12
00040    READ M (X)
00050    NEXT X
00060    PRINT "IS THIS A LEAP YEAR 1 = YES, 2 = NO";
00070    INPUT A
00080    IF A = 1 THEN M(2) = 28
00090    PRINT "INPUT THE FIRST DATE NUMERI-
         CALLY IN THIS FORM: DAY, MONTH"
00100    INPUT D1, M1
00110    PRINT "INPUT THE SECOND DATE IN THE
         SAME FORM"
00120    INPUT D2, M2
00125    IF M1=M2 THEN DA=D2−D1:GOTO 200
00130    EM=M(M1)−D1
00140    IF M1+1=M2 THEN 190
00150    FOR X=M1+1 TO M2−1
00160    DA=DA+M(X)
00170    NEXT X
00190    DA=DA+EM+D2
00200    PRINT "THE NUMBER OF DAYS = "; DA
00210    END
00220    DATA 31, 29, 31, 30, 31, 30, 31, 31, 30, 31, 30, 31
```

WRITING A SMALL BUSINESS ACCOUNTING SYSTEM

The following is an outline of a small business accounting system designed for use on a small computer with a printer, high-level language, and mass storage facilities (e.g. cassettes or floppy disks). The program is intended for use by an individual proprietorship or a small partnership. For such a business, tax returns are prepared (either form 1040 schedule C or form 1065), bookkeeping is done, and balance sheets are produced for management and banking purposes. Advantages of computerizing such information include time-saving and error detection.

The most desirable bookkeeping system is called the double entry system; each transaction is entered twice to different accounts, and thus, the system is self-checking. With the double entry system, each transaction is first recorded as money coming from some account and then recorded as money going to some account. Debits, abbreviated as "DR" for computer use, represent an addition to your account or to an expense; credits, abbreviated "CR" represent a subtraction from one of these. To check whether the bookkeeping of accounts has been done correctly, check that the debits always equal the credits. For example, if you paid a bill for $50 and received a check for $100 for services performed, the bookkeeping entries would be as follows:

a. Debit (subtract from what you owe) accounts payable for $50.
b. Credit (subtract from what you have) cash on hand for $50.
c. Debit (add to what you have) cash on hand for $100.
d. Credit (add to revenue) income or revenue for $100.

The continual up-keep of the status of each account for a business is the purpose of the bookkeeping program. An example of the account files along with a suggested computer abbreviation for each is listed here:

EXPENSES: (debit to add, credit to subtract)

Return and allowances	RTN	(goods returned for refund)
Depreciation	DEP	(for equipment owned)
Business taxes	TAX	
Rent	RNT	
Repairs	RPR	
Bad debts	BDB	(for the charge-off accounting method)
Professional fees	PRF	
Amortization	AMT	(charge partial costs of organization expense, research/development, etc.)
Fuel	FUL	
Telephone	FON	
Electricity	PWR	
Salaries and wages	SAL	(does not include wages included in cost of goods sold)
Interest	INT	(interest paid, only)
Labor/production costs	LAB	
Purchases	PUR	

Insurance	INS	
Pension/profit sharing	PEN	
Depletion	DPL	(used for such assets as mines/oil fields)
Materials/supplies	MAT	
Miscellaneous	MIS	
Cost of goods sold	CGS	(includes: : purchases, materials/supplies, labor/production costs, other costs)

ASSETS: (debit to add, credit to subtract)

Cash	CSH	(usually checking acct. balances)
Receivables	RBL	(amounts owed by customers on accounts)
Inventory	INV	
Prepaid expenses	PPD	
Supplies	SUP	
Equipment	EQT	
Investments	IVS	
Miscellaneous	ETC	

LIABILITIES AND EQUITY:

Payables	PBL	(amounts owed on an account)
Notes	NOT	(borrowed money)
Long term payables	LTP	
Proprietor	PRP	(amount invested in business and net income)
Drawing	DRW	(account from which owner may use money for personal expenses)

REVENUES: (credit to add, debit to subtract)

Gross receipts	RCP
Other revenue	REV

The IRS requires reports in the following areas: depreciation, business taxes, repairs, amortization.

The various reports which may be generated by the system include the balance sheet; a sample balance sheet is listed below:

ASSETS:		LIABILITIES:	
Equipment	5000.	Notes	2000.
Receivables	500.	Payables	3500.
Cash	3000.	Total	5500.
Total	8500.		

EQUITY:

Proprietor   3000

Total (Liabilities + Equity) = 8500.

Assets represent what the businessman has, liabilities represent the amounts owed, and equities are amounts contributed or earned by the owners.

The next report is termed the "income statement," which illustrates the income and expense of the business during a certain length of time (a period); it may be used to fill out tax forms 1040C or 1065. To generate this report, total income is computed and total expenses are subtracted from this figure. Income for accounts may be stated on an accrual basis, which is to say future expenses or revenues are included if the exact amount is known and certain (e.g. the amounts customers owe may be stated on an accrual basis). Business owners may prefer to prepare a tax return report on a cash basis in which the only revenue is considered to be cash in and the only expenses considered are cash out. To prepare such a report, eliminate payables, receivables, prepaid expenses, and supplies not yet part of the cost of goods sold; the revenue and expense accounts should be adjusted accordingly to reflect this change.

The next report is the "ledger" of which may be two types: summary and detailed. The detailed ledger is a complete listing of each account transaction (name, amount, etc.) that has been inputted within a certain period of time (usually done on a weekly or monthly basis). The balances up to the time of the beginning of the report have been stored from prior ledgers and are read into the computer. Thus, a report listing each transaction and the remaining balance in each account is generated. The summary ledger report only lists the remaining balances after adding and subtracting all transaction for a given period of time.

The balance sheet is the final report necessary on a small accounting system. The sum of the liabilities is subtracted from the sum of the assets to determine the balance or net profit for the business owner. This balance is credited to the proprietor (PRP) account and thus, the assets plus net income will balance (equal) with the liabilities.

Additional functions of the accounting system could include: forecasting income using trend-line analysis of previous balance sheets, forecasting other accounts using previous records, preparation of amortization schedules, determination of depreciation amounts (simple depreciation = (2/total life of item)*(initial cost-previous depreciation)), and cash budgeting based on forecasted cash on hand and cash payable.

The accounting system flowchart is shown in Fig. 2-1.

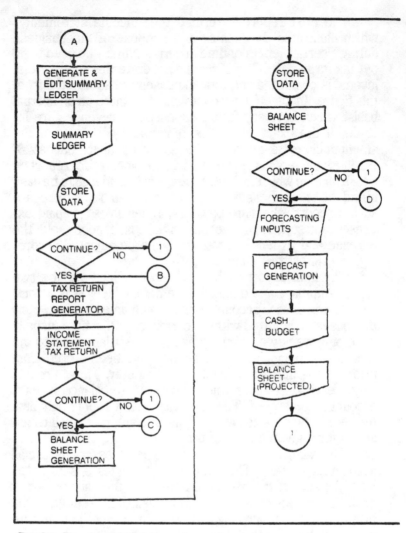

Fig. 2-1. Flowchart for the accounting system program.

Sample computer/operator dialogue for inputting data:
(c = computer, 0 = operator)

c: ENTER ACCOUNT CODE DEBITED, AMOUNT, REMARKS
o: sal, 150.00, check #1045
c: ENTER ACCOUNT CODE CREDITED, AMOUNT,

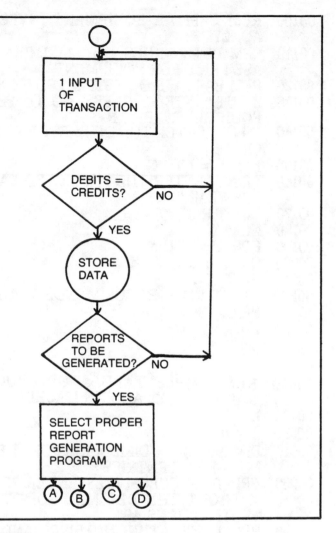

REMARKS
o: csh, 15.00, April
c: CREDITS DO NOT EQUAL DEBITS—CORRECT ER-
RORS
c: csh, 150.00, April
c: ENTER ACCOUNT CODE DEBITED, AMOUNT, RE-
MARKS

.
.
.

```
00100   REM CAPITAL EQUIPMENT INVESTMENT
        ANALYSIS
00110   REM DETERMINES THE MAXIMUM PURCH-
        ASE PRICE FOR EQUIPMENT
00120   REM BASED UPON ESTIMATED PROFITS
00130   INPUT "ENTER THE EST. NO. OF YEARS OF
        EQUIPMENT LIFE"; N
00140   INPUT "ENTER THE INTEREST RATE IN DE-
        CIMAL"; I
00150   FOR X = 1 TO N
00160   PRINT "ENTER THE PROJECTED EARNINGS
        FOR YEAR:"; X
00170   INPUT R (X)
00180   NEXT X
00190   FOR X = 1 TO N
00200   Q = Q + R (X)/I↑X
00210   NEXT X
00220   PRINT "THE RECOMMENDED PURCHASE
        PRICE IS: $"; Q
00230   END
```

```
00010   REM SIMPLE TABULATOR PROGRAM—
        SIMULATES AN ADDING MACHINE
00020   X = 1
00030   T = 0
00040   DIM A (500)      'DIMENSION FOR THE TOTAL
        NUMBER OF ENTRIES
00050   PRINT "SUCCESSIVELY ENTER NUMBERS
        WITHOUT THE DECIMAL POINT. ENTER
        SUBTRACTIONS AS"
00060   PRINT "NEGATIVE NUMBERS AND ENTER
        '9999' TO END."
00070   PRINT
00080   INPUT A (X)
00090   IF A (X) = 9999 THEN 120
00100   A (X) = A (X)*.01      'INSERT DECIMAL POINT
00110   X = X+1: GOTO 80
00120   PRINT "NUMBER", "AMOUNT", "BALANCE"
00130   FOR B = 1 TO X − 1
00140   T = T + A (B)
```

```
00150   PRINT B, A (B), T
00160   NEXT B
00170   PRINT: PRINT
00180   END
```

```
00100   REM CALCULATION OF THE FUTURE VALUE
        OF AN INVESTMENT
00110   CLS 'CLEAR SCREEN
00120   DEFDBL F, D, E, B, C, A
00130   INPUT "ENTER THE CONSUMER PRICE
        INDEX FOR PREVIOUS YEAR"; F
00140   INPUT "ENTER THE CONSUMER PRICE
        INDEX FOR CURRENT YEAR"; E
00150   INPUT "ENTER THE PRESENT VALUE OF THE
        INVESTMENT (OR PRODUCT/SALARY)"; C
00160   INPUT "ENTER THE NUMBER OF PERIODS TO
        BE CALCULATED"; B
00170   A = (100*(E − F)/F)/100
00180   D=INT( (C*(A+1) ↑ B)*100+.5)/100
00190   PRINT
00200   PRINT "THE FUTURE VALUE IS: $"; D
00210   PRINT
00220   END
```

Chapter 3
Mathematical Applications

Mathematical Applications

One of the biggests assets of the computer is its ability to perform complicated and tedious mathematical calculations with unerring diligence. From a simple adding machine to solving complicated simultaneous equations, your home computer can handle them all.

SOPHISTICATED CALCULATOR

A program could be written to simulate the functions of an ordinary or RPN calculator. The computer would be used as a simple business or scientific calculator for filling in a tax form or analyzing data. Additionally, functions not provided on an ordinary calculator could easily be included (e.g. solution to the quadratic equation).

PROGRAM—RPN CALCULATOR

RPN stands for Reverse Polish Notation and is a system of representing mathematical equations. Some of the advanced scientific calculators use the RPN system because fewer keystrokes are required in complex calculations as compared to a regular calculator. The purpose of this program is to emulate an RPN calculator, providing about fifty mathematical functions.

In the RPN system there are no parentheses or "=" keys. Only two numbers are worked with at one time. A sample calculation would proceed as follows:

Step	Input	Display	Comments
1.	2.5	2.5 0 0 0	Enter first number
2.	4	4 2.5 0 0	Enter second number
3.	x	10 4 2.5 0	"x" stands for multiplication. The answer to 2.5 × 4 was calculated and put in the first position in the display
4.	10	10 10 4 2.5	enter third number
5.	5	5 10 10 4	enter fourth number
6.	/	2 5̄ 10 1̄0̄	"/" stands for division. The following calculation was performed and the answer stored in the first display position: 10/5=2

7.	+	12	The "+" sign instructed
		2	that the last two previous
		5	results were to be added:
		10	10+2=12; the answer was
			stored in the first position.

The functions available in this program are listed and described below:

command /function	description
*	multiplication
+	addition
/	division
—	subtraction
↑	powers(e.g. x↑y stands for x^y and x↑.5 stands for $\sqrt{x}$)
INV	inverse (e.g. 1/x)
C	clear display/registers
SIN	compute the sine of x
ASIN	compute the arcsine of x
COS	compute the cosine of x
ACOS	compute the arccosine of x
TAN	compute the tangent of x
ATAN	compute the arctangent of x
SEC	compute the secant of x
ASEC	compute the arcsecant of x
COT	compute the cotangent of x
ACOT	compute the arccotangent of x
CSC	compute the cosecant of x
ACSC	compute the arccosecant of x
PI	place the value of π in the register
E	compute the exponential of x (e.g. e^x)
LOG	compute the logarithm of x
MEM+	add a number to the memory register
MEM−	delete a number from the memory register
%	change x to a percentage value
N!	compute the factorial of x
SD	compute the standard deviation for a set of scores
HYP	compute the value for a hypotenuse of a triangle given the two sides

102

SIDE	compute the value for a side of a triangle given the hypotenuse and another side
DEG	change x from radians to degrees
RAD	change x from degrees to radians
POLR	compute polar coordinates given rectangular coordinates
RECT	compute rectangular coordinates given polar coordinates
MET	compute metric conversions—a subprogram
HSIN	compute the hyperbolic sine of x
HCOS	compute the hyperbolic cosine ot x
HTAN	compute the hyperbolic tangent of x
HSEC	compute the hyperbolic secant of x
HCSC	compute the hyperbolic cosecant of x
HCOT	compute the hyperbolic contangent of x
#SIN	inverse hyperbolic sine of x
#COS	inverse hyperbolic cosine of x
#TAN	inverse hyperbolic tangent of x
#SEC	inverse hyperbolic cosecant of x
#CSC	inverse hyperbolic contangent ot x
#COT	inverse hyperbolic secant of x
SZ	switch the z registers
RZ	rotate the registers
QUAD	compute solutions to quadratic equations with the quadratic equation
?	put computer in monitor mode so that ordinary calculations may be made of the form PRINT 5*1.6. Type CONT in some BASICs to continue with the program

```
10  REM RPN CALCULATOR
20  REM (C) 1978 MARK R. SAWUSCH—MAY NOT BE
    SOLD.
25  CLS 'CLEAR THE SCREEN
30  DIM A(100), M$(21)
35  L=2
40  DEFDBL B, A, X, C, Z
50  PRINT "MAXI-CAL"
55  G=1:F=1
56  REM LINE 60 CONTAINS ALL FUNCTIONS
    AVAILABLE
60 D$="* + / -    INV C SIN ASINCOS ACOSTAN
   ATANSEC ASECCOT ACOTCSC ACSCPI E LOG
```

```
        MEM + MEM−1% N! SD HYP SIDEDEG RAD P
        OLRRECTMENT H  SIN HC OSH TANHSECHCS
        CHCOT#SIN#COS#TAN#SEC#CSC#COTSZRZ
        QUAD?"
70   REM EACH COMMAND/FUNCTION IN LINE  60
        MUST CONTAIN 4 LETTERS AND/OR SPACES
        FOR PROPER OPERATION
99   D=1
100  REM ASK FOR COMMAND/VALUES
110
111  INPUTC$
112  O=0
115  IFVAL (C$)= 0 THEN130 'IS IT A COMMAND OR A
        NUMBER?
120  A(G)=VAL(C$):A(G)=CDBL(A(G)):X=A(G):IFF
        (1)=2THENF(2)=2ELSEF(1)=2
121  L=G
122  IFG=1THENG=2ELSEG=1
123  GOTO3005
125  GOTO111
130  A(G)=L1:IFF(1)=1THENF(2)=1ELSEF(1)=1
134  REM SEARCH TO FIND THE COMMAND
135  FOR I=1 TO LEN(D$)-LEN(C$)+1
136  IF C$=MID$(D$, I, LEN(C$)) THEN 140
137  NEXT I
139  PRINT "ILLEGAL FUNCTION":PRINT: GOTO111
140  IF I=1 THEN 150
145  ON (I-1)/4 GOTO 200, 250, 300, 350, 400, 500, 550,
        600, 650, 700, 750, 800, 850, 900, 950, 1000, 1050,
        1100, 1150, 1200, 1250, 1300, 1350, 1400, 1450,
        1500, 1550, 1600, 1650, 1700, 1750, 1800, 1850,
        1910, 1950, 2000, 2050, 2100, 2150, 2200, 2250,
        2300, 2350
146  ON ((I-1)/4-44)GOTO 2400, 2450, 2500, 2550, 2600
        2700
147  REM CALCULATE *
150  IFF(1)=F(2)ANDF(1)=1THENX=Z1*Z4ELSEX=
        Z1*Z2
160  GOTO3005
199  REM CALCULATE+
200  IFF(1)=F(2)ANDF(1)=1THENX=Z1+Z4ELSEX=Z1
        +Z2
210  GOTO3005
```

```
249  REM CALCULATE/
250  IFF(1)=F(2)ANDF(1)=1THENX=Z4/Z1ELSEX=Z2
     /Z1
260  GOTO3005
299  REM CALCULATE —
300  IFF(1)=F(2)ANDF(1)=1THENX=X4—X1ELSEX=
     Z2—Z1
260  GOTO3005
349  REM CALCULATE POWERS
350  X=Z2↑Z1:GOTO3005
399  REM CALCULATE INVERSES
400  Z1=1/Z1:GOTO3010
499  REM CLEAR REGISTERS
500  Z1=0:Z2=0:Z3=0:Z4=0:GOTO3010
549  REM CALCULATE SIN
550  A(L)=SIN(A(L)*.0174533)
560  GOTO 3000
599  REM CALCULATE ARC SIN
600  A(L)=ATN(A(L)/SQR(-A(L)*A(L)+1))*57.29578
610  GOTO 3000
649  REM CALCULATE COSINE
650  A(L)=COS(A(L)*. 0174533)
660  GOTO 3000
699  REM CALCULATE ARC COSINE
700  A(L)=(-ATN(A(L)/SQR(-A(L)*A(L)+1))+1.5708)
     *57.29578
710  GOTO 3000
749  REM CALCULATE TANGENT
750  A(L)=TAN(A(L)*.0174533)
760  GOTO 3000
799  REM CALCULATE ARC TANGENT
800  A(L)=ATN(A(L))*57.29578
810  GOTO 3000
849  REM CALCULATE SECANT
850  A(L)=1/COS(A(L)*.0174533)
860  GOTO 3000
899  REM CALCULATE ARC SECANT
900  A(L)=(ATN(SQR(A(L)*A(L)-1))+(SGN(A(L)-1)
     *1.5708))*57.29578
910  GOTO 3000
949  REM CALCULATE COTANGENT
```

```
 950   A(L)=1/TAN(A(L)*.0174533)
 960   GOTO 3000
 999   REM CALCULATE ARC COTANGENT
1000   A(L)=(-ATN(A(L)+1.5708))*57.29578
1010   GOTO 3000
1049   REM CALCULATE COSECANT
1050   A(L)=1/SIN(A(L)*.0174533)
1060   GOTO 3000
1099   REM CALCULATE ARC COSECANT
1100   A(L)=(ATN(1/SQR(A(L)*A(L)-1))+(SGN(A(L)-1)
       *1.5708))*57.29578
1120   GOTO 3000
1149   REM VALUE FOR PI
1150   Z1=3.141592654:GOTO3010
1160   GOTO 3000
1199   REM CALCULATE NATURAL LOGARITHM
1200   A(L)=EXP(A(L))
1210   GOTO 3000
1249   REM CALCULATE LOGARITHM
1250   A(L)=LOG(A(L))
1260   GOTO 3000
1299   REM MEMORY ADDITION
1300   DD=DD+1
1310   INPUT "WHICH REGISTER";D
1320   IFD=1THEN M$(DD)=STR$(Z1)ELSEIFD=2THEN
       M$(DD)=STR$(Z2)ELSEIFD=3 THEN M$(DD)=
       STR$(Z3)ELSEM$(DD)=STR$(Z4)
1330   INPUT "DESCRIPTION";C$
1340   M$(DD) = M $ (DD) +" "+ C$
1345   GOTO111
1349   REM MEMORY LISTING
1350   FORD=1TODD
1360   PRINTM$(D)
1370   NEXTD
1380   GOTO111
1399   REM CONV. FOR%
1400   A(L)=A(L)*.01
1410   GOTO 3000
1449   REM COMPUTE FACTORIAL
1450   FOR YY=1 TO A(L)
1470   A(L)=A(L)*(A(L)-YY)
```

```
1480    NEXT YY: GOTO3000
1499    REM STATISTICS
1500    PRINT "IN STATISTICAL MODE"
1501    PRINT
1502    PRINT "ENTER VALUES SEPARATELY AND
        ENTER 9999 WHEN DONE"
1505    B=0:C=0:D=1
1510    INPUT K(D)
1520    IF K(D)=9999 THEN 1541
1530    B=B+K(D): C=C+K(D)↑2: D=D+1
1540    GOTO 1510
1541    PRINT "SCORES:":FOR H%=1TOD-1
1542    PRINT K(H%);
1543    NEXT H%:PRINT
1544    PRINT "SUM OF SCORES", "NUMBER OF
        SCORES"
1545    PRINT B, D-1
1546    PRINT:: PRINT "MEAN", "VARIANCE"
1547    PRINTB/(D-1),C-(B/(D-1))↑2
1548    PRINT "STANDARD DEVIATION =";SQR(C-
        (B/(D-1))↑2)
1549    REM COMPUTE HYPOTENUSE
1550    X=SQR(Z1↑2+Z2↑2)
1560    GOTO3005
1599    REM COMPUTE SIDE OF TRIANGLE
1600    X=SQR(ABS(Z1↑2-Z2↑2)):GOTO3005
1649    REM CONV. TO DEGREES
1650    A(L)=A(L)*57.2957791
1670    GOTO3000
1699    REM CONV. TO RADIANS
1700    A(L)=.017453292*A(L)
1720    GOTO 3000
1749    REM RECT. TO POLAR CONV.
1750    Z1=SQR(Z1*Z1+Z2*Z2)
1760    A=Z2/Z1
1770    Z2=(ATN(A/SQR(−A*A+1) ) )*57.29578
1790    GOTO3010
1799    REM POLAR TO RECT. CONV.
1800    B=Z1*SIN(Z2*.0174533):Z2=Z1*COS(Z2*.0174533)
        :Z1=B:GOTO3010
1850    A(G)=Z1:PRINT "M E N U:"
1852    PRINT "USE THE NEGATIVE OF THE MENU #
```

```
              TO CONV. VICE-VERSA)"
1855   PRINT "1) FEET TO METERS"
1856   PRINT "2) INCHES TO CENTIMETERS"
1857   PRINT "3) MILES TO KILOMETERS"
1858   PRINT "4) GALLONS TO LITERS"
1859   PRINT "5) FARENHEIGHT TO CENTIGRADE"
1860   PRINT "6) POUNDS TO KILOGRAMS"
1861   PRINT "7) END CONVERSIONS"
1864   INPUT "SELECT"; H
1865   IF H<0 GOTO 1867
1866   ON H GOTO 1870, 1876, 1882, 1888, 1894, 1900,
       110
1867   ON -H GOTO 1873, 1879, 1885, 1891, 1897, 1903
1870   X=.33047851*A(G): GOTO 4000
1873   X=A(G)*3.281:GOTO 4000
1876   X=A(G)*2.54: GOTO 4000
1879   X=A(G)*.3937:GOTO4000
1882   X=A(G)*1.609:GOTO 4000
1885   X=A(G)*.6215: GOTO 4000
1888   X=3.7853*A(G): GOTO 4000
1891   X=.2642*A(G): GOTO4000
1894   X=.5555555*(A(G)—32): GOTO 4000
1897   X=1.8*A(G)+32: GOTO 4000
1900   X=.4536*A(G): GOTO 4000
1903   X=2.2046*A(G): GOTO 4000
1909   REM COMPUTE HYPERBOLIC SINE
1910   A(L)=(EXP(A(L))-EXP(-A(L))) /2
1920   GOTO 3000
1945   REM COMPUTE HYPERBOLIC COSINE
1950   A(L)=(EXP(A(L))+EXP(-A(L)))/2
1960   GOTO 3000
1999   REM COMPUTE HYPERBOLIC TANGENT
2000   A(L)=-EXP(-A(L))/ (EXP(A(L))+EXP(-A(L))*2+1
2010   GOTO 3000
2049   REM COMPUTE HYPERBOLIC SECANT
2050   A(L)=2/ (EXP(A(L))+EXP(-A(L)))
2060   GOTO 3000
2099   REM COMPUTE HYPERBOLIC COSECANT
2100   A(L)=2/ (EXP(A(L))—EXP(-A(L)))
2110   GOTO 3000
2149   REM COMPUTE HYPERBOLIC COTANGENT
2150   A(L)=EXP(-A(L))/(EXP(A(L))-EXP(-A(L)))*2+1
```

```
2160    GOTO 3000
2199    REM COMPUTE INV. HYPERBOLIC SINE
2200    A(L)=LOG(A(L)+SQR(A(L)*A(L)+1))
2210    GOTO 3000
2249    REM COMPUTE INV. HYPERBOLIC COSINE
2250    A(L)=LOG(A(L)+SQR(A(L)*A(L)-1))
2260    GOTO 3000
2299    REM COMPUTE INV. HYPERBOLIC TANGENT
2300    A(L)=LOG((1+A(L))/(1-A(L)))/2
2310    GOTO 3000
2349    REM COMPUTE INV. HYPERBOLIC SECANT
2350    A(L)=LOG((SQR(-A(L)*A(L)+1)+1)/A(L))
2360    GOTO 3000
2399    REM COMPUTE INV. HYPERBOLIC COSECANT
2400    A(L)=LOG((SGN(A(L))*SQR(A(L)*A(L)+1)+1)/A
        (L))
2410    GOTO 3000
2449    REM COMPUTE INV. HYPERBOLIC COTAN-
        GENT
2450    A(L)=LOG((A(L)+1)/(A(L)-1))/2
2460    GOTO 3000
2500    B=Z2:Z2=Z1:Z1=B:GOTO3010
2550    B=Z4:Z4=Z3:Z2=Z1:Z1=B:GOTO3010
2600    B=-Z2*Z2+SQR(Z2*Z2-4*Z3*Z1)/2*Z3
2610    Z1=-Z2*Z2-SQR(Z2*Z2-4*Z3*Z1)/2*Z3
2620    Z2=B
2650    GOTO3010
2700    PRINT "ENTERING MONITOR MODE"
2710    STOP
2720    GOTO111
3000    Z1=A(L):GOTO3010
3005    Z4=Z3:Z3=Z2:Z2=Z1:Z1=X
3010    PRINT"Z1:";Z1
3011    PRINT "Z2:";Z2
3013    PRINT "Z3:"; Z3
3015    PRINT"Z4:";Z4
3090    PRINT:PRINT
3999    GOTO 110
4000    PRINT "=";X:PRINT:PRINT:GOTO1850
```

STATISTICS

Basic statistics for one or two variables—The mean,

variance, standard deviation, and standard error may be found for a set of observations on one variable. For two variable sets, the above statistics could be determined for each and the covariance and correlation coefficient calculated.

$$\text{Mean} = \overline{X} = \frac{1}{n} \sum_{i=1}^{n} X_i$$

$$\text{Variance} = S^2 = \frac{1}{n-1} \left[\sum_{i=1}^{n} X_i^2 - n(\overline{X})^2 \right]$$

Standard Deviation = S

$$\text{Covariance} = S_{xy} = \frac{1}{n-1} \sum_{i=1}^{n} (X_i - \overline{X})(Y_i - \overline{Y})$$

$$\text{Coefficient of Correlation} = V_{xy} = \frac{S_{xy}}{S_x S_y}$$

$$S_x = \frac{1}{n-1} \left(\sum_{i=1}^{n} X_i^2 - \frac{(\sum_{i=1}^{n} X_i)^2}{n} \right)$$

$$S_y = \frac{1}{n-1} \left(\sum_{i=1}^{n} Y_i^2 - \frac{(\sum_{i=1}^{n} Y_i)^2}{n} \right)$$

Means and moments—For grouped or ungrouped data the arithmetic, geometric, and harmonic means may be determined; the second, third, and fourth moments about the mean and the coefficients of skewness and kurtosis may also be calculated.

$$\text{Geometric mean} = \sqrt[n]{X_1 \cdot X_2 \cdot X_3 \ldots \cdot X_n}$$

$$\text{Harmonic mean} = \frac{n}{\sum_{i=1}^{n} \frac{1}{X_i}}$$

$$\text{Third Moment} = M_3 = \frac{1}{n} \sum_{i=1}^{n} X_i^3 - \frac{3}{n} \overline{X} \sum_{i=1}^{n} X_i^2 + 2(\overline{X})^3$$

$$\text{Fourth Moment} = M_x = \frac{1}{n} \sum_{i=1}^{n} X_i^4 - \frac{4}{n} \overline{X} \sum_{i=1}^{n} X_i^3 + \frac{6}{n}$$

$$(\overline{X})^2 \sum_{i=1}^{n} X_i^2 - 3(\overline{X})^4$$

Moment Coefficient of Skewness $\dfrac{M_3}{S^3}$

Moment Coefficient of Kurtosis $= \dfrac{M_4}{S^4}$

One and two way analysis of variance—The mean and variance for two treatment groups, and for the entire sample, may be calculated and an F statistic applied to the differences between populations.

Contingency table analysis—The chi-square statistic may be used to test independence between row and column classifications of a contingency table.

Linear regression—A set of observations may be fit to a straight line by linear regression; the coefficient of determination, the standard error of y on x, and standard error for the coefficients may also be computed. Multiple linear regression fits, and polynomial regression could also be performed.

Linear Regression and Correlation Coefficient
for the linear equation $y = mx + b$

$$M = \frac{\sum\limits_{i=1}^{n} (X_i - \overline{X})(Y_i - \overline{Y})}{\sum\limits_{i=1}^{n} (X_i - \overline{X})^2} \qquad b = \overline{Y} - M\overline{X}$$

Correlation coefficient $= r$

$$r = \frac{\sum\limits_{i=1}^{n} (X_i - \overline{X})(Y_i - \overline{Y})}{\sqrt{\sum\limits_{i=1}^{n} (X_i - \overline{X})^2 \cdot \sum\limits_{i=1}^{n} (Y_i - \overline{Y})^2}}$$

Normal distribution—The values of $f(x)$ and $P(x)$ may be calculated for a given x or the value of x may be found for a given $P(x)$, assuming that the sample is of a normal distribution.

Chi-square, t, and F distributions—The most commonly used distributions could be calculated by a useful program. The area under the curve of the distribution could be determined at any point.

Survey analysis—The following statistical parameters could be calculated by a complete survey analysis program: multivariate analysis, regression analysis, time-series analysis, variance determination, factor analysis, descriptions, and tabulations.

Generation of frequency tables—For a large sample, a sorting program could output a standard or relative frequency table.

Hypothesis testing—A useful program could determine confidence intervals for a given sample, which may then be used in testing hypotheses. Statistical hypothesis testing is used to answer such questions as, "A businessman claimed that 20% of the public prefer his products; if 100 people were asked their opinion, what percentage would have to respond negatively for this claim to be refutable?"

PROGRAM—STATISTICAL ANALYSIS

This statistical analysis program has a wide range of applications in business, stock analysis, and the sciences. The program consists of six subprograms: statistics with one variable, statistics with two variables, area under a curve computation, cumulative binomial probabilities calculation, bar graphing, and exponential smoothing calculation.

The first subprogram, statistics with one variable, is used to find basic descriptions for a set of data (e.g. mean and standard deviation). The second subprogram analyzes two sets of data in relation to each other (x, y pairs). For example, the relationship between the price of a stock (x) to the Dow Jones Industrial Average (y) could be determined by inputting pairs of values for the two. The third subprogram computes the area under a normal curve between two points. A normal curve is used to describe many phenomena; it is shaped like this:

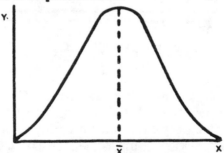

The area under the curve is equal to one; the average of a set of data $(\bar{x})$ is the point at which the curve peaks. If two values on the x axis are picked, the area under the curve between these two points is equal to the probability of a data value being between those points; this subprogram computes that ing between that area. The fourth subprogram computes the cumulative by nominal probability for a certain data valve occurring. The fifth subprogram plots data described in subprogram one in simple bar-graph format. This section could be improved to plot data on an x, y axis or create a labeled histogram. The sixth subprogram expotentially smoothes a set of data. Data values are inputted and an expotential is used to predict future values. This smoothing constant should be adjusted such that the outputted error is minimized.

```
10   REM STATISTICAL ANALYSIS PROGRAM
20   REM FOR BUSINESS AND STOCK ANALYSIS
25   DIM X(105), A(105), Y(105)
27   CLEAR 2000
30   PRINT "MENU:" :CLEAR 2000
40   PRINT "1)STATISTICS FOR 1 VARIABLE"
50   PRINT "2)STATISTICS FOR 2 VARIABLES"
60   PRINT "3)AREA UNDER A CURVE COMPUTATION
62   PRINT "4)CUMULATIVE BINOMIAL PROBABIL-
     ITY CALCULATION"
64   PRINT "5)PLOT DATA"
66   PRINT"6)EXPONENTIAL SMOOTHING PROG-
     RAM"
68   INPUT A: ON A GOTO 70, 1400, 900, 4000, 5000, 6000
69   GOTO 30
70   REM ONE VARIABLE CALCULATIONS
80   PRINT "ENTER SUCCESSIVE VALUES SEPA-
     RATELY, '9999' TO END"
90   D=1: C=0: B=0: E=0
100  INPUT A(D)
120  GOTO 150
130  INPUT A(D)
140  IF A(D)=9999 THEN 500
150  B=B+A(D)
160  C=C+A(D)*A(D)
170  D=D+1
180  GOTO 130
500  D=D-1:M=B/D
505  CLS ' CLEAR SCREEN
```

```
510   PRINT "NO. SCORES", "SUM OF SCORES"
520   PRINT D, B
525   PRINT
540   FOR H=1 TO D
550   G=G+A(H)−M
551   SG=SG+(A(H)−M)*(A(H)−M)
560   NEXT H
562   SG=SG/(D-1):SG=SQR (SG)
580   PRINT "MEAN", "VARIANCE", "MEAN AVE.
      DEV."
590   PRINT M,SG*SG,SG,G
600   PRINT:PRINT "PROBABLE ERROR", "COEFFI-
      CIENT OF VARIATION"
610   PRINT .6745*SG, D/M
615   PRINT
620   PRINT "STANDARD ERROR FOR THE MEAN
      =";SQR(SG*SG/D)
625   PRINT
670   FOR I= 1 TO D-1
672   FOR J=1 TO D-1
674   X=A(J):Y=A(J+1)
684   IF A(J)<=A(J+1) THEN 688
686   A(J)=Y:A (J+1) =X
688   NEXT J, I
689   INPUT "TYPE ENTER TO CONTINUE";A$: CLS
690   PRINT "# MEASURE FREQ REL FREQ DEV
      FROM AVE  DEV SQUARED  STD DEV"
754   J9=0
755   FOR J8=1 TO D
760   H=1
770   FR=1
790   J=1
800   IF A (J8)=A(J8+J) THEN FR=FR+1 ELSE 830
810   J=J+1
820   GOTO 800
830   J9=J9+1
840   A2$="## ####. ### ######. ##### ####.
      #### ########. ### #####. #####"
850   PRINT USING A2$; J9; A(J8); FR; FR*1/D;
      M−A(J8); (M−A(J8))*(M−A(J8)) ; (A(J8)−M)/SG
860   IF FR>1 THEN J8=J8+FR−1
862   RM=RM+FR*A(J8)*A(J8)
```

114

```
863    NEXT J8
864    PRINT "HIGHEST SCORE", "LOWEST SCORE"
865    PRINT A(D), A(1)
866    PRINT "ROOT MEAN SQUARE=";SQR(RM)
870    PRINT "THUS  X=";M; " PLUS/MINUS";SG/
       SQR(D)
880    INPUT "TYPE ENTER TO CONTINUE"; A$:
       GOTO 30
900    REM AREA UNDER NORMAL CURVE
910    PRINT"ENTER THE STANDARD Z VALUE";BE
920    INPUT BE
930    PRINT
940    PRINT "X VALUE  AREA TO LEFT  AREA TO
       RIGHT"
950    A=BE
970    C=0:E=1:H=BE:D=0:G=BE*BE:F=.398942*
       EXP(-.5*G)
1030   J=H/E
1040   C=C+J: IF J/C<. 000001 THEN 1120
1052   L=1: E=1: D=D+1: H=G*H
1060   FOR K=1 TO D
1070   E=E+2:L=L*E
1080   NEXT K
1100   E=L: GOTO 1030
1120   M=F*C+. 5:N=1-M
1130   PRINT A,M,N
1140   GOTO 1370
1160   BE=BE/1.14142:O=BE*BE: P=EXP(-O)*
       .56419/BE: O=. 5*O
1200   P1=O*O:M=O*P:P2=0:P3=0
1240   P5=1:P4=1
1260   P2=P2+2
1270   IF P3=P THEN 1320 ELSE P3=P
1280   P=P5:P4=O*P4*(P2-1)+P5:
       M=P2*M*P1*(P2+1)
1310   GOTO 1260
1320   P6=P*.5:Q=1-P6
1330   PRINT A, Q, P6
1350   BE=A+10
1360   GOTO 950
1370   PRINT
```

```
1380    GOTO 30
1400    D=1:PRINT "REGRESSION AND CORRELATION
        ANALYSIS":PRINT
1410    PRINT "ENTER X, Y VALUES AS PAIRS SEPA-
        RATED BY COMMAS"
1415    PRINT "TYPE 9999, 9999 WHEN DONE"
1420    INPUT X(D), Y(D)
1430    IF X(D)=9999 AND Y(D)=9999 THEN 1510
1440    Q9=Q9+X(D):R9=R9+Y(D)
1450    Q8=Q8+X(D)*X(D):R8=R8+Y(D)*Y(D)
1480    R6=R6+X(D)*Y(D):D=D+1
1500    GOTO 1420
1510    D=D-1:N=D:Q7=Q9/D:R7=R9/D
1540    A9=Q8-Q9*Q7:A8=R8-R9*R7
1560    B9=R6-Q9*R7:B8=B9/A9:B7=R7-B8*G7
1590    A7=A8-B8*B9:A6=A7/(D-2)
1610    FOR I=1 TO N
1620    B(I)=Y(I):A(I)=X(I)
1640    NEXT I
1650    GOSUB 3000
1660    PRINT
1670    PRINT "AVE. OF X", "AVE. OF Y"
1680    PRINT A1, A2
1690    PRINT "STD. DEV X", "STD DEV Y"
1700    PRINT D1, D2
1710    PRINT "CORRELATION COEFFICIENT X-Y:";
        C9
1720    PRINT:A9=A2
1730    INPUT "TYPE ENTER WHEN READY";Z9
1740    PRINT "THE FOLLOWING EQUATIONS EX-
        PRESS THE X, Y RELATIONSHIPS"
1750    PRINT: PRINT "EQUATION 1"
1770    PRINT "Y=";S9;"X+"; I9
1780    PRINT "% ACCURACY OF Y VARIANCE DE-
        SCRIPTION=";P9
1782    PRINT "Y-INTERCEPT ="; I9
1784    PRINT "SLOPE= "; S9
1785    PRINT "F-RATIO = "; S9/(A6/(D-2))
1790    PRINT
1800    FOR I=1 TO D
1810    IF X(I) <=0 THEN 1890
1820    A(I)=LOG(X(I))
```

```
1830   NEXT I
1840   GOSUB 3000
1850   PRINT: PRINT "EQUATION 2"
1860   PRINT "Y= ";S9;"*LOG X+";I9
1870   PRINT"% ACCURACY OF DESCRIPTION"; P9:
       PRINT
1890   FOR I=1 TO N
1900   A(I)=X(I): IF Y(I)<=0 THEN 2010
1920   B(I)=LOG(Y(I))
1930   NEXT I
1940   GOSUB 3000
1950   GOSUB 3500
1954   PRINT
1955   INPUT "TYPE ENTER WHEN READY"; Z9
1960   PRINT "EQUATION 3"
1970   PRINT "LOG Y=";S9;"*X +";I9 :PRINT" OR"
1990   PRINT "Y="; EXP(S9); "fX+"; EXP(I9)
2000   PRINT" % ACCURACY OF DESCRIPTION";P9
2010   FOR I=1 TO N
2020   IF A(I)<=0 THEN 3600ELSE A(I)=LOG(X(I))
2030   NEXT I
2040   GOSUB 3000
2050   GOSUB 3500
2060   PRINT "EQUATION 4"
2070   PRINT "LOG Y="; S9; "*LOG X +"; I9 : PRINT
       OR"
2080   PRINT "Y="; EXP(I9); "*Xf"; S9
2090   PRINT "% ACCURACY DESCRIPTION";P9
2100   GOTO 3600
3000   S1=0:S2=0:S3=0:S4=0:S5=0: FOR I=1 TO N
3010 S1=S1+A(I) :S2=S2+B(I):S3=S3+A(I)*A(I)
3040   S4=S4+B(I)*B(I):S5=S5+A(I)*B(I)
3050   NEXT I
3070   A1=S1/N:A2=S2/N:V1=(S3- (D*(A1*A1)))/(N-1)
3110   V2=(S4—(D*(A2*A2)))/(N-1): D1= SQR(V1)
3120   D2=SQR(ABS(V2)):DO=N*S3-S1*S1:I9=((S2*S3)
       -(S1*S5))/DO
3130   S9=((N*S5)-(S1*S2))/DO:P9=((S9*S9)*V1)/V2:C9
       =SQR(P9)
3140   P9=100*P9:RETURN
3500   S7=0:S8=0
3520   FOR I=1 TO N
```

```
3530   E=EXP(I9+S9*A(I)):S8=S8+(Y(I)-E)↑2:S7=S7+
       (Y(I)-A9)↑2
3560   NEXT I
3570   P9=100*(1-S8/S7):RETURN
3600   INPUT "TYPE ENTER WHEN READY"; Z9
3740   GOTO 30
4000   REM CUMULATIVE BINOMIAL PROBABILITIES
4010   F=0
4020   INPUT "ENTER THE # SUCCESSES, # TRIALS
       (F(Y, N,P)), PROB SUCCESS/TRIAL";Y,N,P
4030   S1=1: FOR I=1 TO N
4040   S1=S1*I:NEXT I
4050   FOR X=0 TO Y
4060   S2=1:S3=1
4070   FOR I=1 TO X
4080   S2=S2*I:NEXT I
4090   FOR I=1 TO N-X
4100   S3=S3*I:NEXT I
4110   F=F+S1/(S2*S3)*P↑X*(1-P)↑(N-X)
4120   NEXT X
4130   PRINT "THE CUMULATIVE BINOMIAL PROBA-
       BILITY =";F
4140   PRINT"FOR F(Y;N,,P) WHERE Y=";Y; "N=";N;
       "P=";P
4150   GOTO 30
5000   CLS : REM CLEAR SCREEN
5005   PRINT" ------------------------------------------"
5015   DX=55/A(D)
5020   FOR X=D TO 1 STEP -1
5025   IF A (X)= A(X-1) THEN NEXT X: GOTO 5200
5030   A$="####. ##": PRINT USING A$; A(X);
       :PRINT " I";
5040   PRINT STRING$(DX*A(X), "+")
5050   NEXT X
5060   PRINT " ------------------------------------------"
5070   GOTO 30
6000   REM EXPONENTIAL SMOOTHING
6010   DIM Y(100,2), S(3,2)
6020   GOSUB 6500
6040   GOSUB 7000
6050   GOSUB 8000
6060   GOTO 30
```

```
6500   INPUT "ENTER SMOOTHING CONSTANT (0-
       1)";A
6510   INPUT "ENTER  PREDICTION  PERIOD
       LENGTH"; T
6520   INPUT "ENTER THE FIRST DATA SET";Y(1,
       1):Y(2,2)=Y(1,1)
6530   S(1,0)=Y(1,1):S(2,0)=Y(1,1):S(3,0)=Y(1,1):N=2:
       RETURN
7000   REM
7001   PRINT N; :INPUT Y(N,1)
7003   IF Y(N,1)=9999 GOTO 7200
7030   S(1, 1)=A*Y(N, 1)+(1−A)*S(1, 0):S(2, 1)=(1−
       A)*S(2, 0)+S(1, 1)*A
7050   S(3,1)=(1−A)*S(3,0)+S(2,1)*A:P1=6*(1−A)*(1−A)
       +(6−5*A)*A*T+(A*T)*(A*T)
7070   P2=S(1,1)/(2*(1−A)*(1−A)):P3=6*(1−A)*(1−A)+2
       *(5−4*A)*A*T+2*(A*T)*(A*T)
7090   P4=S(2,1)/(2*(1−A)*(1−A))
7100   P5=2*(1−A)↑2+(4−3*A)*A*T+(A*T)↑2:P6=S(3,
       1)/(2*(1−A)*(1−A))
7110   Y(N+1,2)=P1*P2−P3*P4+P5*P6:S(1,0)=S(1,1):S
       (2,0)=S(2,1)
7120   S(3,0)=S(3,1):N=N+1: GOTO 7001
7200   RETURN
8000   PRINT:PRINT" PERIOD OBSERVATION PRE-
       DICTION  ERROR"
8001   A$="    ###        ####. ###      ###.
       ###    ##. ##"
8010   PRINT USING A$; 1; Y(1,1)
8020   FOR J=2 TO N−1
8030   PRINT USING A$; J; Y(J, 1); Y(J, 2); Y(J, 2)−Y(J, 1)
8040   IF J/12 <> INT (J/12) THEN 8100
8050   PRINT: INPUT"TYPE ENTER TO CON-
       TINUE";A$
8060   CLS: PRINT" PERIOD OBSERVATION PREDIC-
       TION ERROR"
8100   NEXT J
8110   GOTO 30
```

MATHEMATICS

   Solution of quadratic and cubic equations—Given the
coefficients of either a quadractic or cubic equation, a prog-

ram could solve for both real and complex roots; equations of other degrees, although not commonly used, could also be solved for.

Roots of f(x)—A program could find the roots of a user defined function using the bisection method or Newton's method.

Vector operations—Given two vectors in three dimensions, a program could calculate their magnitudes, the angle between them, and their dot and cross product.

```
00010   REM VECTOR ADDITION
00020   INPUT"INPUT THE DATA FOR THE FIRST
        VECTOR IN THIS FORM: MAGNITUDE, ANG-
        LE";M1,A1
00030   X1=M1*COS(A1)
00040   Y1=M1*SIN(A1)
00050   INPUT"INPUT THE DATA FOR THE SECOND
        VECTOR IN THE SAME FORMAT.";M2,A2
00060   X2=M2*COS(A2)

00070   Y2=M2*SIN(A2)
00080   X =X1 + X2: Y =Y1 + Y2
00090   A=ATN (Y/X)
00100   M=SQR (X*X+Y*Y)
00110   PRINT "NEW VECTOR MAGNITUDE=";M;"
        UNITS."
00120   PRINT "AT AN ANGLE OF ";A;" DEGREES."
00130   PRINT "(X,Y) COORDINATE AT
        ENDPOINT=(";X;", ";Y;")."
00140   PRINT
00150   END
```

Triangle solution—For a triangle with three known parts, the lengths of the sides, angles between sides, and the area could be computed.

Curve solution—The arc length, central angle, radius, chord length, and tangent length for a curve could be calculated given two known parts; the area enclosed by these parts could also be calculated.

Arithmetic, geometric, and harmonic progressions—A table of elements for the above three progressions could be generated. The element and the sum of the first n elements could also be determined.

Factors of integers, GCD, LCM—The prime factors of an integer, greatest common divisor (GCD), or least common multiple (LCM) of two integers could be determined.

Function value table—A useful program could print the values for a user-defined function over a specified interval.

Prime number table—A table of prime numbers or a test for primes in a specified interval could be generated.

Partial sums and products—The partial sum or product of a user defined function could be computed.

Solution of simultaneous equations—The number of equations that may be analyzed at one time should be limited only by memory.

Interpolation between known values—Lagrange polynomial interpolation, or Newton divided difference interpolation may be performed to interpolate values of a function.

Gaussian integration—The integral of a user-defined function may be determined by Gaussian quadrature.

Solutions of differential equations—First-order differential equations may be solved by a program using the Runge-Kutta method; a step size may be determined to yield results within a specific error tolerance.

Polynomial arithmetic—Addition, subtraction, multiplication, and division of polynomials may be accomplished.

Polynomial evaluation—A polynomial $(Px) = a_0 + a_1 x + a_2 x^2 + \ldots + a_n x^n$ may be evaluated at a point x with complex coefficients.

```
00100   REM POLYNOMIAL EVALUATION PROGRAM
00110   REM COMPUTES VALUE AT A GIVEN PT. &
        1ST & 2ND DERIVATIVES
00120   DIM B(50), Z(509), C(50,2)
00130   LET E=0
00140   PRINT "ENTER THE DEGREE OF THE
        POLYNOMIAL";
00150   INPUT X
00160   PRINT "ENTER THE COEFFICIENTS SEPA-
        RATELY";
00170   FOR D=0 TO X
00180   INPUT B(D)
```

```
00190   NEXT D
00200   PRINT "ENTER THE NO. OF VALUES TO BE
        EVALUATED";
00210   INPUT N: N1=N
00220   PRINT "ENTER THE POINTS SEPARATELY ";
00230   FOR D=1 TO N
00240   INPUT Z(D)
00250   NEXT D
00260   GOSUB 00340
00270   GOSUB 00450
00280   E=E+1
00290   GOSUB 00340
00300   GOSUB 00450
00310   E=E+1
00320   GOSUB 00340
00330   GOTO 00500
00340   FOR F=1 TO N1
00350   N=Z(F)
00360   GOSUB 00400
00370   C(F,E)=H
00380   NEXT F
00390   RETURN
00400   H=0
00410   FOR D=0 TO X
00420   H=B(D)+N*H
00430   NEXT D
00440   RETURN
00450   FOR D=0 TO X
00460   B(D) = (X-D)*B(D)
00470   NEXT D
00480   X=X-1
00490   RETURN
00500   PRINT
00510   PRINT "POINT OF EVAL.", "EVAL.", "DER 1",
        "DER 2"
00520   PRINT
00530   FOR F=1 TO N1
00540   PRINT Z(F), C(F,0), C(F,1),C(F,2)
00550   NEXT F
00560   PRINT
00570   END
```

Polynomial root finding—Barstow's method is well suited for computer evaluation of quadric factors for polynomials of degree n.

Factors of a polynomial—Polynomial of degree n may be constructed or reduced by factors X^{-a}.

Complex arithmetic—Addition, subtraction, multiplication, division, squares, inverses, etc. may be performed using complex numbers.

Complex trigonometric functions—Common trigonometric functions may be evaluated using complex numbers.

Base conversions—A useful program could transform numbers of any real base to another base.

Graphing calculations—The intervals to use for proportional axes given the minimum/maximum values and number of major divisions could be calculated and used for plotting data manually. Additionally, conversion routines between radians, quadrants, revolutions, and degrees could be provided.

PROGRAM—SIMULTANEOUS EQUATION SOLVER

The solution to a set of simultaneous equations is a mathematical operation with applications in many areas including business and sciences. An example of two equations to be solved simultaneously are as follows:

$$5X = 4Y + 24$$
$$2.5Y = 6X - 4$$

If the equations are solved simultaneously a value will be found for X and Y such that both equations will be correct. The number of simultaneous equations which can be solved by this program is only limited by the available memory in the computer.

```
100   REM SIMULTANEOUS EQUATION SOLVER
110   REM NO. OF VARIABLES=NO. OF EQNS.
120   REM THERE MUST BE MORE THAN 1 EQN.
130   REM THE ARRAYS MAY BE REDIMENTIONED TO
140   REM ACCOMMODATE ANY NO. OF EQUATIONS
150   REM LIMITED ONY BY AVAILABLE MEMORY
160   DIM M(30,30),P(30),L(30)
170   INPUT"ENTER NO. OF VARIABLES";Z
180   FORE=1TOZ:FOR D=1 TO Z
190   PRINT"EQUATION #";E;", VARIABLE #";D;
```

```
200    INPUT M(E,D)
210    NEXT D:PRINT"CONSTANT FOR EQN #";E;
220    INPUT L(E):NEXT E
230    FORE=1TOZ−1
240    L=ABS(M(E,E)):B=E
250    FORD=E+1TOZ
260    IF ABS(M(D,E)) < L THEN 280
270    B=D:L=ABS(M(D,E))
280    NEXT D
290    IFL=0THEN550
300    IFB=E THEN 390
310    FORD=1TOZ
320    G=M(B,D)
330    M(B,D)=M(E,D)
340    M(E,D)=G
350    NEXT D
360    V=L(B)
370    L(B)=L(E)
380    L(E)=V
390    FORC=E+1TOZ
400    T=M(D,E) /M(E,E)
410    FORC=E+1TOZ
420    M(D,C)=M(D,C)−T*M(E,C)
430    NEXT C
440    L(D)=L(D)−T*L(E)
450    NEXT D
460    NEXT E
470    IF M(Z,Z)=0THEN550
480    E=Z−1:P(Z)=L(Z) /M(Z,Z)
490    U=0:FORD=E+1TOZ
500    U=U+M(E,D)*P(D)
510    NEXT D
520    P(E)=L(E)−U) /M(E,E)
530    E=E−1:IFE > 0THEN490
540    GOTO570
550    PRINT:PRINT"EQNS ARE UNSOLVABLE"
560    GOTO610
570    PRINT:PRINT
580    FORE=1TOZ
590    PRINT"VARIABLE #";E;"=";P(E)
600    NEXT E:PRINT
610    INPUT"TRY AGAIN (1=YES,  2=NO)";N
```

```
620   PRINT:PRINT
630   IF N=1 THEN PRINT:GOTO 170:ELSE END
```

PROGRAM/PLOTTER

This program is a general purpose plotting routine designed for use with a printer peripheral. Three types of plots may be made: two-dimensional, three-dimensional, and simultaneous plots. Lines 40-80 explain how functions to be plotted are to be entered in the program.

```
10    REM PLOTR
20    REM PLOT FUNCTIONS IN 2D, 3D OR SIMUL-
      TANEOUSLY
30    REM ROTATE OUTPUT 90 DEGREES FOR AC-
      TUAL PLOT
40    PRINT "IF THE FUNCTIONS DEFINED IN LINES
      1000, 2000, 3000 ARE TO"
50    PRINT "BE CHANGED, STOP THE PROGRAM AND
      ENTER FUNCTIONS IN THIS FORMAT:"
60    PRINT "FUNCT. #1- 1000 Y=SIN(X) (Y IN TERMS
      OF X)"
70    PRINT "FUNCT. #2- 2000 Y1=COS(X) (Y1 IN TERMS
      OF X) (Y1 IN TERMS OF X– FOR SIMUL. PLOT"
80    PRINT " FUNCT. #3- 3000 Z=EXP(Z) (Z IN TERMS
      OF Z– FOR 3D PLOTS"
90    PRINT
100   PRINT
110   PRINT
120   PRINT "SELECT: 1) 2D PLOT, 2) 3D PLOT, 3)
      END"
130   INPUT A
140   ON A GOTO 160, 520, 150
150   END
160   PRINT "SELECT: 1)PLOT 1 FUNCTION, 2) PLOT 2
      FUNCTIONS SIMULTANEOUSLY"
170   INPUT A
180   F1 = A
190   PRINT "ENTER MIN. X VALUE, MAX. X VALUE,
      X INCREMENT (SEPARATED BY COMMAS)";
```

```
200   INPUT E,F,D
210   PRINT "ENTER MIN.Y VALUE,MAX. Y VALUE";
220   INPUT H,G
230 Y1=56/(G−H)
240   PRINT "Y MIN:"; H;" Y MAX: ";G;" INCRE-
      MENT:";YI
250   PRINT
260   PRINT TAB(5); H; TAB(56); G
270   FOR B=1 TO 58
280   PRINT "+";
290   NEXT B
300   PRINT
304   A$ ="####.##"
310   FOR X=E TO F STEP D
320   PRINT USING A$; X ; PRINT ":";
330   GOSUB 1000
340   IF F1=1 THEN 380
350   GOSUB 2000
360   IF Y >Y1 THEN PRINT TAB(YI*Y1); "*";
      TAB(Y*YI); "#" ELSE PRINT TAB (Y*YI);"#";
      TAB(YI*Y1);"*"
370   GOTO 390
380   PRINT TAB (Y* YI); "*"
390   NEXT X
400   GOTO 120
520   REM 3D PLOT ROUTINE
525   A$="*"
530   E=5
540   V=25
550   G=.707106
560   C=961
570   PRINT "ENTER X INCREMENT";
580   INPUT IN
590   FOR X= −31 TO 31 STEP IN
600   A=0
610   B=1
620   D1=E*INT(SQR(C −X*X)/E)
630   FOR Y=D1 TO −D1 STEP −E
640   Z=SQR(X*X+Y*Y)
650   GOSUB 3000
655   Z=INT (V+Z −G*Y )
```

126

```
660   IF A$="*" THEN A$="+" ELSE A$="*"
670   IF Z< = A GOTO 730
680   A=Z
690.  IF Z B IF Z=F THEN IF A$= "*" THEN A$="+"
      ELSE A$="*"
700   PRINT TAB (Z) A$;
710   IF B LET F=Z
720   B=0
730   NEXT Y
740   PRINT " "
750   NEXT X
770   GOTO 120
1000  Y= ABS(SIN(X))
1001  RETURN
2000  Y1 =ABS(COS(X))
2001  RETURN
3000  Z=30*(EXP( -Z*Z/100) : RETURN
3001  RETURN
```

PROGRAM—EQUATION OF A LINE

This program not only has applications in pure mathematics, but practical mathematics as well. The program accepts (x,y) data points and determines the equation of a line which best fits (describes) the data. Applications are numerous. For instance, if you were on a weight-loss plan and inputted values for your weight vs amount of exercise or calorie intake, the program could find the equation of a line that best fits this data. Thus, you could input a value for one variable (e.g. calorie intake) and receive a corresponding value (e.g. weight) for the other variable. Other analyses include stock price vs Dow Index, miles traveled vs gallons used, distance vs time, heating costs vs outside temperature, etc.

```
1    REM LINE EQUATION CALCULATOR
2    REM MAY BE USED TO DESCRIBE A SET OF DATA
3    REM AND DETERMINE A CORRESPONDING
     POINT FOR
4    REM ANY ENTERED POINT
5    CLS 'CLEAR SCREEN
10   INPUT "ENTER A NAME FOR THE FIRST SET OF
     DTAT"; A$
```

```
20    INPUT "ENTER A NAME FOR THE SECOND SET
      OF DATA"; B$
72    PRINT "ENTER X, Y PAIRS SUCCESSIVELY,
      SEPARATED BY COMMAS"
75    PRINT "ENTER 0,0 TO END"
76    N=1
80    INPUT X, Y
90    IF (X=0) AND (Y=0) THEN 200
110   N=N+1
120   PRINT "SET NO.:"; N
130   A=A+X
140   B=B+X*X
150   C=C+Y*Y
160   D=D+Y
170   E=E+X*Y
180   GOTO 80
200   N=N −1:M=(E*N −D*A)/(B*N−A*A)
210   V=(D*B− E*A)/(B*N−A*A)
220   CLS 'CLEAR SCREEN
230   PRINT "Y="; M; "X+";V
240   PRINT "ENTER A VALUE FOR"; A$; "TO RE-
      CEIVE A CORRESPONDING"
250   PRINT "VALUE FOR "; B$
260   INPUT "ENTER 9999 IF YOU WANT VICE-
      VERSA";A
270   IF A=9999 THEN GOTO 350
280   PRINT
290   PRINT "Y="; M*A+V
300   GOTO240
350   REM
390   CLS 'CLEAR SCREEN
400   PRINT:PRINT "X="; −1/M; "*Y + "; V/M
419   PRINT "ENTER A VALUE FOR "; B$; " TO RE-
      CEIVE A CORRESPONDING"
429   PRINT "VALUE FOR "; A$
439   PRINT "ENTER 9999 FOR VICE-VERSA"
449   INPUT A
460   IF A=9999 THEN 350
470   PRINT "THE VALUE FOR X="; (A −V)/M
480   PRINT
490   GOTO 419
```

Chapter 4
Technical and
Scientific Applications

Technical and Scientific Applications

In the science fields, the computer has provided scientists with the ability to analyze problems that would have taken a lifetime to solve by normal methods. However, with the modern-day computer many of these problems are solved in minutes. Even the home computer has eliminated much of the mathematical drudgery.

MATHEMATICAL RECREATIONS

Interesting mathematical problems/ideas to implement on your computer include:

1. Use of probability to forecast the outcome of a sporting event—For example, an equation expressing the probability that a stronger team will win in a seven-game series is

$$p^4 + 4p^4q + 10p^3q^2x + 10p^2q^2(1-x)p$$

where p=probability that stronger team will win(=>.5)

q=probability that weaker team will win(=1-p)

x=conditional probability particular to a sport (e.g. for basketball this value has been calculated to be =.408)

2. Solve mathematical puzzles—Puzzles such as the following can probably be solved with the use of brute-force, trial and error computer techniques only, if they can be solved at all:

- Find three distinct right triangles with the following properties
    1. Are pythagorean (all three sides are integers)
    2. The perimeters of the three triangles are equivalent

3. The areas of the triangles are in arithmetic progression
- Find the smallest solution in positive integers x and y of $x^2 - n \cdot y^2 = 1$ where n = 61
- In how many ways can the integer 10,000 be expressed as a sum of distinct positive integers (ignoring permutations)
- Find the minimum value of the gamma function gamma $(n) = (n-1)!$ for integer n in the range $1 < n < 2$

Puzzles of simpler solution include such popular logic games as:
- "Instant Insanity"™ blocks (five blocks with different clolors on each side) must be arranged such that all five blocks put in a row have the same colors on each side. The computer could determine all possible solutions (720 total combinations of the blocks are possible).
- The "High I.Q. Game" board is in the shape of a cross, with markers in every hole except the center hole. The player jumps markers with adjacent markers as in checkers and then removes the one jumped over. Markers may not move unless a jump is possible. The object of the game is to jump all markers on the board, leaving one final marker; this is difficult to accomplish. The computer could determine how the game may be won and the number of different ways possible to win (is there only one method?).

3. Compute Pi, e, solutions for high-degree equations, mathematical oddities. Many mathematicians take delight in computing values for irrational expressions, determining equations for special mathematical circumstances, and discovering unusual properties of specific numbers. The computer is, of course, useful in such computations.

Calculation of the value of Pi to any number of decimal places may be accomplished by this BASIC program:

```
1  REM PI CALCULATION PROGRAM
2  REM DEMONSTRATES ITERATIVE TECHNIQUES
   (REQUIRES 30,000
3  REM LOOPS TO CALCULATE TO FIVE DECIMAL
   PLACES.)
5  DEFINT D
```

```
10   S=0:V=-1:R=1
11   FOR D=1 TO 10000
20   L=10000
30   T=2*R-1
40   V=-1*V
50   S=S+V/T
60   N=N+1:R=R+1
70   L=L+10000: IF L>110000 GOTO 30
80   PRINTN, 4*S
90   NEXT D
100  END
```

Pi is calculated using this formula:

$$\pi = 4 - 4/3 + 4/5 - 4/7 + 4/9 - 4/11 + \ldots$$

Similarly, the value of the natural log e may be calculated using this formula:

$$e^x = 1 + x + \frac{x^2}{2!} + \frac{x^3}{3!} + \frac{x^4}{4!} + \ldots$$

Programs to compute a Fibonacci Sequence are also popular. The sequence is created by adding each previous term to the term before that:

1,1, 2, 3, 5, 8, 13...

4. Games. Interesting mathematical games for your computer include:

•The four color map problem—A recreation which has interested mathematicians for many years is to prove that only four colors are needed to color any map such that no bordering countries are of the same color. The proof was accomplished with the use of a computer.

A game based on this fact could involve two players attempting to force each other into coloring two bordering countries the same color. In each turn, a player would choose any color to apply to any country on a map of random boundaries. Proper logic will insure that one player will lose.

•Magic squares game—The magic squares game pits the computer against a human in an attempt to complete a magic square, while blocking an opponent. A magic square is composed of smaller squares, each with a separate number inside. The numbers in the smaller squares in horizontal, vertical, and diagonal rows sum to the same amount. Opposing players could attempt to complete a magic square in opposing directions.

• The maze game—The maze game involves a randomly generated maze and a computer controlled mouse which learns to find its way through the maze.

• Exacto—A game for young people Exacto involves two five-digit numbers which have been randomly selected by the computer. Players are instructed to transform the first number into the second through multiplication, division, addition, or subtraction of any other number within a specified range. The computer would keep track of all computations at each stage. The players are scored according to speed or number of operations required to finish.

• Euclid—Let (p,q) be a pair of positive numbers such that p is greater than q; let A and B signify the two players. Players alternate turns. Each turn consists of replacing the larger of the two numbers given to a player by any positive number obtained by subtracting a positive multiple of the smaller number from the larger number (all numbers are integers). The first player to obtain zero for the (new) smaller number is declared winner.

A sample game is shown below; (51,30) is the starting pair of numbers:
A:(30,21) B:(21,9) A:(9,3) B:(3,0) B wins, or the game could have been-
A:(30,21) B:(21,9) A: (12, 9) B:(9,3) A:(3,0) A wins

WEATHER FORECASTING

Forecasting the weather is usually thought to be a task for large computers only. However, local weather forecasting can be accomplished with surprising accuracy by taking note of wind direction and barometric changes. A chart in use by local weather bureaus has been based upon these two parameters and could easily be computerized.

Wind Change		Barometric condition	Forecast code
FROM	TO		
S	SW	7	L
S	SE	3	E
		4	F
		9	M

Wind Direction	Barometric Condition	Forecast
NE SE	3	G
	4	H
	5	J
	6	K
	9	M
N E	3	I
	4	A
	9	N
to the West	8	O
NW SW	1	C
	2	B
	3	D
	7	L

If a forecast is not listed for the proper barometric condition, other factors must be used to provide the forecast.

Barometric Conditions:

1. 30.1 or more and steady
2. 30.1-30.2 rising rapidly
3. 30.1 or more falling slowly
4. 30.1 or more falling rapidly
5. 30.0 or less falling slowly
6. 30.0 or less falling rapidly
7. 30.0 or less rising slowly
8. 29.8 or less rising rapidly
9. 29.8 or less falling rapidly

A rapid change is considered to be over .06"/hour.

Forecasts

A. Summer-Rain probable/12-24 hours. Winter-Rain or snow, increasing wind; often sets in when barometer begins to fall and winds sets in from NE.
B. Fair, followed within two days by rain.
C. Continued fair, no decided temperature change.
D. Fair for two days with slowly rising temperatures.
E. Rain within 24 hours.
F. Wind increasing, rain within 24 hours.
G. Rain within 12-18 hours.
H. Wind increasing, rain within 12 hours.

I. Summer-Light winds, rain may not fall for several days. Winter-Rain within 24 hours.
J. Rain will continue for 1 to 2 days.
K. Rain, with high wind, followed within 36 hours by clearing, and in winter by colder.
L. Clearing within a few hours, fair for several days.
M. Severe storm imminent, followed within 24 hours by clearing, and in winter by colder.
N. Severe northeast gale and heavy precipitation. In winter, heavy snow followed by a cold wave.
O. Clearing and colder.

A cloud chart with forecasts included is also useful. The forecast data for the various types of clouds could be stored and a comparison made between this forecast and a forecast from the above chart.

Other statistics best suited to be calculated by the computer include: wind chill factor, temperature humidity index and relative humidity.

Wind Chill Factor

$$H = (.14 + .47\sqrt{V})(36.5\text{-}T)$$

where H = chill in calories lost per sq. cm. skin per second
V = wind velocity (m/sec)
T = Temperature (°C)

ENERGY EFFICIENCY COMPUTATION

A computer-statistical comparison between the water temperature in a solar energy system and the outside temperature, angle of the sun, etc. could serve to evaluate the efficiency of a home solar energy system. A/D converters could also be used to gather the information automatically.

For those considering the installation of a solar system, another statistical analysis of heating requirements for your home based on Btu/hr times the number of hours of your furnace operation during the heating season. The size of a solar system necessary to heat your house may then be calculated using this data and the manufacturer's efficiency data.

In the central U.S. on June 21, the maximum solar energy striking the earth is 290 Btu/square foot (approximately 15 hours in the day). On December 21, the solar energy is a maximum of 220 Btu/square foot (approximately

9 hours in the day). Thus, one must compute average values for the variables in the formula below.

Solar collector Btu output =

$$\frac{\text{Btu/sq. ft. *hrs/day*sq. ft. of collector*max. efficiency}}{2}$$

Keep in mind that it takes 500 Btu to heat water at ground temperature (40°F) to 100°F and that the desired water temperature for home use is 120°F.

The answer to "How much fuel can be saved by turning the thermostat down at night from 70°F to 60°F?" may be determined using this equation:

$$A = \frac{.0625 \ (n-1)W}{Z}$$

Where A=amount of heat (Btu)
W=the normal heat loss/hr. (Btu)
n=the number of hours of discontinued heating
z=the number of hours from the beginning of re-heating until the house is at an acceptable temperature

To find the heat loss of your home:

$$H = \frac{kA(t-t^1)T}{d}$$

where H=heat transmission (Btus)
K=coefficient of thermal conduction (Values for the type of construction of your home may be found in builder's manuals)
A=exposed area
$(t-t^1)$=temperature difference between inside and outside (°F)
T=duration of exposure (hours)
d=thickness of walls (inches)

To calculate fuel requirements

$$C = \frac{H(t_a - t_b)N \times S \times q}{100,000 \times (t_i - t_o)}$$

where C=fuel cost
H=heat loss/hr.

t_o=outside temperature
t_i=inside temperature
t_a=average inside temperature
t_b=average outside temperature
N=number of hours of heating required
S=number of units of fuel
q=cost per unit of fuel

Additional formulas available in building manuals may be used to compute the savings of installing insulation or the area of a solar collector necessary to heat a house of certain dimensions and construction.

TECHNICAL AND SCIENTIFIC CALCULATION

Aviation—The private or business pilot will find the following calculations useful. Some are designed for portable programmable calculators so that programs may be used while in flight.

1. Flight plan with wind. Calculation of the heading, speed, fuel, ETA, etc. for a trip of multiple legs could be done.
2. Long-range flight plan. Calculations could be done for great circle routes: distance, time, fuel, source.
3. Atmosphere, speed, temperature and altitude. From pressure altitude, a program could calculate the speed of sound, temperature, pressure and density relative to standard sea level.
4. Prediction freezing level and lowest usable flight level.
5. Wind components and average vector. Crosswind and tail/head wind components of a single wind vector could be calculated.
6. Dead reckoning of position.
7. Great circle flying navigation.
8. Course correction to fly correct path.
9. Rhumbline navigation.
10. Unit conversions. Length, volume weight, English and metric temperature conversions.

$$°F=(9/5)(°C + 32°)$$
$$°C=(5/9)(°F-32°)$$

Marine Navigation—Some of the following applications are designed for use with programmable calculators due to their portability.

1. Time-speed-distance with current sailing. A useful program could solve time-speed-distance equations and consider the current in determining the proper course to steer and speed through the water necessary to reach a given destination in a specified length of time.
2. Distance short of, beyond, or to a horizon. A program could calculate the distance to the apparent horizon as well as the distance to and visibility of an object of known height.
3. Velocity, VMG, and current vectors. Given two of the following, 1) drift and set of the current, 2) speed and course through the water, 3) speed and course made good, a program could calculate the unknown value.
4. Running fix from two objects. A program could calculate a fix of a vessel from bearings of two objects.
5. Planet location. A program could estimate the altitude and azimuth of the four navigational planets. The GMT of twilight could also be calculated, or manually inputted.
6. Rhumbline navigation calculation.
7. Sight reduction calculation.
8. Length conversions. (e.g. nautical miles to statute miles)
9. Vector addition.
10. Estimated time of arrival.

Medical calculations

1. Conversions of weight, length, volume to other units, or English to metric conversion.
2. Lung diffusion calculations.
3. Blood acid-base status determination.
4. Beer's law calculation
5. Protein electrophoresis. Given integration counts of a number of protein fractions, the percentage of each may be found.
6. Body surface area estimation.
7. Oxygen saturation and content. Oxygen content and saturation in the blood may be found given pO_2, pCO_2, pH, and body temperature.

Surveying Calculations

1. Azimuth/bearing traverse. Given reference coordinates, leg length, and azimuth or bearing and quadrant, the endpoint coordinates, departure, latitude, and total distance may be computed.
2. Slope reduction determinations.
3. Point of intersection calculation.

Chemistry

1. Calculation of requirements to produce a given solution.

```
00010   REM STOCK SOLUTION COMPUTATION
00020   REM COMPUTES THE AMOUNT OF STOCK
        SOLUTION AND WATER NECESSARY TO
00030   REM PRODUCE A GIVEN SOLUTION
00040   PRINT "ENTER THESE VALUES: CONCENT-
        RATION OF WORKING SOLUTION, CON-
        CENTRATION OF"
00050   INPUT "STOCK SOLUTION, TOTAL AMOUNT
        OF SOLUTION.";PW, PS, QT
00060   OS=(PW*QT)/PS
00070   W=QT−OS
00080   PRINT "THE QUANTITY OF STOCK SOLU-
        TION=";OS
00090   PRINT "THE QUANTITY OF WATER TO
        ADD=";W
00100   PRINT:PRINT
00110   END
```

2. Calculations of the following parameters, given adequate inputs: pH, molality, total atomic weights, gas density and pressure, electron energies, gravimetric factors, liquid pressure, degree of saturation.
3. Plotting/simulation of reaction rates, electron distribution, etc.

Physics

1. Plotting of potential energy functions, lab data, etc.
2. Conversions of units

3. Solutions to elementary equations: velocity, acceleration, momentum, work, power, etc.

Additional Applications
1. Statistical analysis of data. Useful statistical applications include: curve fitting and plotting, Chi-square tests, analysis of variance and standard deviation, solution to equations, correlation coefficients.
2. Calculation of tables for a specific application. Functions which are commonly referred to, yet do not have reference tables, could be calculated for a number of values, and the results displayed in table form for easy reference.
3. Interfacing microcomputers to lab instrumentation can result in automatic data log and aquisition systems.
4. A voice input interface could accept data called off by a lab technician too busy to manually record data.

ENGINEERING

Professionals and hobbyists as well will have use for computer programs in the following engineering fields.

• Electrical engineering

1. Active high-and low-pass filter design. High-and low-pass filters may be designed for given center frequency, gain, and Q values for the resistors and capacitors in the infinite-gain multiple-feedback circuit.

```
00100  REM LOW PASS FILTER DESIGN PROGRAM
00110  REM SHUNT M-DERIVED FILTER
00120  INPUT "ENTER THE CUTOFF FREQUEN-
       CY";F1
00130  INPUT "ENTER THE FREQUENCY OF RE-
       MOTE CUTOFF";F2
00140  INPUT "ENTER THE TERMINATING RESIS-
       TANCE";R
00150  L=SQR(1-(F1*F1/(F2*F2)))*R/(3.14159*F1)
00160  C1=(1-(SQR(1-(F1*F1/(F2*F2))))-2)/(4*3.14159*
       SQR(1-F1*F1/(F2*F2))*F1*R)
00170  C2=SQR(1-(F1*F1/(F2*F2)))/(3.14159*R*F2)
```

```
00180   PRINT "THE VALUE FOR L=";L
00190   PRINT "THE VALUE FOR C1=";C1
00200   PRINT "THE VALUE FOR C2=";C2
00210   PRINT
00220   END
```

2. Active bandpass filter design. Second-order active bandpass filters may be designed using a multiple-feedback network. Both high-Q and low-Q circuits could be realized. Standard values may be selected for easy implementation.

3. Chebyshev and Butterworth filter design. Chebyshev and Butterworth low-pass filters may be designed for specified filter order, termination resistance, and corner frequency.

4. Resonant circuits. The impedance and resonant frequency could be calculated by a program for series or parallel resonant circuits whose component values are specified.

5. Attentuators. Component values for T and Pi impedance matching circuits may be found for specified input/output impedances and desired loss. Minimum-loss pad matching may be performed for given impedances.

6. T to Pi transformations. T(Pi) networks may be transformed to Pi(T) networks having the same characteristics.

```
00100   REM T-NETWORK DESIGN PROGRAM
00105   REM PROVIDES A GRAPHIC REPRESENTA-
        TION OF THE CIRCUIT
00110   INPUT "ENTER THE RESISTANCE OF THE
        CIRCUIT WITH OUTPUT TERMINALS UN-
        LOADED";RI
00120   INPUT "ENTER THE OUTPUT RESISTANCE
        WITH THE INPUT TERMINALS UNLOAD-
        ED";RO
00130   INPUT "ENTER THE RESISTANCE WITH THE
        OUTPUT TERMINALS SHORTCIRCUITED";
        RN
00140   A=-1
00150   B=RO+1
```

```
00160   C=RO*RN−RI
00170   Q1=(−B+SQR(B*B−4*A*C))/(2*A)
00180   Q2=(−B−SQR(B*B−4*A*C))/(2*A)
00190   IF Q1>=0 THEN R3=Q1 ELSE R3=Q2
00200   R2=RO−R3
00210   RI=RI−R3
00220   PRINT: PRINT: PRINT
00230   PRINT "T-NETWORK CIRCUIT"
00240   PRINT : PRINT"          R1          R2          "
00250   PRINT"_____     _____     _____"
00260   FOR X = 1 TO 3
00270   PRINT"!           !          !          "
00280   NEXT X
00290   PRINT" R-IN_____  _____R OUT"
00300   PRINT"_____  _____"; R3; "OHM"
00310   PRINT"_____"
00320   FOR X=1 TO 3
00330   PRINT "!                !          !"
00340   NEXT X : PRINT"_____"
00350   PRINT : PRINT
00360   END
```

7. Ladder network analysis. The input impedance for a ladder network could be calculated; the network may be composed of any combination of resistors, capacitors, and inductors.

8. Coil properties. The inductance or number of turns for a single or multi-layer coil may be found given wire diameter and dimensions of the coil.

Inductance of Two Parallel, Round Wires One Forming Return Circuit:

$$L = .0041[2.303 \log_{10} (2 D/d − D/1)]$$

where L = inductance (μH)

D = distance in cm. between centers of wires

d = diameter of wire (cm)

l = length of conductor (cm)

9. Power transformer design. Core weight may be calculated for a specified power requirement. For a specified core area, flux density and frequency, the number of primary and secondary turns is found.

10. Rectifier circuits. Full-wave or half-wave rectifier circuits may be evaluated for given component values, input voltage, and frequency. The DC output voltage and peak-to-peak ripple may also be calculated.

11. S and Y parameter transformations. A set of S(Y) parameters expressed as magnitudes and angles may be transformed to a set of Y(S) parameters.

12. Phase-locked loops. Natural frequency, damping factor, and loop noise bandwidth may be found for either passive or active phase-locked loops. Loop gain and component values for the circuits are required for input.

13. Transistor amplifier design. Collector current and sensitivity factors may be computed for transistor circuits for specified current gain, supply voltage, and resistor values.

14. Fourier series. Fourier coefficients may be computed for discrete values for a periodic function. Sine and cosine coefficients may be found and could be used to calculate new values of the function.

15. Reactive L-Network impedance matching. Networks which will match any two complex impedances may be determined.

16. Bilateral design, stability factor, maximum gain, and optimum matching. A program could compute the maximum gain available and the load and source reflection coefficients which yield the maximum gain.

17. Transistor configuration conversion.

18. Resistive attenuator design.

19. Smith chart conversions.

20. Phase shift oscillator design.

21. DC bias analysis.

22. Waveform limits determination.

23. Plotting of waveforms.

24. Gain vs. frequency circuit analysis.

Frequency Conversions:

$T = 1/f$

$w = 2\pi f$

$\lambda = v/f$

$f = 1/T$

$f = w/2\pi$

$f = v/\lambda$

where T= period
     f= frequency
     w= radian frequency
     λ= wavelength
     V= propagation velocity

25.   555 timer circuit design. Given the frequency duty cycle and either the timing capacitor or resistor, a program could calculate the other timing component, charge time, discharge time, and period of the commonly used 555 stable multivibrator circuit.

26.   Plate resistance-transconductance calculations.

27.   Resonance calculations. Resonant frequency of inductance-capacitance circuit:

$$f_r = \frac{L - R_L{}^2 C}{2\pi\sqrt{LC}\ (L - R_c{}^2 C)}$$

where $L = 1/(4\pi^2 f^2 C)$
    $C = 1/(4\pi^2 f^2 L)$
    R_L=series resistance of inductor
    R_c=effective series resistance of capacitor
    f_r =resonant frequency

28.   Gauss calculations.

29.   Antenna design. A given frequency could be inputted to a program which would calculate the antenna dimensions for a dipole, Yagi, or cubical-quad antenna.

30.   Reactance chart calculations.

31.   Decibel conversion and voltage to dBm conversion. Voltage ratio in Decibels:

$$N_{dB} = 20\ \log_{10}\ (E_{OUT}/E_{IN})$$

where E_{out} = output voltage
    E_{IN}= input voltage

Such computations would be helpful to the serious audiophile. Also of interest to the audiophile would be a formula used to compute the inductance of a straight wound speaker wire:

$$L = .002l[2.303\ \log_{10}\ (4l/d) - .75]$$

where L= inductance (μH)
    d= diameter of wire (cm)
    l= length of conductor (cm)

32. Design of controlled rectifier circuits.
33. Integrated-circuit current-source design.
34. Solution of resistive networks.
35. Resistive voltage divider design.
36. RF amplifier analysis.
37. Bipolar junction transistor analysis.
38. Complex matrix calculations as used in electrical engineering.
39. Evaluation routine for a program of Boolean functions. AND, OR, NOT, etc. logic statements could be evaluated as a program; the circuit status at each step would be outputted.
40. Ohm's law calculation. Determine the unknown value.

$I = E/R$
$E = IR$
$R = E/I$

where R = resistance (ohms)
E = voltage
I = current

41. Wheatstone bridge design.
42. Resistor or capacitor color codes. An ideal program for the novice in electronics would output the value for a resistor or capacitor; the color codes would be inputted.
43. Inductance Bridge calculation.

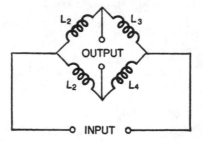

if any three values are known the fourth may be calculated:

$L_1 = L_2L_3/L_2$
$L_2 = L_1L_4/L_3$
$L_3 = L_1L_4/L_2$
$L_4 = L_2L_3/L_1$

```
00100   REM RL EQUIVALENT IMPEDANCE
00110   REM ANSWERS A QUESTION SUCH AS 'WHAT
        IS THE EQUIVALENT
```

```
00120  REM IMPEDANCE OF A 300 OHM RESISTOR
       AND A 30 MILLIHENRY
00130  REM INDUCTOR AT A FREQUENCY OF 2000
       HERTZ?'
00140  INPUT "ENTER RESISTANCE IN OHMS"; R
00150  INPUT "ENTER INDUCTANCE IN MILLIHEN-
       RIES"; IND
00160  INPUT "ENTER FREQUENCY";FREQ
00170  EQU=(2*3.141582*FREQ*IND*.001)*(1/(SIN
       (ATN((2*3.141592*FREQ*IND*.001)/R)))
00180  PRINT"THE EQUIVALENT IMPEDANCE=";
       EQU
```

```
00100  REM A/C VOLTAGE DIVIDER CALCULATIONS
00110  REM DETERMINES THE MODULUS AND
       PHASE
00120  INPUT "ENTER THE ANGULAR FREQUEN-
       CY";A
00130  R1=1E6: R2=0: I1=0: I2 =1/(A *1E − 6)
00140  R=(R2*(R1+R2)+I2 * (I1 + I2)/(R1 + R2) * (R1 +
       R2) + (I1 + I2) * (I1 + I2))
00150  I=(−R2*(I1+I2)+(R1+R1)*I2)/((R1+R1)*(R1+
       R1)+(I1+I2)*(I1+I2))
00160  C=SQR(R*R+I*I)
00170  D = 180*ATN(I/R) /3.14159
00180  PRINT "ANGULAR FREQUENCY", "MOD-
       ULUS", "PHASE"
00190  PRINT A,C,D
00200  PRINT
00210  GOTO120
```

- **Civil engineering**
  1. Moment of inertia calculation
  2. Vector statics
  3. Section properties.
  4. Stress on an element or beam.
  5. Static equilibrium about a point.
- **Chemical engineering**
  1. Ideal gas equation of state
  2. Conservation of energy calculations
  3. Heat exchanger analysis

4. Curve fitting
5. Hydrocarbon combustion calculations.
* **Machine design**
1. Constant acceleration calculations, relation to time and velocity
2. Kinetic energy determination.
3. Critical shaft speed calculation
4. Cam design functions
5. Gear and spring calculations/design
6. RPM/torque/power computation

PROGRAM—ANTENNA DESIGN

This program may be used to calculate the dimensions for a yagi antenna to receive television, radio, or amateur radio broadcasts; the antenna is designed for a specific frequency. Such an antenna can often receive signals from distances not previously approached. If the mathematical specifications of the antenna design are unclear, reference an electronic manual for a picture. Construction of the antenna is not difficult and should cost no more than twenty dollars.

```
10  REM YAGI ANTENNA DESIGN PROGRAM
20  INPUT "INPUT THE FREQUENCY TO DESIGN
    THE ANTENNA FOR IN MEGAHERTZ"; F
30  PRINT:PRINT
40  PRINT "FOR"; F; "MEGAHERTZ THE LENGTHS
    OF THE ELEMENTS ARE:"
50  PRINT "ELEMENT NUMBER", "LENGTH IN IN-
    CHES"
51  A=466.667/F: D=A*.05*A: B=11. 52*A
53  W=6*A: X=4. 32*A: E=11. 28*A
55  Y=4. 8*A: G=3. 6*A: L=4. 8*A
57  C=11. 4*A: Z=11. 46*A
59  R=5*W+X+G+Y+L+.333
60  PRINT "1",D
70  PRINT "2", B
80  PRINT "3", C
90  PRINT "4",E
100 PRINT "5",E
110 PRINT "6",A
120 PRINT "7",Z
```

```
130   PRINT "8",E
140   PRINT "9",E
150   PRINT "10",E
160   INPUT "TYPE 'ENTER' TO CONTINUE";A$
165   PRINT:PRINT
170   PRINT "ELEMENT SPACING:"
180   PRINT "ELEMENT NUMBER:", "SPACING IN IN-
      CHES:"
190   PRINTZ"1-2",L
200   PRINT "2-3",X
210   PRINT "3-4",W
220   PRINT "4-5", W
230   PRINT "5-6",W
240   PRINT "6-7", G
250   PRINT "7-8", Y
260   PRINT "8-9",W
270   PRINT "9-10",W
280   PRINT "THE BOOM IS";C; "INCHES LONG (";C/
      12; " FEET LONG)"
290   END
```

PROGRAM—HIGH-ACCURACY PLOTTING PROGRAM

The purpose of this program is to accurately plot a function such that a connecting line may be drawn with the accuracy of a plotter. A portion of the output appears as:

```
01000000000000000
00200000000000000
00040000000000000
00006000000000000
00000900000000000
00000009000000000
```

The numbers other than zero are to be used in plotting the function by hand. The value of the numbers from 1-9 indicates the point at which the line should be drawn through the number. Thus, if the number 1 appeared, a line would be drawn such that it touched the bottom of the 1. If 5 appeared, the line would be drawn through the middle of 5. If 9 appeared, the line would be drawn through the very top of the 9. In this manner, a highly accurate graph may be drawn. This program demonstrates one way to overcome the problem of not having the best peripheral (in this case a plotter) available.

There are several scientific and engineering applications which could make use of this program for the professional with a personal computer.

```
00050   REM HIGH ACCURACY FUNCTION PLOTTING
        ROUTINE-PRESENTLY SET
00070   REM FOR SINE WAVES
00100   DIMU(10),V(10),W(10),T(2000)
00110   MAT T=ZER
00120   PRINT "MEAN VALUE IS SET=75"
00130   INPUT "ENTER THE WIDTH";N
00140   INPUT "ENTER THE NO. OF SINEWAVES TO
        PLOT" ;Z
00150   MAT SIZE T(N)
00160   FOR I=1TOZ
00170   INPUT "ENTER THE STARTING POINT";W1
00180   INPUT "ENTER THE AMPLITUDE";V1
00190   INPUT "ENTER THE PERIOD";U1
00200   V(I)=V1
00210   U(I)=U1
00220   W(I)=W1
00240   NEXT I
00250   FOR J=1 TO N
00260   FOR I=1 TO Z
00270   T(J)=T (J)+V(I)*SIN(2*3.14159/U(I)*(J-1+W(I)))
00280   NEXT I
00290   T(J)=INT(T(J)+75.5)
00300   IF T(J)>0 THEN 00320
00310   T(J)=0
00320   NEXT J
00330   X9=0
00350   MAT PRINT T;
00360   X9=0
00370   INPUT "TO PLOT THE GRAPH TYPE '1',ELSE
        TYPE '0'";X9
00380   IF X9=0 THEN 00880
00390   LET A9=0
00400   LET B9=0
00410   LET C9=0
00420   LET D9=0
00430   FOR I1=1 TO ((N-1)/60)+1
```

```
00440   P1=1+60*(I1-1)
00450   L1=150
00460   FOR I2=1 TO 16
00470   FOR I3=1 TO 4
00480   P4=P1+15*(I3-1)
00490   IF P4>N THEN 00780
00500   Q4=P4+I4
00510   IF Q4 < N THEN 00530
00520   Q4=N
00530   G9=0
00540   FOR I4=P4 TO Q4
00550   IF T(I4)<L1 THEN 00760
00560   T1=T(I4)—L1
00570   IF T1<9 THEN 00590
00580   T1=9
00590   IF T1<> 0 THEN 00610
00600   T1=1
00610   T(I4)=-1
00620   T2=14-G9
00630   T1=T1*10 ↑ T2
00640   ON I3 GOTO 00650, 00680, 00710, 00740
00650   A8=P4
00660   A9=A9+T1
00670   GOTO 00760
00680   B9=B9+T1
00690   B8=P4
00700   GOTO 00760
00710   C9=C9+T1
00720   C8=P4
00730   GOTO 00760
00740   D9=D9+T1
00750   D8=P4
00760   G9=G9+1
00770   NEXT I4
00780   NEXT I3
00790   A$="### ################ ######
        ######## ################"
00800   PRINT USING A$;L1;A9;B9;C9;D9
00810   A9=B9=C9=D9=0
00820   L1=L1-10
00830   NEXT I2
```

```
00840   B$=" ####      XXXXXXXXXX      ####
        XXXXXXXXXX #### XXXXXXXXXX ####"
00850   PRINT USING B$; A8; B8; C8; D8
00860   A8=B8=C8=D8=0
 870    NEXT I1
00880   END
```

PROGRAM—LOGIC CIRCUIT ANALYSIS

The purpose of this program is to simulate the operation of a simple logic circuit. The circuitry (gates and connecting lines or "nodes") is described to the computer along with the input states to the circuit (e.g. on or off are represented as 1 and 0 respectively). Next, the program determines what the resultant states of nodes will be throughout the circuit following all logic "decisions". Essentially, this program allows one to design and test a logic circuit without breadboarding it.

The program recognizes the following gates: AND, OR, INV, NAND, exclusive OR (abbreviated XOR), exclusive NOR (abbreviated XNOR); up to 64 gates and 255 nodes may be used in one circuit. To begin, the program will allow one to input a circuit; answer 1 for a new circuit to the first question. Next, the program will request a "label" for the first gate (which may be any gate in the circuit). This is simply a distinguishing number (any number) for the gate. Now, input the gate type (e.g. AND, OR, etc.) and then input the identifying nodes connected to the gate. For example, to describe the circuit below, the following sequence could be used:

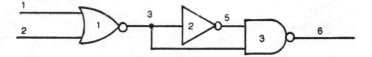

SELECT: 1)NEW CIRCUIT   2)OLD CIRCUIT ?1

ENTER THE LABEL?1
ENTER THE GATE? NOR
ENTER THE NODE?3
ENTER THE NODE?1
ENTER THE NODE?2
ENTER THE NODE?0   (0 is used here to mean "go to
                      next gate")

151

ENTER THE LABEL?2
ENTER THE GATE?INV
ENTER THE NODE?5
ENTER THE NODE?3
ENTER THE NODE?0
ENTER THE LABEL?3
ENTER THE GATE?NAND
ENTER THE NODE?6
ENTER THE NODE?5
ENTER THE NODE?3
ENTER THE NODE?0

Remember to enter the output node for each gate first, followed by input nodes.

After describing the circuit, the logic states of various nodes will be described. Simply type the number of the node and its initial state (1 or 0). Usually, only the input nodes are described.

Finally, the program analyzes the operation of the circuit, outputting the state of each node after the circuit has been completed. The circuit is analyzed according to standard logic tables. In this manner, the professional or hobbyist can test circuit operation without breadboarding.

```
10   REM LOGIC CIRCUIT ANALYSIS PROGRAM
30   DIM F(3000)
40   FOR X=1 TO 8
50   READ X(X)
60   NEXT X: READ A1, A2
65   A(9)=25
70   B$="AND OR   INV NANDNOR XOR XNOR"
80   PRINT
90   PRINT "SELECT:1)ENTER A CIRCUIT"
100  PRINT "        2)ENTER SPECIFIED STATES FOR
     NODES"
110  PRINT"        3)ANALYZE CIRCUIT OPERATION"

120  PRINT"        4)OUTPUT THE STATES OF
     NODES"
130  INPUT "        5)OUTPUT THE CIRCUIT";A3
140  ON A3 GOTO 150, 350, 500, 1300, 1500
150  INPUT "SELECT: 1)NEW CIRCUIT, 2)OLD CIR-
     CUIT";X
155  IF X=2 THEN 190
160  FOR A4=8 TO 511
```

```
170   F(A2+A4)=0
180   NEXT A4
190   PRINT
200   INPUT "ENTER THE LABEL";A5:A5=8*A5
205   IF A5=<0 THEN 80
210   FOR A4=0 TO 7
220   F(A5+A4+A2)=0
230   NEXT A4:   A6=0
240   INPUT "ENTER THE GATE"; W$
250   IF W$="REDO" THEN 190
260   IF W$="AND" THEN A6=1
261   IF W$ = "OR" THEN A6=2
262   IF W$="INV" THEN A6=3
263   IF W$="NAND" THEN A6=4
264   IF W$="NOR" THEN A6=5
265   IF W$="XOR" THEN A6=6
266   IF W$="XNOR" THEN A6=7
270   IF A6=0 THEN 240
300   F(A2+A5)=A6: A5=A5+1
310   INPUT "ENTER THE NODE";A6
320   IF A6 <>0 THEN 300 ELSE 200
350   INPUT "SELECT: 1)REDO OR BEGIN 2 )CON-
      TINUE";X
360   IF X=2 THEN 400
370   PRINT: FOR A4=1 TO 255
380   F(A1+A4)=255
390   NEXT A4
400   INPUT "ENTER THE NODE";A6
405   IF A6<=0 THEN 80
410   INPUT "ENTER THE STATE";A7
420   F(A1+A6)=A7
430   GOTO 400
500   A8=0
520   A8=A8+1:PRINT "NO.";A8
525   A9=0
530   FOR A4=1 TO 63
540   A6=F(A4*8+A2)
545   IF A6=0 THEN 950
550   ON A6 GOTO 600, 650, 700, 750, 800, 850, 900
600   B=0: GOSUB 1180
610   GOTO 920
650   B=1: GOSUB 1180
```

```
660    GOTO920
700    B1=F(A1+F(A2+2+8*A4))
710    GOSUB 980
720    GOTO 920

750    B=0: GOSUB 1180
760    GOSUB 980
770    GOTO 920

800    B=1: GOSUB 1180
810    GOSUB 980
820    GOTO 920

850    GOSUB 1110
860    GOTO 920

900    GOSUB 1110
910    GOSUB 980
920    IF B1=F(A1+F(8*A4+1+A2)) THEN 950
930    A9=1
940    F(A1+F(A2+8*A4+1))=B1
950    NEXT A4
960    IF A9=1 THEN 520
970    GOTO 80
980    IF B1 > 1 THEN 1000
990    B1=1-B1:RETURN
1000   B1=257-B1: RETURN
1110   B2=F(A1+F(8*A4+2+A2))
1120   B3=F (A1+F(8*A4+3+A2))
1130   IF B2<>0 AND B<>0 THEN 1140 ELSE
       B1=B2+B3: RETURN
1140   IF B2-1<>0 AND B3-1<>0 THEN 1150 ELSE
       B1=B3*B2: GOSUB 980
1145   RETURN
1150   B1=1
1160   IF B3=B2 THEN B1=0
1170   RETURN
1180   B1=1-B
1190   FOR B4=2 TO 7
1200   B2=F(8*A4+B4+A2)
1210   IF B2=0 THEN 1260
1220   B5=F(B2+A1)
1230   IF B5<>B THEN 1240 ELSE B1=B: RETURN
1240   IF B1+B5<>257 THEN 1250 ELSE B1=B: RE-
       TURN
1250   IF B5=1-B THEN 1260 ELSE B1=B5
```

```
1260    NEXT B4
1270    RETURN
1300    A9=1
1310    FOR A4=1 TO 255
1320    IF F(A4+A1)>1 THEN 1400
1330    PRINT A4; ": " ;F(A4+A1)
1400    NEXT A4
1410    PRINT
1420    GOTO 90
1500    FOR A4=1 TO 63
1510    A6=F(8*A4+A2)
1520    IF A6=0 THEN 1700
1530    PRINT A4; TAB(4);
1540    A9=10 : PRINT MID$(B$,A6*4-3,4);
1550    FOR B4=1 TO 7
1560    A6=F(8*A4+A2+B4)
1570    IF A6=0 THEN 1610
1580    PRINT TAB(A9);A6;
1590    A9=4+A9
1600    NEXT B4
1610    PRINT
1700    NEXT A4
1710    GOTO 90
2000    DATA 1,4,6,9,13,16,19,23
2001    DATA 768,1025
```

TACHOMETER/DWELL METER CALCULATION

Your oscilloscope may be converted into a tachometer and dwell meter in conjunction with your computer. The following information must be inputted to the computer to determine engine RPM and dwell angle:

a. Number of cylinders in the engine
b. Interval in milliseconds for open ignition points
c. Interval in milliseconds for closed ignition points

Factors a and b are determined using the oscilloscope. RPM may also be calculated using the factors of tire diameter, gear ratio, and vehicle speed.

$$\text{ignition pulse frequency} = \frac{\text{RPM} \times \text{No. Cylinders}}{120}$$

STATISTICS FOR THE SOCIAL SCIENCES

Analysis of social science research usually requires numerous statistical computations, best accomplished with the use of the computer. Often universities and other research centers do not provide adequate computer facilities for social science analysis, leaving only one option—let your personal computer do the job. Non-professionals may also desire to do this type of analysis as well. Possibilities are numerous; here are a few:

Questionnaire analysis—Clubs and other organizations may find this useful in surveying their membership; politicians use such to determine voter dispositions; businessmen will find questionnaire analysis useful to survey their markets.

Confidence interval determination—A confidence interval may be used to answer such questions as: "From a sample of 1000 washing machines sold, 400 were white; does this necessarily imply that more than one-third of all customers prefer white?"

Graphing results of data and curve fitting(e.g. answer the question—"Does the data describe a normal curve?")

Research—Leading national newspapers print approximately 500 column inches of text each day in main news sections. Some of these inches can be identified as politically oriented—favorable/unfavorable to Republicans or Democrats or third party members; others are neutral. In theory, material that reflects the political leanings of a newspaper's editors should only be found in the editorial section. But, in practice, the amount of text space allotted to a candidate or party reflects the paper's views, however inconspicuously. A school of journalism will be using a small computer to record and plot the ratios of column inches which apply to the possible categories for the fifteen national newspapers (1978). Such research is now becoming popular with the advent of small, inexpensive computers; you or your organization may wish to conduct such research.

ADDITIONAL SCIENTIFIC PROGRAMS
Temperature Humidity Index Calculator

```
00010   REM TEMPERATURE HUMIDITY INDEX CAL-
        CULATOR
00020   REM DETERMINES THE EFFECTIVE TEMP-
        ERATURE
00030   INPUT "ENTER THE RELATIVE HUMIDITY";H
```

```
00040   IF H>94 THEN A=0 ELSE IF H>89 AND H<95
        THEN A=2
00050   IF H>79 AND H<90 THEN A=4 ELSE IF H>69
        AND H<80 THEN A=6
00060   IF H>59 AND H<70 THEN A=10 ELSE A=14
00070   INPUT "ENTER THE TEMPERATURE (IN DE-
        GREES F)";T
00080   TH=.8*T+15-A
00090   PRINT "THE TEMPERATURE HUMIDITY
        INDEX =";TH
00100   PRINT
00110   END
```

Air Conditioning Requirements

```
00010   REM AIR CONDITIONING REQUIREMENT
        CALCULATION
00020   REM DETERMINES THE BTU RATING FOR AN
        AIR COND./HEATER FOR YOUR HOME
00030   INPUT "ENTER THE ESTIMATED TOTAL
        SQUARE FEET OF EXTERIOR WALL AREA
        FOR YOUR HOUSE";W
00040   INPUT "ENTER THE ESTIMATED TOTAL
        GLASS AREA FOR YOUR HOUSE";G
00050   INPUT "ENTER THE ESTIMATED TOTAL
        AREA WITHIN THE ROOF CROSS-SECTION";R
00060   INPUT "ENTER THE NUMBER OF OCCUP-
        ANTS";N
00070   BTU=W*5+G*35+R*12+N*100+2000
00080   PRINT "THE ESTIMATED BTU NECESSARY
        TO AIR CONDITION YOUR HOME=";BTU
00090   PRINT
00100   END
```

House Heating Evaluation

```
00100   REM HOUSE HEATING EVALUATION PROG-
        RAM
00110   PRINT "THIS PURPOSE OF THIS PROGRAM IS
        TO COMPUTE THE"
```

```
00120    PRINT "RELATIVE EFFICIENCY OF HEATING
         A HOME WITH"
00130    PRINT "ELECTRICITY, NATURAL GAS, OR
         OIL. IT WILL BE"
00140    PRINT "NECESSARY TO CONTACT YOUR
         LOCAL DISTRIBUTORS OF"
00150    PRINT "THE ABOVE FUELS TO MAKE A COST
         COMPARISON."
00160    PRINT "THERE ARE OTHER FACTORS TO
         CONSIDER WHEN EVALUATING"
00170    PRINT "THE COST FOR HEATING (I.E. THE
         AMOUNT OF IN-"
00180    PRINT "SULATION YOU HAVE), BUT THE
         RATIOS BETWEEN DIFFERENT"
00190    PRINT "FUELS SHOULD BE CONSISTENT."
00195    PRINT "USE THE COST EFFICIENCIES THE
         PROGRAM OUTPUTS ALONG WITH"
00196    PRINT "THE COST OF THE HEATING SYSTEM
         TO DETERMINE WHICH YOU"
00197    PRINT "SHOULD CHOOSE."
00200    INPUT"ENTER ESTIMATED HEAT LOSS PER
         HOUR";H
00205    REM THIS MAY BE APPROXIMATED USING
         FORMULA ON PAGE 136 OR WITH BUILDERS
         MANUALS
00210    PRINT "IF YOU KNOW THE EFFICIENCY OF
         THE OIL BURNING SYSTEM"
00220    PRINT "PLEASE ENTER THE VALUE,";
00230    INPUT "OTHERWISE ENTER '0'";B
00240    IF B=0 THEN B=. 8 ELSE B=B*.01
00250    INPUT "ENTER THE AVE. NO. OF MONTHS OF
         COLD SEASON PER YEAR";C
00260    C=C*720
00270    INPUT "AT WHAT TEMPERATURE WILL YOU
         SET THE THERMOSTAT";D
00280    INPUT "WHAT IS THE AVERAGE WINTER
         TEMPERATURE";E
00290    REM COMPUTE HEAT LOSS PER HOUR
00300    X=((D−E)/70)*((H*C)/(140000*B))
00310    PRINT "WHAT IS THE AVE. PRICE OF OIL IN
         YOUR AREA PER GALLON-"
00320    INPUT "IF NOT KNOWN TYPE '0'";F
```

```
00330   IF F=0 THEN F=.50
00340   PRINT "YOU WILL REQUIRE AN ESTIMATED
        ";X; "GALLONS OF OIL-COST="X *F
00350   INPUT "ENTER THE COST PER KILOWATT
        HR. IN YOUR AREA IN DOLLARS";G
00360   PRINT "ELECTRICITY TO RUN THE OIL PUMP
        MAY COST UP TO ";206*G;" DOLLARS"
00370   PRINT "IF YOU KNOW THE EFFICIENCY OF
        THE NATURAL GAS HEATER PLEASE"
00380   INPUT "ENTER, OTHERWISE ENTER '0'";B
00390   IF B=0 THEN B=.8 ELSE B=B*.01
00400   Y=((D-E)/70)*((H*C)/(100000*B))
00410   INPUT "WHAT IS THE COST PER THERM IN
        YOUR AREA";I
00420   PRINT "YOU WILL REQUIRE AN ESTIMATED
        ";Y;"THERMS TO HEAT/COST=$";I*Y
00430   Z=((D-E)/70)*(H*C)/3405
00440   PRINT "AND AN ESTIMATED";Z; "KWH WILL
        BE REQUIRED TO HEAT WITH"
00450   PRINT "ELECTRICITY-COST=$";Z*G
00460   PRINT "SUMMARY:"
00470   PRINT "MEDIUM", "AMOUNT","COST"
00480   PRINT "OIL",X,X*F
00490   PRINT "NATURAL GAS",Y, I*Y
00500   PRINT "ELECTRICITY", Z,Z*G
00510   PRINT "REMEMBER THAT THESE VALUES
        ARE ONLY ESTIMATES"
00520   PRINT "AND WILL DIFFER ACCORDING TO
        THE INSULATION, BUILDING"
00530   PRINT "MATERIAL, FURNISHINGS,AND CLI-
        MATE."
00540   PRINT "THE VALUES GIVEN ARE MOST USE-
        FUL IN DETERMINING THE"
00550   PRINT "MOST INEXPENSIVE METHOD OF
        HEATING FOR YOUR HOME."
00560   PRINT "THUS, THE PROCUREMENT COSTS
        FOR THE VARIOUS SYSTEMS"
00570   PRINT "SHOULD BE ANALYZED ALONG WITH
        THE ABOVE COSTS TO"
00580   PRINT "ARRIVE AT A FINAL FIGURE."
00590   REM A COMPLETE PROGRAM COULD BE
```

WRITTEN WITHOUT MUCH DIFFICULTY
00600 REM TO CONSIDER THE ABOVE FACTORS...

Chapter 5
Educational Applications

Educational Applications

CAI stands for "Computer Assisted Instruction," and is an excellent application for your home computer. Possibilities for using the computer to instruct yourself, your children, friends, or to sell includes:

1. A program describing how to program computers in BASIC (or assembly language, FORTRAN, etc.) with step-by-step examples.

2. Story building program for youngsters in which the computer randomly selects individual story parts and combines them to produce a different story each time. Questions could be asked to test reading comprehension, grammar, and writing skills. For example, the program could produce a personalized story for a child using his/her name. Occasionally, questions such as this would be prompted—Johnny, should I write the next sentence as:

1. "Johnny and I went to the park."

or

2. "I and Johnny went to the park."

If the child answers correctly, the computer reply could be "O.K., that's correct," and a wrong answer could be explained—"NO, that's wrong. The person who is talking should place the "I" last, after the names of other people."

3. I.Q. builder program to familiarize people with the types of questions and problem solving methods for the Scholastic Aptitude test, Civil Service tests, American Col-

lege Assessment test, etc. Research has shown that familiarization with the tests can improve performance considerably.

Example of an I.Q. building computer dialogue:

Which does not belong?

genius

imbecile

idiot

fool

cretin

intellectual

ANSWER: "cretin"—this term is biologically specific, the other terms are behavioral judgements.

4. Future potential evaluation program designed to quiz high school/college students about their talents/interests/abilities could direct them toward promising occupational careers based upon this information.

5. Psychological quiz to help people understand themselves, such as those appearing in books and magazines, and test some personal characteristic. Tests particularly suited to be computerized are those requiring tedious calculation to analyze.

Example quiz to test your "happiness quotient":

Answer each question as "true" or "false"

1. My work is usually fulfilling or interesting
2. I have a good ability to relax
3. I can enjoy happiness in little things easily
4. I seldom envy other people
5. My moods have great fluctuation
6. I have a great desire to change either my location, family situation, or job
7. I usually sleep well and don't feel tired in the morning
8. I periodically "blow my top" without knowing the real reason

9. I am usually a pessimistic person
10. I cannot have happiness without others being around me

Scoring:
Start with zero, add one point to each true answer to questions 1, 2, 3, 4, 7 and subtract one point for each false answer to questions 5, 6, 8, 9, 10. Subtract one point for each true answer to questions 5, 6, 8, 9, 10 and multiply the total by 10 to determine percentage happiness (average score is approximately 50).

Additionally, an analysis of ones problems, based upon his answers, could be similar to this: (referred to question number in parentheses)

If you don't derive much pleasure from "little things" or if you regularly lose your temper (3 & 8), you should give some attention to your attitudes. Is your social situation the cause of the trouble (6) or what about your job situation (1)? Often, the simple recognition of this difficulty will serve to clear up the situation. The person who is truly happy can find happiness while alone (10) and isn't envious (4). The moody person (5 & 9) can often benefit from the advise of a counselor.

PROGRAM—COMPUTER ASSISTED INSTRUCTION

Computer assisted instruction (CAI) refers to the use of a computer to teach with the use of graphics, readings, or questions. The simple program presented here is designed to ask questions on any subject, wait for a response by the operator, determine whether the answer was correct or not, and keep track of progress. Two incorrect answers are allowed before the answer is given; change line 100 if this is not desired.

Sample data for a quiz about computers could be as follows:

```
300 DATA IS YOUR COMPUTER CONSIDERED A
    MICROCOMPUTER OR MINI COMPUTER, MIC-
    ROCOMPUTER
310 DATA WHAT DOES CPU STAND FOR, CENTRAL
    PROCESSING UNIT
```

The question comes first and is immediately followed by the answer.

```
00001   REM GENERAL CAI PROGRAM-QUESTIONS
        AND ANSWERS ARE CONTAINED
00002   REM IN THE DATA STATEMENTS
00003   PRINT "CAI- TO STOP AT ANY POINT TYPE
        'STOP' AS AN ANSWER"
00005   Y = 0: Z = 0: N = 25 'N = THE NUMBER OF
        QUESTIONS IN THE DATA STATEMENTS
00010   CLEAR 1000 'ADJUST TO YOUR REQUIRE-
        MENTS
00015   FOR A = 1 TO N: Y=1
00020   READ A$, B$
00030   PRINT A$
00040   INPUT C$ : IF C$ = "STOP" THEN 150
00050   IF C$ = B$ THEN NEXT A ELSE 100
00060   GOTO 150
00100   IF Y =2 THEN 130
00110   PRINT "INCORRECT ANSWER... PLEASE TRY
        AGAIN": Y = Y + 1
00120   GOTO 40
00130   PRINT "THE ANSWER WAS:" : PRINT B$: Z = Z
        + 1
00140   NEXT A
00150   PRINT "YOU ANSWERED"; A-Z; OR; 100 − (
        (A-Z)/N*100); "% QUESTIONS CORRECT"
00170   PRINT "AND"; Z; " QUESTIONS WERE
        ANSWERED INCORRECTLY"
00180   INPUT "TRY AGAIN"; A$
00190   IF A$ = "YES" THEN 5
00200   END
00210   DATA 'ENTER YOUR QUESTIONS AND
        ANSWERS HERE SEQUENTIALLY
00220   DATA . . .
```

COMPUTER TUTOR

The memorization of lists, vocabulary words, and other types of abstract information may be assisted with your personal computer. For instance, the computer could quiz you from a list of vocabulary words, displaying each randomly selected word individually. Once you have glanced at a word, and attempted to recite the definition, type the "enter" key.

The definition could be automatically displayed afterwards. If you did not know the correct definition, type "w" ("wrong") to indicate this mistake, and the word and definition could be stored for a requiz later. Otherwise, the next word would be displayed after typing the "enter" key. Additionally, the number and percentage of correct answers could be maintained.

The highschool or college student should find computerized quizzes helpful in memorizing such information as:

1. Historical names, dates, and places
2. Parts and functions of the anatomy
3. Mathematical or chemical formulas
4. Verses in literature
5. Spellings or definitions of difficult words
6. Trigonometric identities
7. Geography
8. Technical and scientific terminology

EDUCATIONAL SIMULATIONS

Because of the rapid computational ability of the computer, educational and mathematical simulations are advantageous applications. Possible simulations for educating young people include:

1. The "Manhattan Indian Problem" teaches the principle of compounded interest. As the story goes, the new world settlers paid the Indians $24 for the entire island of Manhattan in 1626. Today, this property is worth millions of dollars. But, what if the settlers had deposited the $24 in a savings account compounded daily; how much would that account be worth today? A computer generated chart listing the value of the account after each decade would serve to illustrate the geometrical growth rate involved and the surprising answer to the "Manhattan Indian Problem."

2. Simulate the growth of a colony of amoebas (one-celled organisms) in a jar with a limited food supply. The amoeba's reproduction rate will cause the colony population to double per unit time. However, pollution and limited food supply will decrease colony size at an increasing rate. A numerical listing or plot of the population vs time could be generated by the computer. Will the colony reach equilibrium

(stable state)? Along parallel lines, simulations of a larger scale (e.g. ecological balance in a forest) could be undertaken.

3. Demonstration of some laws of physics could take the form of a graphical illustration of planetary orbits, acceleration due to gravity, motion of a pendulum, etc. A popular physics demonstration program is called "lunar lander", in which one must control the flight of an Apollo moon lander under the influence of gravity (limits on oxygen, food, and fuel supply must be contended with also). Similar programs have been written to graphically simulate the piloting of an airplane.

```
010  PRINT "LUNAR LANDING SIMULATION"
020  PRINT "---------------------- "
030  PRINT
040  PRINT "DO YOU WANT INSTRUCTIONS? (YES OR
     NO)"
050  INPUT A$
060  IF A$ = "NO" THEN 00300
070  PRINT
080  PRINT "YOU ARE LANDING ON THE MOON AND
     HAVE TAKEN OVER MANUAL"
090  PRINT "CONTROL 500 FEET ABOVE A GOOD
     LANDING SPOT. YOU HAVE A"
100  PRINT "DOWNWARD VELOCITY OF 50 FT/SEC."
110  PRINT "120 UNITS OF FUEL REMAIN."
120  PRINT
130  PRINT "HERE ARE THE RULES THAT GOVERN
     YOUR SPACE VEHICLE:"
140  PRINT "(1) AFTER EACH SECOND, THE HEIGHT,
     VELOCITY, AND REMAINING"
150  PRINT "FUEL WILL BE REPORTED:"
160  PRINT "(2) AFTER THE REPORT, A > ? < WILL
     BE TYPED. ENTER THE"
170  PRINT "NUMBER OF UNITS OF FUEL YOU WISH
     TO BURN DURING THE"
180  PRINT "NEXT SECOND. EACH UNIT OF FUEL
     WILL SLOW YOUR DESCENT"
190  PRINT "BY 1 FT/SEC."
200  PRINT "(3) THE MAXIMUM THRUST OF YOUR
     ENGINE IS 30 FT/SEC/SEC OR"
210  PRINT "30 UNITS OF FUEL PER SECOND."
220  PRINT "(4) WHEN YOU CONTACT THE LUNAR
     SURFACE, YOUR DESCENT"
```

```
230   PRINT "ENGINE WILL AUTOMATICALLY CUT
      OFF AND YOU WILL BE"
240   PRINT "GIVEN A REPORT OF YOUR LANDING
      SPEED AND REMAINING"
250   PRINT "FUEL."
260   PRINT "(5) IF YOU RUN OUT OF FUEL, THE > ? <
      WILL NO LONGER APPEAR,"
270   PRINT "BUT YOUR SECOND BY SECOND RE-
      PORT WILL CONTINUE UNTIL"
280   PRINT "YOU CONTACT THE LUNAR SURFACE."
290   PRINT
300   PRINT "BEGIN LANDING PROCEDURE........."
310   PRINT "G O O D   L U C K"
320   PRINT
330   PRINT "SEC FEET SPEED FUEL PLOT of DIS-
      TANCE"
340   PRINT
350   T = 0
360   H = 500
370   V = 50
380   F = 120
390   IF B = 0 THEN 00420
400   PRINT T; TAB (4); H; TAB (12); V; TAB (20); F;
      TAB (29); "I"; TAB (H/12 + 28); "**"
410   GO TO 00430
420   PRINT T; TAB (4); H; TAB (12); V; TAB (20); F;
      TAB (29); "I"; TAB (H/12 + 29); "**"
430   INPUT B
440   IF B < 0 THEN 00600
450   IF B > 30 THEN 00600
460   IF B > F THEN 00480
470   GO TO 00500
480   B = F
500   V1 = V - B + 5
510   F = F - B
520   H = H - . 5*(V + V1)
530   IF H < = 0 THEN 00620
540   T = T + 1
550   V = V1
560   IF F > 0 THEN 00390
570   IF B = 0 THEN 00590
580   PRINT "*** OUT OF FUEL ***"
```

```
590   PRINT T; TAB (4); H; TAB (12); V; TAB (20); F;
      TAB (29); "I"; TAB (H/12 + 29); "**"
600   B = 0
610   GO TO 00500
620   PRINT "*** CONTACT ***"
630   H = H + .5* (V + V1)
640   IF B = 5 THEN 00670
650   D = ( -V + SQR (V*V + H* (10 - 2*B) ) )/(5 - B)
660   GO TO 00680
670   D = H/V
680   V1 = V + (5 - B)*D
690   PRINT "TOUCHDOWN AT"; T + D; "SECONDS."
700   PRINT "LANDING VELOCITY = "; V1; "FT/SEC."
710   PRINT F; "UNITS OF FUEL REMAINING."
720   IF V1 > < 0 THEN 00750
730   PRINT "CONGRATULATIONS     A PERFECT
      LANDING"
740   PRINT "YOUR LICENSE WILL BE RENEWED . . .
      . . . LATER."
750   IF ABS (V1) <5 THEN 00780
760   PRINT "*** SORRY, BUT YOU BLEW IT ***"
770   PRINT "APPROPRIATE CONDOLENCES WILL BE
      SENT TO YOUR NEXT OF KIN."
780   PRINT "ANOTHER MISSION?"
790   INPUT A$
800   IF A$ = "YES" THEN 00300
810   PRINT
820   PRINT "CONTROL OUT."
830   PRINT
840   END
```

Simulations to satisfy scientific curiosity:

1. Accoustics of a room could be mathematically simulated if such parameters as dampening effects of the walls, shape of the room and its contents, location of the sound source, etc. were provided; this could be useful to the architect or stereo-listening perfectionist.

2. Simulation of world dynamics, similar to Jay Forrester's "Limits to Growth" computer simulation, could be accomplished on a smaller scale. World dynamics involves the interaction of population, pollution, resources, etc. to predict future outcomes.

3. A simulation of astronomical theories could possibly be accomplished with a personal computer system. Of course, the memory requirements would be very large and simulation time could be hundreds of hours.

4. A simulation of automotive fuel economy could be accomplished with such variables as: fuel injection, fuel additives, pollution monitors, etc.

ADDITIONAL CAI IDEAS

Examples of teaching programs for young children to adult level are listed below.

Basic Math "Flashcards". Programs designed to increase speed and efficiency in basic mathematics (e.g. addition and multiplication) in which a time limit would be set for answering a question.

Word Problems. A program designed to output "random" word problems in mathematics for practice.

Fractions. A drill program in recognizing common denominators and adding/multiplying fractions.

Spell. A program which teaches one to recognize commonly misspelled words.

Roots. A guessing/learning game in which one must guess the square or cube root of a random number.

Kinema. A program in physics which helps one learn to calculate the path of a projectile.

Gasvol. A plotting/calculating program which draws pressure/volume diagrams of a gas (chemistry and physics use).

Balance. A drill program on balancing chemical equations.

Metric. An exercise in converting between the English and metric systems of units.

Bases. A demonstration program in converting from one numerical base system to another.

```
10   REM MULTIPLICATION DRILL PROGRAM
20   PRINT "MULTIPLICATION DRILL- WOULD YOU
     LIKE INSTRUCTIONS";
30   INPUT Z$
40   IF Z$ = "NO" THEN 90
```

```
50   PRINT "I'M GOING TO SEE HOW WELL YOU CAN
     MULTIPLY. WHEN I SHOW YOU"
60   PRINT "A PROBLEM. TYPE IN THE ANSWER AND
     THEN HIT THE 'RETURN' KEY."
70   PRINT "I'LL TELL YOU IF YOU ARE RIGHT AND
     WILL GIVE YOU A SCORE AFTER"
80   INPUT "TEN QUESTIONS. O.K."; Z$
90   A$="#########.": B$="########."
95   REM
100  FOR X = 1 TO 10: X1 = X1 + 1
110  A = RND (10): B = RND (10)
120  PRINT
130  E = 0: PRINT "PROBLEM #";X1
135  GOSUB 140: NEXT X
137  GOTO 420
140  PRINT USING A$; A
150  PRINT "X"; : PRINT USING B$; B
160  C = A*B
170  PRINT "---------------------------------------------------"
180  INPUT " =      "; D
190  IF D = C THEN 300
193  M = M + 1 : E = E + 1
195  IF E = 2 THEN PRINT "THE ANSWER WAS:"; C:
     GOTO 240
200  PRINT "YOU GOOFED . . . TRY AGAIN."
220  GOTO 140
240  F = F + 1
250  A (F) = A
260  B (F) = B
270  RETURN
280  REM
290  REM
300  X2 = X2 + 1: R = RND (5)
310  ON R GOTO 320, 340, 360, 380, 400
320  PRINT "RIGHT ON!!!"
330  RETURN
340  PRINT "FINE . . ."
350  RETURN
360  PRINT "GOOD WORK!!!"
370  RETURN
380  PRINT "KEEP IT UP!"
390  RETURN
```

```
400   PRINT "EXCELLENT!"
410   RETURN
420   PRINT "YOUR SCORE IS NOW"; X2; "CORRECT
      AND";M;" ERRORS.(";INT(100−(M/X2)*100);"%"
430   INPUT "DO YOU WANT TO CONTINUE"; Z$
440   IF Z$ = "YES" THEN 500
450   PRINT "THANKS FOR PLAYING WITH ME . . ."
460   END
500   G = 0: FOR X = 1 TO 10
510   IF (A (X) > 0) OR (B (X) > 0) THEN G = G + 1
520   NEXT X
530   IF G = 0 THEN 100
540   PRINT "I DIDN'T FORGET YOU MISSED THESE:"
550   FOR X = 1 TO G
560   A = A (X): B = B (X)
570   GOSUB 140
580   NEXT X
590   GOTO 100
```

Chapter 6
Hobby Applications

Hobby Applications

It does not seem possible that a computer can create original art work until one considers the mathematics as well as randomness of some art forms. This is one personal computer application in which possibilities are numerous, and many are yet undiscovered. A few possibilities:

Mathematical Functions—Plotting or graphing a mathematical function can often produce interesting geometrical designs. Color terminals equipped to plot a grid in full color, each color indicative of the value of the function at each individual point, produces fantastic geometrics. If, however, you only have an ordinary printer available, a program to plot points indicating the function value for a one-character-sized interval may be used. Manually connecting the points with line segments afterwards will produce a similar plot.

Alteration of a Design—A given design (e.g. drawing of a human face, American flag, etc.) transformed into a series of points on a grid may be manipulated with a mathematical algorithm to produce "modern art" effects. Once again, output is best done by a plotter. Additionally, one design may be gradually transformed into another, through a series of plots, producing a fascinating result.

Random Art Patterns—If your video display module provides graphics, an algorithm combined with a random number generator could produce a constantly changing graphical pattern. The Conway "game of life" is an example of such an algorithm.

A/D Converters—Use of an A/D converter to digitize real-world events and transform them with the computer can produce interesting results. For example, one hobbyist interfaced a human dancer to his computer by applying a dozen mercury switches to the dancer's body. The dancer's movements caused the switches to open and close, producing digital signals for the computer. The computer, in turn, created "choreographed music" from the signals.

Amorphic Art—Amorphic art is designed such that a normal picture will appear only if a cylindrical mirror is placed on top of it. The mathematics necessary to transform a set of points on an x, y grid may be accomplished easily by the computer. This art form, popular centuries ago, is now becoming popular once again, and the computer is here to help.

Crossword Poetry—An interesting "crossword" of the words from a piece of literature may be created by the computer. A program to create such "art" would scan each word, and determine how that word could fit in crossword form with adjacent words:

```
WHO                BUT
  A                WHEN THE LEAVES
  SEEN               A    R
                     N    R
THE                  G    E
  WIND?                   M
  E                       B
  I                       I   THE WIND
  T                       N        S
  H        I              G
  E                           PASSING
  R                           THROUGH
NOR   YOU
```

READ AS "Who has seen the wind?
　　　　　Neither I nor you.

　　　　　But when the leaves hang trembling,
　　　　　The wind is passing through."

```
10 REM COMPUTER TEXTILE GENERATOR
20 REM CREATES RANDOM 'TEXTILE' PATTERNS
30 REM FOR OUTPUT ON A VIDEO SCREEN OR
40 REM GRAPIC PRINTER. REQUIRES A TVT
50 REM WHICH HAS GRAPHIC CHARACTER BLOCKS
60 REM ACCESSABLE USING 'CHR$(X)'
```

```
70 REM
80 RANDOM
90 N = RND(9) + 1
100 FOR X=1 TO N
110 A$(X) = CHR$(RND(62)+129)
120 NEXT X
130 CLS' CLEARS SCREEN
140 FOR M=1 TO 6
150 FOR X=1 TO N
160 FOR Y=1 TO 64 'ADJUST TO YOUR LINE LENGTH
170 PRINT A$(X);
180 NEXT Y
190 NEXT X
200 NEXT M
210 GO TO 90
```

Perspective Drawing Aid—Given a set of points describing the (x,y,z) dimensions of objects in a picture, the computer could use matrix manipulations to produce a new set of points describing the picture from another perspective viewpoint (Fig. 6-1). Additionally, if video graphics or plotting capabilities are available, the new picture could be plotted. Perspective transformations are useful in technical illustration and other art forms as well.

As an example of the perspective transformations that may be accomplished on a large array of points, let (x,y) be a coordinate pair under the "old" coordinate system. Let (x_θ, y_θ) be the center coordinates of the new system rotated through angle θ in relation to the old system. The new coordinates (x',y') may be calculated with these equations:

$x' = (x - x_\theta) \cos\theta + (y - y_\theta)\sin\theta$

$y' = -(x - x_\theta)\sin\theta + (y - y_{\theta'}) \cos\theta$

MORSE CODE

Computerists interested in passing the Morse code test to become amateur radio operators could use their machines to quiz themselves both visually and audibly. The visual representation of Morse code is, of course, a series of dots and

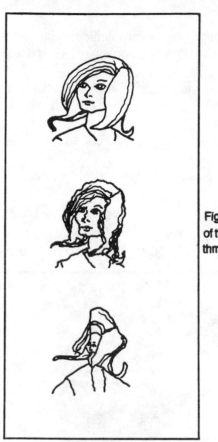

Fig. 6-1. Computer plotted examples of the use of a mathematical algon - thms to alter a drawing.

dashes—.-. --- .... The audible representation could be obtained in two ways:

1. Use of an interfaced tone output speaker
2. Use of timing loops to generate tones of a certain duration on an AM radio placed next to the CPU.

The standard method of learning Morse code is to first study the visual representations, and second, to transcribe an audio transmission at a gradually increasing rate. A program similar to the "computer tutor" described on page 165 could be used to requiz you on the codes you have missed.

MUSIC

Possible applications for your personal computer to assist with learning music:

1. Graphic flash-card type quizzes could display notes on the scale for identification, and thus, one may learn to read music.

2. Learning the pronunciations and definitions of foreign terms used with music (e.g. stacco, andante, diatonic).

3. Learning the notes in commonly used chords (for piano, organ, guitar, etc.).

4. Learning names and pronunciations of famous composers/pieces.

PATTERN GENERATOR

A color graphics terminal programmed to display a function such as $y=30*(EXP(-x*x/100)+SIN(x/5))$ in various

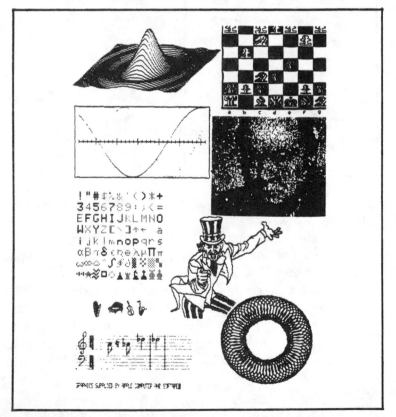

Fig. 6-2. Example of capabilities of a graphic printer.

color patterns(according to the value of the function at each point on the display) often displays amazingly beautiful patterns (Fig. 6-2). Such designs could be used in knitting, embroidering or for producing a geometical painting.

ANIMATED FILMS

Although most microcomputers are not fast enough to display real-time animation, a time-lapse film could be made with the end result being equivalent to realtime graphics. The graphic resolution should be a minimum of 200 by 200 individually definable blocks. 3-D rotation of an object is an interesting film subject. Much better, although much more expensive, would be a system equipped with a plotter to draw all of the figures necessary to produce an animated film sequence.

ASTRONOMY

Potential applications for your personal computer in amateur astronomy:

1. Locate and identify stars—Calculation of declination, sidereal hour angle from observed altitude, azimuth, and time are necessary.

2. Make records of observations efficiently in computer format for quick retrieval.

3. Interface telescope drive mechanics to a microprocessor controller for automatic photographic observations.

4. Calculate and plot orbits of satellites and planets.

```
10   REM ASTRONOMY DEMO PROGRAM
20   REM CALC. RELATIVE POSITION OF VENUS &
     SUN
25   REM CALC. NO. DAYS SINCE 12-31-49:
30   INPUT"ENTER THIS YEAR AS TWO DIGITS (E.G.
     '82' FOR 1982)";Y
35   INPUT"ENTER NO. DAYS SINCE DEC. 31 OF
     LAST YEAR";DA
37   REM E.G. FEB. 5 WOULD BE 36 DAYS
40   X=364*INT((Y-50)/4)+365((Y-50)
     -INT((Y-50)/4))+DA
```

```
50    PI=3.141592:A=PI/180:C=A*.9856:B=180/PI:
      D=99.2*A:E=D+C*X
55    IF E < PI*2 THEN 70
60    E=E−PI*2:GOTO 55
70    E=SIN(E−A*105)*1.9*A+E:F=A*1.602:
      G=A*80.85:H=G+F*X
80    IFH < PI*2THEN100ELSEH=H−PI*2:GOTO80
100   H=H+SIN(H−A*135)*.8*A
110   J=SIN(H−A*232)*.0055+.7233
120   K=H−E:I=SIN(E−A*195)*.016+1:M=−PI/2
130   L=SQR(J*J+I*I−2*J*I*COS(K))
135   N=SIN(K)*(J/L)+SIN(M)
140   IFN < 0THENM=PI/3600+M:GOTO135:
      ELSER=M*12/PI
170   PRINT"THE RELATIVE LOCATION OF VENUS
      IS";M*B;" DEGREES FROM THE SUN"
180   PRINT"= TO";R;" HOURS FROM THE SUN":END
```

GARDENING

Writing a garden analysis program for one time use would not be a practical idea, but your friends and neighbors could use such a program, and you may be able to sell the completed software to a local garden supply store. A complete analysis program is more complicated than it appears on the surface. These are some of the factors to consider:

1. pH, water, soil density, and sunshine levels of the plot.

2. Desired pH, water, soil density, and sunshine levels for the vegetables to be planted.

3. Nitrogen, phosphorus, and potassium contents in the soil compared to plant requirements.

4. The size of the garden.

Proper planning dictates positioning certain vegetables which ward off insects next to others. The space allotted between each plant should also be considered. Specific requirements and harvest times of the vegetables should be outputted along with a graphic presentation of the garden plot:

```
BEETS      ••••••••••••••••••••••••••••••••••••••••••••
CORN       − − − − − − − −·− − − − − − − − − −
RADISHES:::::::::::::::::::::::::::::::::::::::::::::::::::
TOMATOES------------------------------------------------
```

Additional outputs could explain how to form a compost heap and the use of fertilizer.

ANALYSIS OF LITERATURE

Several universities have utilized the computer to analyze the words of a particular writer, such as Shakespeare. Interesting congruencies have been found (e.g. the fact that a large percentage of the words Shakespeare wrote were only used once in all of his writings). Other than providing word counts, the computer may be used to analyze sentence structure typical of one writer (to determine whether all of a famous work was written by one person only) and to index/cross-reference/access particular segments of a manuscript. At least one hobbyist is attempting to transcribe the Bible onto his system. He intends to attempt the above analyses and have verses of one topic available instantly.

COLLECTION NARRATOR

Hobbyists with collections will find that their personal computer with video display makes an excellent visual narrator of a collection. For example, a stamp collector created a file of his entire collection, with information on each item randomly accessible. His narrations were similar to:

Decade of Space Achievement Issue
Issued: August 2, 1969 Purchased: September 1, 1969
Purchase price: .16   Value: .60

This stamp pair depicts the ascent of man upon the surface of the moon.

Interested persons are instructed how to obtain information on a particular item or otherwise the computer would present a continuous display of each item in sequence; this saves you from monotonous repetition of information to visitors at an exhibition. Businessmen at expositions could put their personal computer to similar use in explaining products.

MODEL RAILROADING

Model railroading enthusiasts with a large layout may wish to automate the trains, lights, switches, etc. with a controlling microprocessor. One hobbyist went so far as to print train schedules, tickets, and analyze freight business on his personal computer.

ASTROLOGY

Determination of the alignments of the planets and sorting of astrological data are best done with the computer. Horoscopes, interpolation midpoints, aspects, Placidus house and astropoints calculation may be done. Tarot, I-Ching, Numerology may be accomplished similarly.

GAMBLING ANALYSIS AND ADVISING

Your computer could become a helpful advisor for poker and various other card games. All information available (e.g. the cards in your hand, the amount of the bet, etc.) would be inputted each round and an analysis based upon the laws of probability could determine your best move (perhaps your opponents would object to this advantage!). For example, these are the probabilities for obtaining sample poker and bridge hands:

Royal flush	649,739 to 1
Straight flush	72,192 to 1
Full house	693 to 1
Flush	508 to 1
One pair	1.37 to 1
Straight	254 to 1
13 card suit	158,753,389,899 to 1
12 card suit	367,484,698 to 1
Nine honors	104 to 1
Yarborough— no honors	1,827 to 1
Four aces	378 to 1

Other forms of gambling (eg. football and jai-alai) may be computer analyzed based upon past performances of the opponents and a confidence level established to conservatively pick the winner/point spread.
A complete computer analysis of hundreds of games played from any one sport could yield a system for predicting future outcomes.

DESIGN RECREATIONAL VEHICLES

A hang glider enthusiast considering designing a new hang glider aerofoil could find a detailed computer simulated wind-tunnel test beneficial. The proposed design would be mathematically described to the computer and an aerodynamic simulation of flight characteristics made. Obviously, a simulation of this magnitude could only be done by someone with a good background in aerodynamics. Similar simulations could be applied to boats and other recreational vehicles.

FISHERMAN'S HELPER

Potential applications for serious fishermen include:

1. Analysis of weather patterns and times to forecast the ideal time to fish.

2. Analysis of depth, temperature, location, time, etc. gathered when an ideal location is found. Use this data for future reference. A portable microcomputer with an A/D converter could gather this data automatically.

3. Computation of high and low tide times and time of sunrise/sunset.

SPORTS

A file of team and player statistics, player's names and numbers, and other sports information could be stored on the computer (preferably on floppy disk) for quick retrieval by the television sports fan. Sports statistics could be compiled, graphed, and analyzed. Probability forecasting of score and point spread based upon past performance of opposing teams could be accomplished. The computer could also "learn" from its mistakes, retaining the outcomes of many games in memory.

At local sporting events a microcomputer could be useful in maintaining scores, team records, and player records or statistics as the game progresses (for use by the announcer, or for permanent records).

A series of elapsed time computations could be accomplished efficiently with the proper program. A programmable calculator could serve as digital stopwatch as well.

Bowling, golf and related sports involving tedious calculation of averages and other statistics for a league are well suited for computer bookkeeping. Sell such a computer service or offer it gratuitously to your local bowling alley or golf course.

GENEOLOGICAL STOREHOUSE

A few hobbyists have obtained a sufficient amount of geneological information such that a personal computer is necessary to file and update the information. Having specified characteristics of each family member instantly available eases the task of further genological research as well.

AMATEUR RADIO

The ham radio or citizen's band radio enthusiast could use a personal computer to assist with his hobby in these ways:

1. Morse code decoder/sender interface between radio and computer. Received and sent messages would be displayed on a video monitor in English, allowing the computer to translate Morse code (or some other code).

2. Message monitor—The computer would monitor a specified frequency for a particular audio signal or coded message. Transmissions immediately following such would be recorded digitally or on cassette tape. Thus, one need not attend to the radio constantly to receive a message for himself. Received messages could also be forwarded automatically on another frequency to another station in a network.

3. Message relay—A stored message could be sent at the proper time if the station operator was unable to send it personally.

4. Add intelligence to your test equipment/radio with a controlling microprocessor. Test sequences could be done automatically.

5. Maintain your station log automatically—All entries could be stored, classified, and special reports generated (e.g. How many countries have been contacted? Have there been any repeat contacts?).

6. Error correcting codes could be automatically generated to improve communications.

7. Several ham radio contests have utilized small computers to keep track of all contacts.

COMPUTE TIMES OF SUNRISE/SUNSET/TIDES

Pilots as well as fishermen will find a sunrise/sunset calculating program useful. To keep such a program as simple as possible, tide or sunrise data from previous days could be entered to eliminate highly-technical calculations. The times for future sunrises or sunsets may then be projected by linear regression.

COLLECTION INVENTORY

A list of the items in a large collection could be computerized. Each item would be listed along with specific information concerning it (e.g. for a stamp collection these factors could be entered: denomination, date, country, condition, approximate value, where purchased, purchase price, remarks). With this information, the computer can categorize, cross-index, and generate special lists of the items. A special list could include all items which have a particular characteristic (e.g. a list of all British stamps in a stamp collection). Additionally, a cassette or floppy disk copy of the inventory could be stored in a safe location in the event an insured collection is destroyed.

BIORHYTHM

Biorhythms are supposedly the cycles in emotional, physical, and intellectual states governing everyone's behavior. Dozens of computer programs have been written to generate personalized biorhythm charts, yet interesting additions could be included.
Potentials include:
1. Plotting or numerically comparing the biorhythms of two or more friends or a family.
2. The average of all three biorhythmic cycles could be included.
3. Generate a biorhythm in the form of a standard calendar.
4. Judge the reliability of biorhythms by objectively analyzing your three states at the end of each day and make a computer-statistical comparison and plot this data versus your biorhythm.
5. Investigate the use of histograms and other means of presenting data to output biorhythms in a more favorable format.
6. Compare the reliability of your standard biorhythm to one beginning with your conception.

Fig. 6-3. Example of music generated by a computer.

MUSIC COMPOSITION

In the past, computer programs designed to compose music were based more upon random numbers than musical principles. Thus, the songs that were produced could only be compared to a child randomly hitting piano keys. Lately, progress has been made in developing more complex programs that adhere to the "rules of thumb" for composing particular types of music (Fig. 6-3). One program, which used the following rules, was somewhat successful in composing "pop" music

Basic melody requirements:

1. The first note must be other than a fourth, a flatted fifth, a minor second, or a ninth.

2. An ascending minor second progresses to a second and a decending minor second progresses to the tonic; an ascending flatted fifth progresses to a fifth and a decending fifth progresses to a fourth.

3. Not more than five notes in descention or ascention are allowed without a complementary movement.

4. The melody should consist of 35 to 60 notes.

5. The release begins on a sub-dominant major note.

One of the songs composed was represented as (*see corresponding music in Fig. 6-3*):

/C/F*DA/G8C:8C:F"G/C*AF8G8/G***/DEF"G/ABC:B8
C:8/C:*B8C:8/D*C/F*DA/G8C:8C:F"G/G*AF8G8/G***/
DEF"G/ABC:B8C;8/C:*A*/F***/A**C8CD/FE*/B**C:8E
F"/G***

```
00010   REM MUSIC PROGRAM
00020   REM HARMONIZES AND TRANSPOSES
00030   INPUT "SELECT: 1) TRANSPOSER 2) HAR-
        MONIZER"; A
00040   ON A GOTO 3000, 100
00100   REM HARMONY COMPOSING PROGRAM
00110   REM A FOUR PART HARMONY IS PRODUCED
        FROM A GIVEN MELODY IN THE KEY OF C
00120   DIMB(5,100), Y(6,6), V(100): RESTORE
00130   J$=" ##   +##   +##   +##   +##"
00140   FORT1 = 1TO6: FORT2 = 1TO6:READY(T1,T2)
00150   NEXT T2, T1:R1 = 1
00160   DATA  5,4,1,6,2,3,6,4,2,1,5,3,6,4,3,1,2,5,
               1,5,4,6,3,2,2,6,5
00170   DATA 4, 1, 3, 1, 5, 3, 6, 2, 4, 1, 0, -3, -5, -7
00180   INPUT "ENTER THE NUMBER OF NOTES IN
        THE MELODY",W9
00190   FORE = 0TO4:READB(E,W9):NEXTE
00195   REM INPUTTED MELODIES MUST BE IN THE
        KEY OF C
00200   PRINT "ENTER NOTES INDIVIDUALLY IN
        THE FOLLOWING FORMAT:"
00210   PRINT" MIDDLE C = 0"
00220   PRINT" NOTES ABOVE MIDDLE C ARE +1, +2,
        +3 . . . CORRESPONDING"
00230   PRINT"      TO D, E, F. . ."
00240   PRINT" NOTES BELOW MIDDLE C ARE -1, -2, -3
        . . . CORRESPONDING"
00250   PRINT"      TO B,A,G. . ."
00260   FORT1 = 1TOW9:INPUTV(T1):NEXTT1
00270   PRINT: PRINT "  #    SOPRANO   ALTO
```

TENOR BASS"
```
00280 L2 = 1
00290 FORW=W9TO1STEP-1
00300 IFW=W9 THEN 760 ELSE R1=1
00310 FORR=R1TO6
00320 B=V(W):B(1,W)=B:L2=Y(L1,R):B(0,W)=L2
00330 M=B(4,1+W):M(1)=L2-8:M(2)=L2-15
00340 FORS=1TO2
00350 IF ABS(M(S)−M)<=5 THEN NEXTSELSE A
      =M(3−S):GOTO370
00360 IFB>B(1,W+1)THENA=M(2)ELSEA=M(1)
00370 S=1:B(4,W)=A
00380 FORT=0TO4STEP2
00390 G=B-(T+A):GOSUB790 :IFG=0THEN410
00400 K(S)=A+T:S=S+1
00410 NEXTT
00420 IFS>3 THEN690 ELSEFORU=0TO6
00430 F(3,U)=K(1):F(0,U)=0:F(2,U)=K(2)
00440 K=K(2):J=K(1):K(2)=J+7:K(1)=K
00450 NEXTU
00460 FORU=0TO6
00470 FORE=2TO3
00480 K=F(E,U)
00490 IF ( 5−E*4>K )OR(17−E*4<K)OR(ABS(K−B(E,
      W + 1))>5)THEN610
00500 B(E,W)=K:IFB(2*E-3,W)<=B(2*E-2,W) THEN
      610 ELSENEXTE
00510 IFL1=L2THEN570 ELSEFORE1=1TO4
00520 FORE2=E1+1TO4
00530 M=B(E1,W+1)-B(E2,W+1)
00540 G=M:GOSUB 790 : IF(G=0)OR(G=4) THEN
      550 ELSE560
00550 IFB(E2,W)-B(E2,W+1)=B(E1,W)-B(E1,W+1)
      THEN 610
00560 NEXT E2,E1
00570 FORE=2TO3
00580 M(E)=ABS(B(E,W)-B(E,W+1))
00590 NEXTE
00600 F(0,U)=M(2)+M(3):GOTO620
00610 F(0,U)=88
00620 NEXTU
00630 V=88:FORU=0TO6
00640 V1=F(X,U)
```

```
00650   IFV1>V THEN 660 ELSEV=V1:U9=U
00660   NEXTU
00670   IFV=88THEN690
00680   B(3,W)=F(3,U9):B(2,W)=F(2,U9): GOTO760
00690   NEXTR
00700   W=W+1:   IFW9<>W THEN 710 ELSEPRINT
        "PROGRAM CANNOT CONTINUE":STOP
00710   L1=B(0,W+1):L2=B(0,W)
00720   FORR=1TO6
00730   IFL2=Y(L1,R)THEN750
00740   NEXTR
00750   R1=R+1:GOTO310
00760   PRINTUSINGJ$,W,B(1,W),B(2,W),B(3,W),B(4,W)
00770   L1=L2:NEXTW
00780   END
00790   G=G-INT(G/7)*7:RETURN
03000   REM TRANSPOSER
03010   REM READ HARMONY PROG. DATA FIRST
03015   RESTORE
03020   FOR X=1 TO 36
03030   READ A: NEXT A
03040   DIM A$(17,17),W$(100⌐
03050   FOR B=1 TO 17
03060   FOR C=1 TO 17
03070   READ A$(B,C)
03080   NEXT C,B
03090   INPUT "ENTER THE KEY THAT THE SONG IS
        IN (EG. C#)";B$
03100   FOR X=1 TO 17
03110   IF B$=A$(1,X) THEN 3120 ELSE NEXT X
03120   INPUT "ENTER THE KEY TO TRANSPOSE
        TO";C$
03130   FOR T=1 TO 17
03140   IF C$=A$(1,T) THEN 3150 ELSE NEXT T
03150   PRINT "ENTER THE NOTES OF THE SONG
        SEPARATELY"
03160   PRINT "ENTER 'END' TO END":R=1
03170   INPUT W$(R)
03180   IF W$(R)= "END" THEN 3190 ELSER=R+1:
        GOTO 3170
03190   R=R-1
03200   FORZ=1 TO R
```

189

```
03210   FOR P=1 TO 17
03220   IF W$ (Z)=A$(P,X) THEN 3230 ELSE NEXT P
03230   PRINT A$(P,T);" ";
03240   NEXT Z
03250   DATA C, C#, D', D, D#, E', E, F, F#, G', G, G#,
        A', A, A#, B', B, C#, D
03260   DATA D, D#, E, E, F, G', G, G, G#, A, A, A#, B,
        B, C, D', D, D, D#, E, E, F
03270   DATA G', G, G, G#, A, A, A#, B, B, C, D, D#, E',
        E, F, F, F#, G, G#, A', A, A#
03280   DATA B', B, C, C, C#, D#, E, E, F, F#, G', G, A',
        A, A, A#, B, B, C, C#, D', D
03290   DATA E', E, E, F, F#, G', G, A', A, A, A#, B, B,
        C, C#, D', D, E, F, F, F#, G, G
03300   DATA G#, A, A#, B', B, C, C, C#, D, D, D#, F,
        F#, G', G, G#, A', A, B', B, B, C
03310   DATA C#, D', D, D#, E', E, F#, G, G, G#, A, A,
        A#, B, C, C, C#, D, D, D#, E, E, F
03320   DATA G', G, G, G#, A, A, A#, B, C, C, C#, D, D,
        D#, E, E, F, G, G#, A', A, A#, B'
03330   DATA B, C, C#, D', D, D#, E', E, F, F, F#, G#, A,
        A, A#, B, B, C, D', D, D, D#, E
03340   DATA E, F, F#, G', G, A', A, A, A#, B, B, C, D', D,
        D, D#, E, E, F, F#, G', G
03350   DATA A, A#, B', B, C, C, C#, D, D#, E', E, F, F,
        F#, G, G, G#, A#, B, B, C, C#, D'
03360   DATA D, E', E, E, F, F#, G', G, G#, A', A, B', B, B,
        C, C#, D', D, E', E, E, F, F#
03370   DATA G', G, G#, A', A, B, C, C, C#, D, D, D#, E,
        F, F, F#, G, G, G#, A, A, A#
```

Possibilities with your personal computer include:

1. Produce a stricter set of rules for composition; rely less upon randomness.

2. Develop programs to compose in assorted music styles: classical, rock and roll, children's etc.

3. Develop programs to compose songs for given lyrics by using the timing of each syllable to time the duration of the notes accordingly. The ambitious programmer might try to link a lyric producing program with a music composition program; some unusual results would undoubtedly be produced.

4. Develop programs to compose songs in the style of a given (human) composer. Research of the idiosyncracies of a particular composer would be necessary to produce favorable results. Perhaps program could be written to determine general rules for composing in a particular composer's style by analyzing some of his music.

5. A popular melody could be mathematically transformed to produce a new melody, and this new melody would most likely be favorable. The original melody would be numerically encoded such that every note and note duration has a unique number. With the melody so coded, an algorithm could be applied to each note, translating that note into another. The simplest such algorithm could reflect each note around a central value, transforming high notes into low ones and vice-versa.

6. Given the score of a music piece written for a solo instrument (e.g. the piano), the computer could transpose and analyze melodies, bass, and counter rhythms to produce sheet music versions for other instruments.

7. A microcomputer connected to a player piano via a solenoid interface could digitally record songs you play or song notes you input. The song could be stored on cassette or floppy disk and recalled to be played at normal speed, faster, slower, backwards, with sticato, etc.

8. A microcomputer interfaced with a monophonic electronic synthesizer could theoretically produce a polyphonic effect, add a continuous bass or beat pattern, and perform a sequence of switching/mixing for live performances.

9. From a given music piece a simplified version could be obtained by the computer (the melody is carried by the highest notes, the bass by the lowest). Also, a given piece could be arranged such that all chords are broken up into varying arpeggios.

10. Given a melody, the computer could be programmed to compose a bass counter-melody.

SCUBA DIVING PLAN

A simple program could calculate one of these four parameters, given the other three:
1. time underwater,

2. tank air volume,
3. diving depth,
4. surface air consumption rate.

PHOTOGRAPHY

The serious photographer should investigate the use of the computer to obtain more precise values for development times, light exposures, filterings, etc. through the use of mathematical formulas. For example, the standard exposure meter assumes that 1) for any emulsion, the curve of the density vs. the log of the exposure yields a straight line and is characterized by a single factor—speed, 2) time and intensity of light are interchangeable to provide a certain exposure (reciprocity). Actually, these assumptions are only approximations of true values. In extreme cases, reciprocity does not work; the density vs log of exposure curve is not linear and emulsions have differing contrasts and latitudes. A reference manual describing the mathematical calculations of photography should describe the formulas used to take these factors into account.

Further applications:

1. Exposure compensation is useful in the darkroom to calculate the exposure required to compensate for a change in photo enlargement magnification.

2. Fill-in flash computation is used to determine the correct lens f-stop when a flash is used in the presence of strong ambient light to fill-in undesired shadows.

3. If you intend to do specialized photography requiring homebuilt equipment, the computer could be useful in optical and dimension calculations.

4. Automated control of darkroom equipment (including such features as temperature correction for chemicals, timer, development calculator) could expedite the development process.

5. An inventory of slides/photographs could be computer stored and topics could be indexed/cross-referenced. Thus, to create a slide show of a particular topic, one can use the computer to determine all relevant slides and output a listing of each along with its location and remarks.

6. A simple interface (switching) to a cassette recorder and slide projector could automate a complete audio-

visual slide presentation. An exotic audio-visual light show could be controlled similarly.

7. Focal length conversions from one camera to another, based on the diagonal or horizontal angle of view, could be done.

8. A program could be written to calculate film speed (ASA), flash ECPS value, or flash guide number, given the other two values. Once the flash guide number is known, the maximum f-stop for the distance from the flash to subject, may be calculated.

$$f\text{-stop} = \frac{\text{Guide number}}{\text{distance}}$$

9. Close-up photography values for subject distance, required lense, focus setting, or field of coverage could be calculated given the other three values.

10. The depth of field indicates the distance from some point in front and back for which a given photograph will be acceptably sharp. A computer program could mathematically determine how the desired near and far distances may be obtained, in terms of the f-stop and distance settings to use. Inputs necessary are 1) the distances for the desired depth of field 2)diameter of the circle of confusion on the negative 3) focal length of the camera lens. The required formula is fully described in many photography manuals.

Chapter 7
Games and
Recreational Applications

Games And Recreational Applications

With the computer's ability to solve long and complex equations in a matter of microseconds, many complex and unique games have been implemented, especially on the home computer. From the simple Tic-Tac-Toe to the complex game of Baseball, a computer can provide hours of home enjoyment.

GAMES TO BE COMPUTERIZED

Many popular board and logic games take on an added dimension when computerized, especially if the computer is programmed to be the opponent. Some of the many possibilities:

Tricolor—Tricolor is a game played on a hex board with the hexagonal cells colored red, white, and blue (or different shades). A separate board should be used in the computerized version, since board display on a video screen would be difficult. Each player begins with 18 pieces. Those of one player are white, those of the other black. At the start of the game white places his pieces on hexes 1-18 and black on hexes 44-61.

The pieces are called stacks, as one may place more than one piece together to form a stack. The range of a stack, that is, the maximum number of cells it can traverse in any one direction in a single move, is determined by the number of pieces in the stack, one cell for a single piece, two cells for a stack of two pieces, and three cells for any larger stack.

The combat strength of a stack depends upon both the number of pieces it contains and the color (or shade) of the cell on which it rests. Taking the strength of a single white piece on a white cell as the unit, the strength of a stack of two pieces on a white cell is two units, that of any larger stack on a white cell is three units. The strength of a stack on a black cell is twice this, and a stack on a red cell is three times that of the white cell.

Players take alternate turns, each moving a single stack as far as he wishes within the range of the stack and along a straight line diagonally or horizontally. The entire stack may be moved, or only a portion of it; the number of pieces in the part moved determines the strength of the stack. Occupied cells may not be jumped, but a player may move his stack to a cell occupied by another stack owned by himself or the opponent. If the stack is his own, the stacks are merged. If the opponent owns the other stack, an "attack" has been initiated and the disposition of pieces is as follows: a stack may attack an opposing stack only if it is stronger (contains more pieces). If it is more than twice as strong, the opposing stack is "killed", and all hostile pieces in the stack are removed from play; friendly pieces are added to the winning stack. If the attacking stack is not more than twice as strong, it "captures" the opposing stack by combining it with itself. If a capture or kill can be made in a player's turn, it must be made. The game ends with the capture or killing of all of one player's pieces.

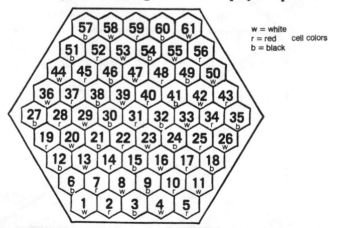

Black Sheep—Black sheep is played on a chess board between two players, one "white" the other "black." White begins the game with four white checkers which are placed on the four black squares on one side of the chess board. Black uses one black checker and places it on either of the middle black squares on the opposite side of the board. The white pieces may only move forward to the opposite side; black may move forward or backwards. Both colors may only move one square at a time and only on the diagonals.

Black moves first and then moves alternate. The object for black is to reach the opposite side of the board without being "trapped" (surrounded by white pieces such that there is no adjacent diagonal unoccupied square to move to). The objective for white is to trap black before it reaches the other side of the board. Apparently, no one has determined a winning strategy for this game, thus it would be challenging to develop a heuristic strategy for the computer to play either side.

Jam—In this simple, yet challenging game, the small circles in the diagram below represent cities; the lines represent roads. Each road has a designated number. Players

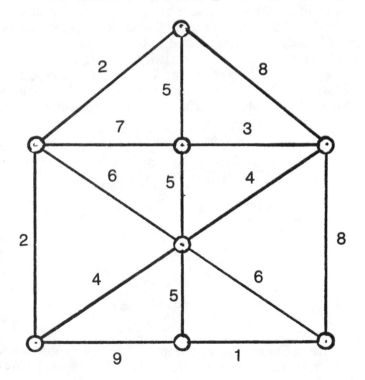

alternate turns choosing one of the nine roads as their own property. The winner is the first to own three roads which connect directly with any one city. The game may be won with a mathematical strategy similar to that employed with "tic-tac-toe."

Hot—"Hot" is a clever variation of tic-tac-toe. The following words are listed on a computer output: TANK, WOES, SHIP, WASP, HOT, BRIM, HEAR, FORM, TIED. Players take alternate turns picking one word from the list; words are removed from the list as they are chosen. The first player to have three words that bear the same single letter is the winner.

The game may be analyzed by the computer in the same manner as tic-tac-toe, if the words are arranged on the board as in this diagram:

SHIP	BRIM	TIED
WASP	HEAR	TANK
WOES	FORM	HOT

By choosing three words in a row horizontally, vertically, or diagonally, one can win the game. Thus, the strategy for play is the same as in tic-tac-toe, except the player that does not know these congruencies is at a disadvantage.

Bridge It—In the game of Bridge-it, the first player is designated as O and the second player as X. Turns alternate with each player putting a connecting line between two horizontally or vertically adjacent markers of that player's symbol. The O player attempts to form a connected "bridge" from the top to bottom of the board while the X player attempts to form a bridge from the left to right side of the board. The first to form a bridge wins the game.

A winning strategy exists for this game. The first player should put his first line between Os at positions 9, 2 and 11, 2 as shown in the diagram. The game may be won by the O player if the following strategy is used. Whenever X draws a

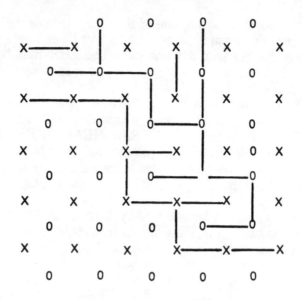

connecting line, the line will touch one of the dotted lines or semicircles in the second diagram. O should draw a connecting line between two O markers such that the line will touch the *end* of the dotted line just mentioned following each X turn. In this manner, O will inevitably win.

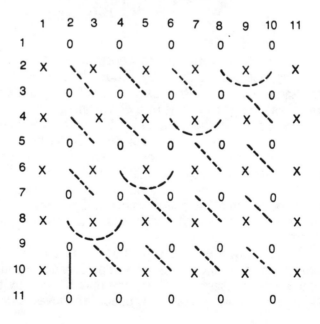

Hex—Hex is a game similar to Bridge-it, but the game has not been solved such that a win is always certain. For this reason, hex would probably be more interesting to play against a computer. A heuristic strategy similar to that used in Bridge-it could be employed.

The game of Hex is played on a board composed of hexagons, with eleven hexagons on each side (although other sizes have been used). Two opposite sides of the board are named black, while the other two are named white. The hexes at the four junctions between sides are neutral. One player has black pieces, the other player has white. Alternate turns are taken with each player placing one of his pieces on any unoccupied hexagon. The object for both players is to complete a continuous chain of his pieces between the two sides labeled by his color. The game is mathematically solvable on boards with certain dimensions.

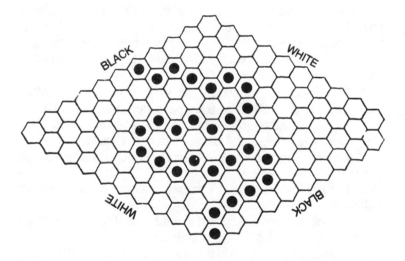

Cross Capture—Cross capture is played on a chess board. At the start of the game, a set of randomly distributed letters (or numbers) is put on the board, with most of the board empty. Players take turns choosing one of the letters, and all other letters on the board which fall under some criteria become property of that player. The criteria may be all the letters in a horizontal, diagonal, or vertical row with the chosen letter or all the letters within a certain proximity to the chosen letter. The player who possesses the most letters at the end of the game is declared the winner.

Tic-Tac-Toe Variation—An interesting tic-tac-toe variation is played as follows. Each player puts his three pieces on a tic-tac-toe board such that piece ownership alternates around the periphery of the board. Following this set-up, each player is allowed to move one of his pieces to an adjacent square. The winner of the game is the first to make three-in-a-row.

Space Games—In recent years complicated outer-space games have become popular. Use of a computer to play the opponent in this type of simulation game is a challenging application. One space game, called "Stellar Conquest" (sold by Metagaming Concepts, Box 15346, Austin, TX 78761) provides a good example of the complexity involved. A summary of the game is included here to suggest improvements to computer space games.

Stellar Conquest is a game of exploration, colonization, industrialization, technical research, and conquest. Two to four players direct complete interstellar societies as they compete for dominance of a star cluster. The sequence of events for each turn is as follows.

1. Ship movement is semi-secret; pieces indicating each ship are face down in the space hex-map provided.

2. Star exploration—star cards determine planetary types and resources, and thus, results are random.

3. Ship-to-ship combat to resolve control of specific star hexes.

4. Ship-to-ship planet combat in conquest assaults on colonies.

5. Colonization—population and industry are offloaded from transports to habitate planets.

6. Industrial unit production—every fourth turn of play changes are made in these factors: population growth, technical research, industrial expansion, ship-building, migration, and others.

7. Next player begins turn.

Tuknanavuhpi—Tuknanavuhpi is a Hopi Indian chase game played on a 4 × 4 board with diagonals drawn in each of the 16 squares. Pieces move on the points where lines meet on the board, not on the squares. There are two players, each of which has 20 pieces placed on the board as indicated in the diagram below. The middle of the board is initially empty.

Players take alternate turns moving their pieces in any direction along the lines on the board, from one intersection to another adjacent intersection. Pieces are captured as in checkers by jumping over any of the opponents pieces. The winner is the player who has captured all of his opponents' pieces.

Many other games exist which are popular in other cultures, but undiscovered in the United States. These games are often well suited to be used as computer games.

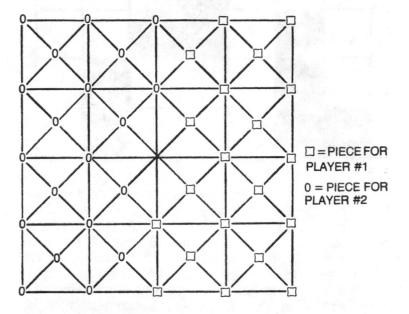

☐ = PIECE FOR
PLAYER #1

0 = PIECE FOR
PLAYER #2

Nim Variations—The game of Nim has become a very popular computer game. The rules are simple. From a pile of any number of items (20 is the usual number), players take turns picking one, two, or three items from the pile. The player forced to pick up the last item loses the game. Here are a few games which may be mathematically analyzed similar to Nim:

- Rectangular dominoes—Players take turns placing dominoes on a chess-type board or arbitrary size (8×8 is fine). The board is of a size such that a domino placed horizontally or vertically on it will cover up exactly two

203

squares. The first player places his dominoes horizontally, the second player places his vertically, and dominoes may not overlap. The winner of the game is the player who makes the last possible move.

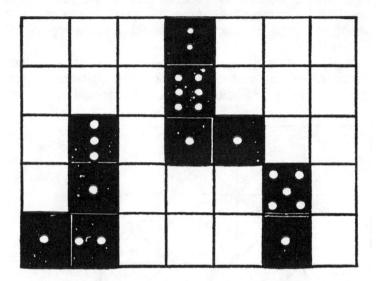

• Welter—The board for this game consists of an arbitrary number of squares in one line (usually about twenty). Any arbitrary number of tokens are randomly placed in the squares, with only one token in each square (there are usually about five tokens). Players take turns moving a single token to any unoccupied square to the left, jumping over other tokens if desired. The player who makes the last move wins the game.

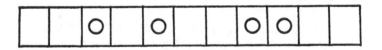

• Traffic Jam—The game board below represents one-way roads between towns. An arbitrary number of vehicles are placed on the board to set-up the game. Players take turns moving one of the vehicles in the proper direction from one town to an adjacent town.

The game continues until a traffic jam develops, in which no further moves are possible; the player who makes the final move is declared the winner.

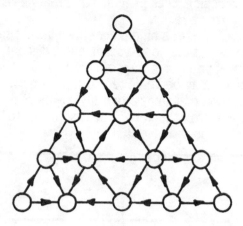

- Innocent Marble Game—In this game, either zero, two, or four markers may be placed in the circles on the gameboard; only one marker may be in any one circle. Players take turns moving any one marker from one circle to adjacent one and in the direction of the arrows. Whenever a marker is moved to a circle already occupied, both markers are removed from play. The winner is the player making the last possible move.

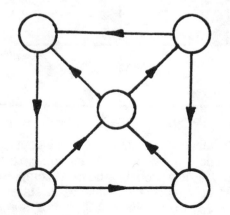

Mill—Mill is a two player game using the board shown below. Players alternate turns placing one of their nine pieces on any of the corners or intersections of lines on the board. The moment one player gets three pieces in line, he may remove an opposing piece provided that that piece is not part of three in a row already.

After each player's nine pieces are placed, they may be moved one at a time to a vacant and adjacent corner or intersection. If any other lines of three are formed, another opposing piece may be removed. If a player has only three pieces on the board, he may move any one piece to any corner or intersection during his turn. The first player to be left with only two pieces is the loser.

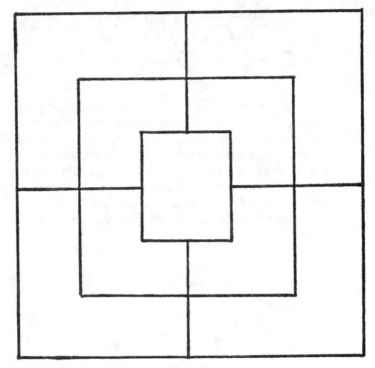

PROGRAM—STAR CHALLENGE

Star Challenge is perhaps the most popular computer game in existence, possibly due to its complexity. The version presented here is probably the most complete version in print. The MAT X = ZER commands in statements 29-39 simply set all the array values = 0. For some BASICS, RND(-1) will have to be changed to RND (0).

```
00001    REM -----------STAR FIGHT---------------
00003    REM
00005    REM
00007    DIM A (5), T (5), R (5), F (5), D (5), H (5), C (5)
00009    LET H1 = F = R = D = D2 = D3 = B1 = B2 = C =
         C1 = P = S = 0
00011    LET B$ = "PHASER BANKS "
00013    LET C$ = "CLOAK ACTIVATED**"
00015    LET K$ = "KLINGON "
00017    LET E$ = "ENGINEERING REPORTS "
00019    LET P$ = " PHOTON TORPEDOES "
00021    LET D$ = ", DAMAGE REPORT-"
00023    LET H$ = "HIGH ENERGY PLASMA BOLT"
00025    LET G$ = " DAMAGED"
00027    MAT C = ZER
00029    MAT H = ZER
00031    MAT R = ZER
00033    MAT A = ZER
00035    MAT D = ZER
00037    MAT T = ZER
00039    MAT F = ZER
00041    LET P3 = 1.5
00043    LET R1 = 1
00045    PRINT "SPACE--THE FINAL FRONTIER.
         THESE ARE THE VOYAGES OF"
00047    PRINT "THE STARSHIP ENTERPRIZE, HER
         FIVE YEAR MISSION--"
00049    PRINT "TO EXPLORE STRANGE NEW
         WORLDS, TO SEEK OUT NEW LIFE AND
         NEW"
00051    PRINT "CIVILIZATION, TO BOLDLY GO
         WHERE NO MAN HAS GONE BEFORE."
00053    PRINT "(SWISH, TRUMPETS)"
00055    PRINT
00057    PRINT
00059    LET Q = INT (10*RND (-1.) )
00061    PRINT "YOU ARE ON PATROL IN ARCTURUS
         SECTOR"; Q; "WHEN YOU"
00063    PRINT "PICK UP UNEXPECTED SENSOR
         READINGS, CONFIGURATION---"
00065    PRINT "            KLINGON BATTLE CRUIS-
         ERS"
```

```
00067   PRINT "DO YOU NEED A SUMMARY OF YOUR
        SHIP'S CAPABILITIES";
00069   INPUT A$
00071   IF A$ = "NO" THEN 00105
00073   PRINT "CAPABILITIES OF THE USS ENTER-
        PRIZE."
00075   PRINT "AFTER THE QUESTION MARK TYPE
        TWO DIGITS SEPARATED BY COMMAS"
00077   PRINT "EXAMPLE: 0,0.    FIRST DIGIT IS
        THE OPTION."
00079   PRINT "         SECOND DIGIT IS THE SHIP
        TO ATTACK."
00081   PRINT "COMMAND OPTIONS:  1 FIRES PHAS-
        ERS."
00083   PRINT "         2 FIRES SECRET WEAPON."
00085   PRINT "         3 FIRES FRONT PHOTON
        TORPEDOES."
00087   PRINT "         4 FIRES REAR PHOTON
        TORPEDOES."
00089   PRINT "         5 FIRES HIGH ENERGY
        PLASMA BOLT."
00091   PRINT "         6 ACTIVATES SELF DE-
        STRUCT."
00093   PRINT "         7 FOR CHANGE OF WARP
        SPEED."
00095   PRINT "         11 ACTIVATES CLOAK DE-
        VICE."
00097   PRINT "         12 DEACTIVATES CLOAK
        DEVICE."
00099   PRINT "         13 TURNS SHIP 180 DE-
        GREES."
00101   PRINT "         14 DIVERTS POWER TO RE-
        PAIRS."
00103   PRINT "         15 DIVERTS POWER TO
        WEAPONS."
00105   PRINT
00107   PRINT
00109   PRINT "HOW MANY KLINGONS DO YOU WANT
        TO TAKE ON";
00111   INPUT N1
00113   LET N1 = INT (N1)
00115   IF N1 > 0 THEN 00121
```

```
00117    PRINT "THE KLINGONS";
00119    GOTO 00125
00121    IF N1 < 6 THEN 00129
00123    PRINT "THE KLINGONS ONLY"
00125    PRINT "HAVE 5 BATLE CRUISERS IN THIS
         QUADRANT"
00127    GOTO 00109
00129    IF N1 = 1 THEN 00139
00131    IF N1 > 2 THEN 00135
00133    LET S = H (1) = H (2) = –1
00135    PRINT N1; "KLINGONS";
00137    GOTO 00143
00139    PRINT N1; K$;
00141    LET S = H (1) = –3
00143    PRINT " COMING INTO RANGE--SHIELDS ON"
00145    PRINT
00147    FOR I = 1 TO N1
00149    LET R (I) = 400000. + RND (–1.)*200000.
00151    LET A (I) = 360*RND (–1.)
00153    PRINT "RANGE OF";K$;I; "="; R(I); "KM.AT"; A
         (I); "DEGREES"
00155    NEXT I
00157    LET S = 0
00159    P3 = 1.5
00161    R1 = 1
00163    GO TO 00377
00165    LET M = D1 = N2 = 0
00167    PRINT "YOUR MOVE? DIRECTED AT "; K$;
00169    INPUT M1, K
00171    LET K = INT (K)
00173    LET M1 = INT (M1)
00175    IF M1 > 0 THEN 00181
00177    GOSUB 00975
00179    GOTO 00537
00181    IF M1 > 16 THEN 00387
00183    IF K > N1 THEN 00387
00185    IF M1 < 14 THEN 00189
00187    ON (M1 – 13) GOTO 00363, 00371, 00159
00189    ON M1 GOTO 231, 231, 191, 197, 231, 233, 233,
         231, 233, 233, 233, 341, 349
00191    IF F > = 20 THEN 00407
00193    IF A (K) > 180 THEN 00387
```

```
00195   GOTO 00201
00197   IF R > = 10 THEN 00417
00199   IF A (K) < 180 THEN 00387
00201   IF R (K) < 200000 THEN 00387
00203   IF R (K) > 600000 THEN 00387
00205   IF H1 > = 9 THEN 00387
00207   IF C (K) = 1 THEN 00387
00209   IF N1 < > 1 THEN 00215
00211   LET N2 = 1
00213   GOTO 00233
00215   PRINT "HOW MANY"; P$; "DO YOU WANT TO
        FIRE";
00217   INPUT N2
00219   LET N2 = INT (N2)
00221   IF N2 > (N1*2) −1 THEN 00395
00223   IF N2 < 1 THEN 00395
00225   IF C = 1 THEN 00229
00227   GOTO 00231
00229   IF N2 > 5 THEN 00391
00231   IF C (K) = 1 THEN 00387
00233   ON M1 GOTO 235, 251, 257, 267, 273, 875, 913,
        965, 961, 309, 333
00235   IF R (K) > 300000 THEN 00387
00237   IF A (K) > 180 THEN 00387
00239   IF H1 > = 8 THEN 00387
00241   LET N3 = 2/M1
00243   LET P = P + N3
00245   GOSUB 00975
00247   LET N2 = N3
00249   GOTO 00461
00251   IF R (K) > 300000 THEN 00387
00253   IF A (K) < 180 THEN 00387
00255   GOTO 00239
00257   LET F = F + N2
00259   IF F > 20 THEN 00401
00261   LET P = P + N2
00263   GOSUB 00975
00265   GOTO 00461
00267   LET R = R + N2
00269   IF R > 10 THEN 00411
00271   GOTO 00261
00273   IF H1 > = 8 THEN 00387
```

```
00275   IF C = 1 THEN 00387
00277   IF R (K) < 100000 THEN 00387
00279   IF R (K) > 300000 THEN 00387
00281   LET B1 = B1 + 1
00283   IF B1 > 5 THEN 00421
00285   LET P = P + 3
00287   GOSUB 00975
00289   LET B = RND (−1)
00291   IF B > .7 THEN 00297
00293   IF B > .2 THEN 00303
00295   GOTO 00529
00297   PRINT "DIRECT HIT ON "; K$; K
00299   LET H (K) = H (K) + 4
00301   GOTO 00491
00303   PRINT "HIT ON "; K$; K
00305   LET H (K) = H (K) + 2
00307   GOTO 00491
00309   IF H1 > = 7 THEN 00387
00311   IF H1 < 5 THEN 00387
00313   PRINT "HOW MANY MILLION STROMS DO
        YOU WANT TO USE";
00315   INPUT P1
00317   LET P1 = INT (P1)
00319   IF P1 < 0 THEN 00387
00321   LET P = P + P1
00323   GOSUB 00975
00325   LET H1 = H1 − (P1*.5)
00327   IF H1 > = 5 THEN 00537
00329   PRINT "SHIELDS FIRMING UP"
00331   GOTO 00537
00333   IF C = 1 THEN 00387
00335   LET C = 1
00337   PRINT C$
00339   GOTO 00165
00341   IF C = 0 THEN 00387
00343   PRINT "CLOAK DEACTIVATED"
00345   LET C = 0
00347   GOTO 00167
00349   IF C (K) = 1 THEN 00387
00351   IF A (K) < 180 THEN 00357
00353   LET A (K) = A (K) −180
00355   GOTO 00359
```

211

```
00357   LET A (K) = A (K) + 180
00359   PRINT K$; K; "NOW AT"; A (K); "DEGREES"
00361   GOTO 00167
00363   LET R1 = 2
00365   LET P3 = .5
00367   PRINT "POWER DIVERTED TO REPAIRS"
00369   GOTO 00165
00371   LET P3 = 2.5
00373   PRINT "POWER DIVERTED TO WEAPONS"
00375   GOTO 00165
00377   IF C < > 1 THEN 00381
00379   PRINT C$;
00381   IF P3 = 2.5 THEN 00373
00383   IF P3 = .5 THEN 00367
00385   GOTO 00165
00387   PRINT "MOVE IMPOSSIBLE, TRY AGAIN"
00389   GOTO 00167
00391   PRINT "WITH THE CLOAK ACTIVATED ONLY
        5"; P$; "MAY"
00393   GOTO 00397
00395   PRINT "WITH"; N1; "KLINGONS ONLY"; (N1*2)
        −1; P$; "MAY"
00397   PRINT "BE FIRED AT A TIME"
00399   GOTO 00165
00401   LET F = F − N2
00403   PRINT "ONLY"; 20 − F; "FORWARD"; P$;
        "LEFT"
00405   GOTO 00165
00407   PRINT "OUT OF FORWARD"; P$
00409   GOTO 00167
00411   LET R = R − N2
00413   PRINT "ONLY"; 10 − R; "REAR"; P$; "LEFT"
00415   GOTO 00165
00417   PRINT "OUT OF REAR"; P$
00419   GOTO 00167
00421   PRINT "OUT OF"; H$; "S"
00423   GOTO 00167
00425   PRINT "SECONDARY DILITHIUM CIRCUIT
        FUSED"
00427   PRINT "IMPULSE POWER ONLY—LIMIT 2
        MILLION STROMS"
00429   PRINT "WARNING—IF CAPACITY OF IM-
        PULSE ENGINE IS EXCEEDED, IT"
```

```
00431   PRINT "WILL IMPLODE"
00433   LET C1 = 2
00435   GOTO 00443
00437    PRINT "PRIMARY DILITHIUM CIRCUIT
        FUSED, SWITCHING TO SECONDARY"
00439   PRINT "OVERLOAD CAPACITY FOR THIS CIR-
        CUIT IS 10 MILLION STROMS"
00441   LET C1 = 1
00443   LET P = 0
00445   IF M1 = 5 THEN 00457
00447   IF M1 = 3 THEN 00453
00449   LET R = R − N2
00451   GOTO 00167
00453   LET F = F −N2
00455   GOTO 00167
00457   LET B1 = B1 − 1
00459   GOTO 00167
00461   FOR I = 1 TO N2
00463   LET B = RND (−1)
00465   IF B > (R (K)*5.E −07 + .55) THEN 00473
00467   IF B > (R (K)*5.E − 07 + .25) THEN 00479
00469   LET M = M + 1
00471   GOTO 00483
00473   LET H (K) = H (K) + 2
00475   PRINT "DIRECT HIT**";
00477   GOTO 00483
00479   LET H (K) = H (K) + 1
00481   PRINT "HIT**";
00483   IF H (K) > = 8 THEN 00489
00485   NEXT I
00487   IF M = N2 THEN 00529
00489   PRINT
00491   IF H (K) < 6 THEN 00495
00493   LET F (K) = F (K) + 1
00495    PRINT "DAMAGE TO "; K$; K; "IN THIS
        ATTACK-";
00497   IF H (K) > 8 THEN 00521
00499   ON INT (H (K) ) GOTO 00501, 00501, 00505,
        00505, 00509, 00513, 00517
00501   PRINT "SHIELDS HOLDING, NO DAMAGE"
00503   GOTO 00531
00505   PRINT "SHIELDS WEAKENING, MINOR DAM-
        AGE"
```

```
00507   GOTO 00531
00509   PRINT "ALL SHIELDS DESTROYED"
00511   GOTO 00531
00513   PRINT B$; "DEACTIVATED"
00515   GOTO 00531
00517   PRINT "ALL WEAPONS DEACTIVATED"
00519   GOTO 00531
00521   PRINT
00523   PRINT "*****"; K$; K; "DESTROYED*****"
00525   LET C (K) = 1
00527   GOTO 00537
00529   PRINT " NEAR MISS"
00531   IF F (K) < > 3 THEN 00537
00533   PRINT K$; K; "CAN NO LONGER REPAIR IT-
        SELF"
00535   LET F (K) = 4
00537   IF H1 > = 9 THEN 00543
00539   LET P = P − P3
00541   GOTO 00545
00543   LET P = P − P3 − .5
00545   IF D > 4 THEN 00605
00547   IF P3 = 2.5 THEN 00605
00549   FOR I = 1 TO R1
00551   Z1 = H1 − .5
00553   IF Z1 > −1 THEN 00559
00555   LET H1 = −1
00557   GOTO 00561
00559   LET H1 = H1 − .5
00561   IF H1 = 9.5 THEN 00565
00563   GOTO 00567
00565   IF C1 < > 2 THEN 00577
00567   IF H1 = 8.5 THEN 00581
00569   IF H1 = 7.5 THEN 00593
00571   IF H1 = 6.5 THEN 00597
00573   IF H1 = 4.5 THEN 00601
00575   GOTO 00603
00577   PRINT E$; "WARP ENGINES REPAIRED"
00579   GOTO 00603
00581   IF F < 20 THEN 00585
00583   IF R > = 10 THEN 00589
00585   PRINT E$; P$; "PROJECTORS REPAIRED"
00587   GOTO 00603
```

```
00589  PRINT E$; "NORMAL POWER LEVELS RE-
       STORED"
00591  GOTO 00603
00593  PRINT E$; B$; "REPAIRED"
00595  GOTO 00603
00597  PRINT E$; "SHIELDS RESTORED AT A LOW
       POWER LEVEL"
00599  GOTO 00603
00601  PRINT E$; "SHIELDS FIRMING UP"
00603  NEXT I
00605  FOR K = 1 TO N1
00607  IF C (K) = 1 THEN 00723
00609  IF C = 0 THEN 00617
00611  IF M1 = 0 THEN 00647
00613  IF H (K) > 5 THEN 00651
00615  IF F (K) > 2 THEN 00651
00617  IF R (K) < = 500000. THEN 00621
00619  IF H (K) < 7 THEN 00637
00621  IF R (K) > = 1. E + 06 THEN 00625
00623  IF H (K) > = 7 THEN 00651
00625  IF R (K) > = 200000. THEN 00629
00627  IF H (K) > 6 THEN 00651
00629  IF R (K) > = 300000. THEN 00633
00631  IF H (K) < 6 THEN 00669
00633  IF R (K) > = 200000. THEN 00637
00635  IF T (K) < 10 THEN 00707
00637  IF H (K) < 6 THEN 00641
00639  IF T (K) = 10 THEN 00651
00641  LET R (K) = R (K)/2
00643  PRINT K$; K; "APPROACHING"
00645  GOTO 00725
00647  PRINT K$; K; "DOING NOTHING"
00649  GOTO 00733
00651  IF H (K) > = 7 THEN 00657
00653  LET R (K) = R (K) + 200000. + RND (-1)*100000.
00655  GOTO 00659
00657  LET R (K) = R (K) + 100000. + RND (-1)*50000.
00659  PRINT K$; K; "ATTEMPTING TO BREAK CON-
       TACT"
00661  IF R (K) < 1.E + 06 THEN 00725
00663  PRINT K$; K; "OUT OF SENSOR RANGE-
       CONTACT BROKEN"
```

```
00665    LET C (K) = D (K) = 1
00667    GOTO 00723
00669    IF N1 > 2 THEN 00673
00671    IF RND (−1) <.7 THEN 00677
00673    PRINT K$; K; "FIRES PHASERS AT ENTER-
         PRISE"
00675    GOTO 00803
00677    IF B2 = 10 THEN 00673
00679    IF R(K) < 100000. THEN 00673
00681    LET B2 = B2 + 1
00683    IF B2 = 10 THEN 00689
00685    PRINT K$; K; "LAUNCHES"; H$
00687    GOTO 00691
00689    PRINT K$; K; "LAUNCHES ITS LAST"; H$
00691    LET B = RND (−1)
00693    IF B > .7 + C*.3 THEN 00703
00695    IF B > .2 + C*.4 THEN 00699
00697    GOTO 00811
00699    LET H1 = H1 + 1
00701    GOTO 00821
00703    LET H1 = H1 + 2
00705    GOTO 00815
00707    IF N1 >2 THEN 00711
00709    IF RND (−1) < .4 THEN 00637
00711    LET T (K) = T (K) + 1
00713    IF T (K) = 10 THEN 00719
00715    PRINT K$; K; "FIRES"; P$
00717    GOTO 00803
00719    PRINT K$; K; "FIRES ITS LAST"; P$
00721    GOTO 00803
00723    LET D1 = D1 + 1
00725    IF D < 4 THEN 00733
00727    IF D > 9 THEN 00733
00729    PRINT E$; "FURTHER MAJOR REPAIRS IM-
         POSSIBLE"
00731    LET D = 10
00733    NEXT K
00735    IF D1 = N1 THEN 00993
00737    PRINT
00739    FOR J = 1 TO N1
00741    IF C (J) = 1 THEN 00757
00743    LET R (J) = R (J) − RND (−1)*1000
```

216

```
00745   IF R (J) > 1000 THEN 00749
00747   LET R (J) = R (J) + (RND (−1)*10000)
00749   LET A (J) = A (J) − (5*RND (−1) )
00751   IF A (J) > 10 THEN 00755
00753   LET A (J) = A (J) + (RND (−1)*20)
00755   PRINT "RANGE OF "; K$; J; "="; R (J); "KM.
        AT"; A (J); "DEGREES"
00757   NEXT J
00759   FOR I = 1 TO N1
00761   IF C (I) = 1 THEN 00797
00763   IF F (I) > = 3 THEN 00797
00765   H (I) = H (I) − .5
00767   IF H (I) > S THEN 00771
00769   H (I) = S
00771   IF H (I) < > 6.5 THEN 00775
00773   IF T (I) < 10 THEN 00783
00775   IF H (I) = 5.5 THEN 00787
00777   IF H (I) = 4.5 THEN 00791
00779   IF H (I) = 2.5 THEN 00795
00781   GOTO 00797
00783   PRINT K$; I; "HAS REPAIRED ITS PHOTON
        TORPEDO PROJECTORS"
00785   GOTO 00797
00787   PRINT K$; I; "HAS REPAIRED ITS "; B$
00789   GOTO 00797
00791   PRINT K$; I; "HAS RESTORED ITS SHIELDS AT
        LOW POWER"
00793   GOTO 00797
00795   PRINT K$; I; "HAS RESTORED ITS SHIELDS TO
        FULL POWER"
00797   NEXT I
00799   PRINT "YOUR CURRENT POWER OVERLOAD
        IS "; P; "MILLION STROMS"
00801   GOTO 00377
00803   LET B = RND (−1)
00805   IF B > (R (K)*5.E − 07 + .6 + C*.4) THEN 00815
00807   IF B > (R (K)*5.E − 07 + .3 + C*.2) THEN 00821
00809   IF B > .3 THEN 00827
00811   PRINT " NEAR MISS"
00813   GOTO 00725
00815   PRINT "DIRECT HIT ON USS ENTERPRISE";
        D$;
```

```
00817    LET H1 = H1 + 2
00819    GOTO 00833
00821    PRINT "HIT ON USS ENTERPRISE"; D$;
00823    LET H1 = H1 + 1
00825    GOTO 00833
00827    IF M1 < = 0 THEN 00811
00829    PRINT "YOU OUTMANEUVERED HIM, MISS"
00831    GOTO 00725
00833    IF H1 < 8 THEN 00837
00835    LET D = D + 1
00837    IF H1 > = 11 THEN 00869
00839    IF H1 < 5 THEN 00843
00841    ON INT (H1 − 4) GOTO 00847, 00847, 00851,
         00855, 00859, 00865, 00869
00843    PRINT "SHIELDS HOLDING, NO DAMAGE"
00845    GOTO 00725
00847    PRINT "SHIELDS WEAKENING"
00849    GOTO 00725
00851    PRINT "ALL SHIELDS DESTROYED"
00853    GOTO 00725
00855    PRINT B$; "DEACTIVATED, ";
00857    GOTO 00851
00859    PRINT
00861    PRINT "ALL WEAPONS, SHIELDS DEACTI-
         VATED, POWER DROPPING"
00863    GOTO 00725
00865    PRINT "WARP POWER GONE,"
00867    GOTO 00861
00869    PRINT "USS ENTERPRISE DESTROYED"
00871    LET D2 = 1
00873    GOTO 00993
00875    PRINT TAB (15); "A C T I V A T E D"
00877    LET R1 = 9800*RND (−1) + 200
00879    PRINT "RADIUS OF EXPLOSION ="; R1; "KM."
00881    FOR I = 1 TO N1
00883    IF C (I) = 1 THEN 00905
00885    IF R (I) > R1 THEN 00905
00887    IF R (I) > R1*.8 THEN 00895
00889    PRINT K$; I; "DESTROYED";
00891    LET C (I) = 1
00893    GOTO 00903
00895    LET H (I) = H (I) + 6
```

218

```
00897   IF H (I) > = 8 THEN 00889
00899   LET F (I) = F (I) + 1
00901   PRINT K$; I; "HEAVILY"; G$;
00903   PRINT " BY THE BLAST"
00905   NEXT I
00907   GOTO 00871
00909   PRINT "IMPULSE ENGINE OVERLOAD"
00911   GOTO 00877
00913   IF C1 = 2 THEN 00387
00915   IF H1 > = 10 THEN 00387
00917   PRINT "HOW FAST DO YOU WANT TO GO,
        WARP 1-8";
00919   INPUT W
00921   IF W < 0 THEN 00387
00923   IF W > 8 THEN 00387
00925   LET P = P + W
00927   GOSUB 00975
00929   IF M1 < > 9 THEN 00933
00931   LET W = 2
00933   FOR I = 1 TO N1
00935   IF C (I) = 1 THEN 00957
00937   LET R (I) = R (I) + W*100000. − RND (−1)*50000.
00939   IF R (I) > 1.E + 06 THEN 00947
00941   IF A (I) > 180 THEN 00957
00943   LET A (I) = A (I) + 180
00945   GOTO 00957
00947   LET C (I) = 1
00949   LET D (I) = 2
00951   IF H (I) < 7 THEN 00955
00953   LET D (I) = 1
00955   PRINT "LOST CONTACT WITH "; K$; I
00957   NEXT I
00959   GOTO 00537
00961   LET W = 1
00963   GOTO 00925
00965   LET P = P + 1
00967   GOSUB 00975
00969   LET R (K) = R (K)/2
00971   LET A (K) = A (K)/2
00973   GOTO 00537
00975   IF C < > 1 THEN 00979
00977   LET P = P + 3
```

```
00979   IF P < = 20 THEN 00983
00981   IF C1 = 0 THEN 00437
00983   IF P < = 10 THEN 00987
00985   IF C1 = 1 THEN 00425
00987   IF P < = 2 THEN 00991
00989   IF C1 = 2 THEN 00909
00991   RETURN
00993   PRINT
00995   PRINT
00997   PRINT "RESULTS OF THIS BATTLE:"
00999   PRINT
01001   FOR I = 1 TO N1
01003   IF C (I) < > 1 THEN 01007
01005   IF D (I) = 1 THEN 01031
01007   IF C (I) < > 1 THEN 01011
01009   IF D (I) = 2 THEN 01035
01011   IF C (I) = 1 THEN 01021
01013   IF H (I) > = 6 THEN 01027
01015   IF H (I) > = 3 THEN 01043
01017   PRINT K$; I; "NOT"; G$
01019   GOTO 01045
01021   PRINT K$; I; "DESTROYED"
01023   LET D3 = D3 + 1
01025   GOTO 01045
01027   PRINT K$; I; "HEAVILY"; G$
01029   GOTO 01037
01031   PRINT K$; I; "FORCED TO RETIRE"
01033   GOTO 01023
01035   PRINT "CONTACT LOST WITH "; K$; I
01037   IF H (I) < 6 THEN 01041
01039   IF F (I) > = 3 THEN 01023
01041   GOTO 01045
01043   PRINT K$; I; "LIGHTLY"; G$
01045   NEXT I
01047   PRINT "USS ENTERPRISE ";
01049   IF D2 = 1 THEN 01071
01051   IF C1 = 2 THEN 01067
01053   IF H1 < 5 THEN 01057
01055   ON INT (H1 − 4) GOTO 01063, 01063, 01067,
        01067, 01067, 01067, 01067
01057   IF C1 = 1 THEN 01063
01059   PRINT "NOT"; G$
```

```
01061   GOTO 01073
01063   PRINT "LIGHTLY"; G$
01065   GOTO 01073
01067   PRINT "HEAVILY"; G$
01069   GOTO 01073
01071   PRINT "LOST"
01073   IF D3 < N1/2 THEN 01077
01075   IF D2 = 0 THEN 01087
01077   IF D3 > = N1/2 THEN 01091
01079   IF D2 < > 0 THEN 01083
01081   IF D3 > = 1 THEN 01091
01083   PRINT "THIS BATTLE AWARDED TO THE
        KLINGONS"
01085   GOTO 01105
01087   PRINT "CONGRATULATIONS—YOU HAVE
        WON A MAJOR VICTORY"
01089   GOTO 01093
01091   PRINT "CONGRATULATIONS—YOU HAVE
        WON A TACTICAL VICTORY"
01093   PRINT
01095   PRINT "DO YOU WANT ANOTHER BATTLE";
01097   INPUT Z$
01099   IF Z$ = "NO" THEN 01123
01101   PRINT "REPAIRS COMPLETED"
01103   GOTO 00009
01105   PRINT
01107   PRINT "DO YOU WANT ANOTHER BATTLE";
01109   INPUT Z$
01111   IF Z$ = "NO" THEN 01123
01113   PRINT "HERE'S ANOTHER STARSHIP --- BE
        MORE CAREFUL THIS TIME"
01115   GOTO 00009
01117   LET P3 = 1.5
01119   GOTO 00009
01121   IF D2 = 1 THEN 01125
01123   PRINT "REPORT TO STARBASE" INT (RND
        (−1)*12) + 1
01125   END
```

WORD GAMES AND QUIZZES

Ideas for word games and quiz programs include:
1. Trivia quizzes on science fiction, movies, history,

etc. for enjoyment; the program could calculate your "trivia I.Q."

2. Cryptograms, or coded messages, could be displayed for you to decode; simple clues could be provided.

3. Anagrams, or jumbled words, serve to help one prepare for I.Q. tests and help determine mental abilities.

```
10   REM ANAGRAM CREATOR
20   REM SCRAMBLES WORDS FOR ENTERTAIN-
     MENT
30   N=6 'NUMBER OF WORDS IN DATA STATE-
     MENTS
40   DIM M(N), W$(N), A(20)
50   FORI=1 TO N
60   M(I)=I
70   NEXT I
80   FORI=1 TO N-1
90   R=(N+1-I)*RND(0)
100  R=INT(R)+I
110  T=M(R)
120  M(R)=M(I)
130  M(I)=T
140  NEXT I
150  FORI=1 TO N
160  READ W$ (M(I))
170  NEXT I
180  FOR I = 1 TO N
185  A$=" "
190  A=LEN(W$(I))
200  FOR B=1 TO A
210  A(B)=B
220  NEXT B
230  FORB=1 TO N-1
234  RANDOM
235  S=(A+1-B)*RND(0)
240  S=INT(S)+B
250  C=A(S):A(S)=A(B):A(B)=C
260  NEXT B
270  FORB=1 TO A
280  A$=A$+MID$(W$(I),A(B),1)
290  NEXT B
300  PRINTA$
```

```
310  INPUT C$
320  IF C$=W$(I) THEN PRINT "RIGHT!" ELSE PRINT
     "WRONG, THE ANSWER WAS:"; W$(I)
330  NEXT I
340  END

500  REM DATA STATEMENTS CONTAIN WORDS
     HERE...
510  DATA COMPUTER, TELEVISION, GAME, IN-
     STRUMENT, WRITE, BASIC
```

4. The game of hangman, in which one has ten guesses to determine the letters in a randomly chosen word, serves to familiarize one with vocabulary terms.

5. Word search puzzles ad infinitum may be computer generated. A program to determine locations of all words in the puzzle could also be implemented.

6. Word guessing games, similar to twenty questions, except that the human player asks the questions. Replys must be stored for the many possible questions a human could pose. One such program dialogue went like this:

(c=computer, h=human)

h: Does it grow?
c: To answer that question might be misleading.
h: Can I eat it?
c: Only as food for thought.
h: Do computers have it?
c: Strictly speaking, no.
c: The word is "Knowledge"

Another word game would involve the selection of a three-letter word from a large list by the computer. The player would input a guess as a three-letter word and would be informed as to whether the computer's word contained any of the letters in that word if those letters are in the correct position. The object is to guess the computer's word in the least number of trials.

RECREATIONS WITH THE COMPUTER ITSELF

A hobby computer magazine once listed some suggestions on "busting your computer" to determine the limitations of your BASIC (or other high-level language). The results may surprise you. A few ideas:

1. Determine the maximum number of parentheses that may be used in one statement (don't be surprised if over 100 are allowed!).
2. Determine the maximum allowed dimension for an array.
3. Determine the maximum number of nested DO or FOR loops allowed.

Other challenges include writing a "self-duplicating" program which is not simply composed of verbatim PRINT statements yet prints a duplicate of itself." If you are ambitious, you might attempt to break the record for carrying out Pi to the most decimal places (500,000).

STORY WRITER

Using the combination of a random number generator, a list of words, and simple rules for English grammar, a microcomputer can compose original stories ad infinitum; the results are often amusing. Story writing suggestions:

1. Use of a standard story line in which blanks are left to be filled in with inputted words. The inputted words could consist of personalized information or arbitrary nouns, adjectives, and adverbs (e.g. as are used with Mad Libs"). For example, a story could begin:

Space, the (adjective) frontier.
These are the voyages of the starship (noun),
Its five-year mission:
To seek out new (noun) and new (noun)...

The operator is requested to provide one adjective and three nouns to fill-in the four blanks above. On resultant story:

Space, the nauseating frontier.
These are the voyages of the starship lemon
Its five-year mission:
To seek out new games and new computers...

Also included in this category are "Me Books" for young children. The computer fills the blanks in a story with a child's name, address, and other personalized information. The resultant personalized story often increases a child's interest in reading.

2. A more difficult approach to story writing involves the random selection of words or phrases to compose a series

of sentences which follow standard rules of grammer. A program written in 1960 (before high-level language was in widespread use) called SAGA was designed to produce short scripts for movie westerns. A sample of the output:

Sheriff:

> The Sheriff is at the window
> Sheriff sees robber
> Robber sees Sheriff
> go to door
> wait
> open door
> Sheriff sees robber
> go through door
> robber sees Sheriff
> go to window

Robber:

> take gun from holster with right hand
> aim
> fire
> Sheriff nicked

Sheriff:

> take gun from holster with right hand
> aim
> fire
> robber hit
> blow out barrel
> put gun down at door
> go to table
> pick up glass with right hand...

Writing a program to accomplish the above is more complex than would seem on first impression; the program was considered quite an achievement in 1960. Random numbers were used to determine the sequence of events; the events were selected from a wide range of pre-programmed possibilities. But, the program had to guard against a character firing a gun without first withdrawing it from his holster and similar situations. Also, a routine was necessary to compose "sentences" using the rules of grammar (e.g. "gun takes robber from holster with right hand" would not be allowed, but "robber takes gun from holster with right hand" would be allowed). The use of pre-programmed phrases to select from instead of individual words would simplify this task considerably. In like manner, a science fiction spoof or soap opera dialogue could be written. A professional software house sells a program to produce random, technical double-talk to "fill out business reports that are too short." A sample line produced by the program: "The product configuration requires considerable analysis and trade-off studies to arrive at the total system rationale."

MAGIC

Magic tricks performed by your computer would make an interesting demonstration for your guests. Suggestions:

Micro Mentalist—The computer becomes a mind reader in this trick. The performer, who is the computer operator, is given an item for the audience. The performer inputs a question such as, "What is the item given to me by the audience?" After a brief delay, the computer outputs the name of the item.

The trick is based on a code programmed into the computer, with which the performer inconspicuously indicates to the computer which of approximately twenty items he has been given. The code is contained within the inputted sentence; different sentences stand for different objects (e.g. "What do I have now?" could indicate a watch, and "What am I holding?" could indicate a match folder, etc.). The computer merely matches the inputted question to the item list stored in its memory.

Age Determination—The performer hands a member of the audience a pocket calculator and tells him to enter his age and then subtract his favorite one-digit number. Next, the guest multiplies this result by nine and adds his age to the product. The final result is called out and is inputted to the computer. The determination of the guest's age is accomplished by adding the first two digits in the result to the last (e.g. if the result was 176, add $17 + 6 = 23$, the guest's age).

The Break in the Chain—This trick is performed with a complete set of dominoes (usually 28 pieces). Beforehand, the performer removes one of the dominoes (it may not be a double) and inputs the two numbers on the domino to be stored in the computer. The guests are given the remaining set and are asked to complete a single domino chain as in regular play. Once completed, the numbers on the two ends of the chain are noted and the performer inputs a question such as, "What are the two numbers?" to which the computer replys correctly with the two previously stored numbers. The trick is automatic and will work with any domino chosen, excluding doubles.

COMPUTER LEARNING GAMES

Programs may be written such that a computer can learn from its mistakes. A checkerplaying program has been written which stores the results of all previous moves. Although the time necessary to decide on a move increases as the game progresses, the moves made are much better on the average. Suggestions:

1. NIM is a popular computer game in which players may take 1, 2, or 3 items from a pile of twenty each turn. The object is to force your opponent to take the last item. Although this game is completely solveable, a learning program could also be written as a demonstration of computer "learning."

2. A BASIC game called "Animal" has been written in which the computer plays the game of twenty questions with a human. The computer asks such questions as, "Does it swim?" to try to determine what animal the human is thinking of. If that animal is not in the computer's file, the human is requested to provide information such that a new file on that animal may be created. Thus, the computer "learns". Of course, it may be interesting to use a subject other than animals (e.g. places instead of animals, for young people to learn geography).

COMPUTER AS BOARD DISPLAY
DEVICE, BOOKKEEPER, AND GAME ADVISOR

Certain games designed such that the computer cannot be programmed to be a formidable opponent may utilize the computer in other ways. Suggestions:

1. Board display and bookkeeping for complex board games such as Risk™, Stratego™, Go, Metagames, and Avalon-Hill games can be accomplished (with high-density graphics). Other than displaying the board, the computer could:

A. Generate random numbers to replace spinners, dice, cards.

B. Record each move for later review

C. Compute game status at the end of each turn

D. Compute energy, arsenal, moves, positions, money, statistics for each player.

2. Game advising and bookkeeping for such games as checkers and chess. The computer could store each move, advise against potential checks, skewers, forks, discoveries, and print a listing of the game move by move at the finish. Advising for gambling games such as blackjack could take the form of an odds table for the high cards remaining in the deck, computation of whether to stay or hit, and the safest amount to bet.

DRAWING AND KALEIDOSCOPE PROGRAMS

Programs to create patterns/pictures on a video screen are interesting to computer hobbyists as well as non-hobbyists. Most picture drawing programs utilize the arrow (cursor positioning) keys on the video terminal keyboard to direct a cursor point which leaves a line behind. Several additions could be made to these programs, including animation routines, special standard designs which may be called to the screen, provisions for storing a design on cassette or floppy disk, light pens, and joystick interfaces. The "kaleidoscope effect" refers to a computer algorithm used to alter a design in kaleidoscope fashion in real time.

SIMULATION GAMES

Simulations of real-world situations need not be outputted as complex numerical listings; they may be transformed into games suited for people young and old. Some of the many possibilities:

Pool Table—A pool playing game (displayed with video graphics) could serve to teach the principles of elastic collisions and angular geometry.

Motorcycle Jump—A simulation in which a motorcycle must leap over a certain distance to land safely could illustrate projectile motion. The ramp angle and initial motorcycle velocity would be determined by the person playing the game.

Navigation—A simulation in which the participant must find his way to an island, using a radio direction finder in his sailboat, could teach principles of geometry as well as sailboat handling (e.g. tacking with the wind).

Detective—The participant would assume the role of a detective in this simulation. A valuable gem has been stolen from a museum and five persons are suspected. The use of deductive reasoning is the only way the detective can solve this crime.

Face-off—Be a hockey manager and run your own franchise in this simulation. Of course, scrambling for superstars, trading players, coping with broken contracts, and unexpected expenses are all part of the game. Planning is worthwhile.

World Race—Using a combination of race and rally tactics, players compete to be the first motor from England to New York and back again, navigating their way through Europe, Asia, the far east and South America. Strategy plays a large part as players have to motor through towns in every country in order to pick up points. Out of the way towns score higher than those along main routes. The winner is the player who reaches New York in the least time and with the most points. Rabies in Europe, tropical rains in South America, drought in Africa, etc. deter everyone's progress. The game serves to teach geography.

Wall Street—A stock market simulation, preferably multiplayer, would allow players to buy and sell stocks according to market conditions. A computer determines outcome and price for each stock each round and serves as bookkeeper.

World Conflict—A multiplayer simulation in which each player is head of a nationality. Players must decide whether they should go to war, form cartels, or make concessions/compromises. The computer could determine conflicting situations (e.g. oil embargoes, assassinations, nuclear threats, Communist expansion).

Decision—A simulation corporate management and big business could place each player as a top level executive. Each executive has the authority to produce the product of his choice and sell the product at the best market price. Throughout the game, prices fluctuate according to the law of supply and demand.

Fire—The object of this simulation is to subdue a raging forest fire with chemicals, backfires, and other fire-fighting methods. The success of the player depends upon quick decisions to control a geometrically increasing fire.

Auction—Principles of bidding at an auction could be simulated in a one-or-more player game involving the auction of art. One must be careful of forgeries.

Adventure—The object is survival against time in a desperate attempt to locate buried treasure on an island in this simulation. How does one obtain fresh water on an island surrounded by salt water?

Billionaire—This big-money simulation allows one to plunge into aerospace, oil, chemicals, cattle, and other world-wide industries and demonstrates the power of money. The computer could issue profit and loss statements and receive "sealed bids" from players in competition with others for properties.

Ethics—This simulation, involving the conflict between morals and greed, uses the computer as the judge of ethics. Conflicting situations are provided in which players must decide the outcome. If a pre-programmed decision does not match with a players, that player accumulates "morality deductions." The winner is the player with the most money and fewest deductions.

Careers—This simulation game places one in a new occupation to experience decision making, conflicts, opportunities, or finances from a different viewpoint.

Artillery—This is a simulation in which a fixed implacement must fire a projectile at such a velocity and angle that it will hit a target. The distance the projectile lands from the target could be displayed as the integer of the log to the base 2 of the absolute value of the distance; several other possibilities exist for teaching mathematical principles.

Simulations from Literature—Simulation programs built around the themes of *Lord of the Rings*, *The Aeneid*, *Tales of King Arthur*, or *The Voyages of Sinbad* would be interesting to attempt. One approach to such a simulation could present you with situations in which a decision must be made and action taken.

Grid Search Simulations—A search game of destroyer vs submarine, for example, could be incorporated with a 10x10 grid which must be selectively searched by the ship or submarine to find and attack each other. Similarily, a game played on the same grid could involve a spy searching for hidden documents with hidden enemy agents to watch for as well.

Computer—Based on a large scale computing system, the object of this simulation is to process two complete programs before your opponents. Players who make the best decisions can avoid the jeopardy of power failures, restricted use of I/O channels, bugs, and priority interrupts.

Fief—This game is based upon the medieval-feudal period of history in which players may find themselves playing roles as kings, knights, noblemen, and peasants.

Robotwar—The purpose of this simulation is to teach computer programming. Two opposing players are instructed to secretly design a program written in a custom language for a robot designed to annihilate any other robot. The programs would be entered and a video display of the combat field updated in real-time. The object could be to hit the opposing robot five times to win.

PROGRAM—ROBOT WAR II

Robotwar is a challenging game to play against your computer. You are represented in the game by an " $*$ ", while the computer controls anihilating robots represented by "$+$." An electrified, lethal fence defines the playing field.

The computers robots will destroy you if they come close. However, the robots will destroy themselves if they run into the fence. Your objective is to evade the robots until all have been destroyed by the fence. To move in a desired direction, use the chart below indicating the number to input.

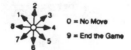

```
00160    REM-----ROBOTWAR II-------
00170    PRINT
00199    REM SET UP THE GAME
00200    DIM A(10, 20), E(21), F(21)
00210     G = 0:Z7 = 1
00220    FOR B = 1 TO 10
00230    FOR C = 1 TO 20
00240    A (B, C) = 0
00250    IF B < > 1 THEN 260
00251    A( B, C) = 1
00260    IF B < > 10 THEN 270
00261    A(B, C) = 1
00270    IF C < > 1 THEN 280
```

```
00271   A(B, C) = 1
00280   IF C < > 20 THEN 290
00281   A(B,C) = 1
00290   NEXT C
00300   NEXT B
00310   FOR D = 1 TO 21
00320    B = INT (RND (Ø) *8) + 2
00330    C= INT (RND (Ø) *18) + 2
00340   IF A(B,C) < > 0 THEN 320
00350    A(B, C) = 1
00360   IF D> = 6 THEN 370
00361    A(B,C) = 2
00370   IF D < > 6 THEN 380
00371    A(B,C) = 3
00380    E(D) = B
00390    F(D) = C
00400   NEXT D
00499   REM PRINT PATTERN
00500   FOR B = 1 TO 10
00510   FOR C = 1 TO 20
00520   IF A(B,C) < > Ø THEN 530
00521   PRINT " ";
00530   IF A(B,C) < > 1 THEN 540
00531   PRINT "X";
00540   IF A(B,C) < > 2 THEN 550
00541   PRINT "+";
00550   IF A(B,C) < >3 THEN 560
00551   PRINT "*";
00560   NEXT C
00570   PRINT
00580   NEXT B
00599   REM MAKE MOVE
00600    B = E (6)
00610    C = F (6)
00620    A(B, C) = 0
00630   INPUT Y
00640   IF Y = 0 THEN 800
00650   ON Y GOTO 660, 660, 660, 690, 680, 680, 680, 690,
        1400
00660    B = B−1
00670   GOTO 690
00680    B = B + 1
```

```
00690    ON Y GOTO 700, 800, 720, 720, 720, 800, 700, 700
00700    C = C-1
00710    GOTO 800
00720    C = C + 1
00799    REM CALCULATE THE RESULTS
00800    IF A(B, C) = 1 THEN 1500
00810    IF A(B,C) = 2 THEN 1600
00820    A(B,C) = 3
00830    E(6) = B
00840    F(6) = C
00850    FOR D = 1 TO 5
00860    IF A (E(D), F(D)) < > 2 THEN 960
00870    A(E(D), F(D)) = 0
00880    IF E (D) > = B THEN 890
00881    E(D) = E(D) + 1
00890    IF E(D) < = B THEN 900
00891    E (D) = E(D) - 1
00900    IF F(D) > = C THEN 910
00901    F(D) = F(D) + 1
00910    IF F(D) < = C THEN 920
00911    F(D) = F(D) - 1
00920    IF A(E(D), F(D)) = 3 THEN 1600
00930    IF A(E(D), F(D)) = 0 THEN 940
00931    G = G + 1
00940    IF A(E(D), F(D)) < > 0 THEN 950
00941    A(E(D), F(D)) = 2
00950    IF G = 5 THEN 1700
00960    NEXT D
00970    PRINT "MAP";
00980    INPUT Y$
00990    IF Y$ = "Y" THEN 500
00995    GOTO 600
01025    Z7 = Z7 + 1
01400    PRINT "SORRY TO SEE YOU QUIT"
01401    Z9 = Z9 + 1
01410    GOTO 1710
01500    PRINT" YOU TOUCHED THE FENCE"
01501    Z9 = Z9 + 1
01510    GOTO 1710
01600    PRINT "YOU HAVE BEEN DESTROYED BY A
         LUCKY COMPUTER"
01601    Z9 = Z9 + 1
01610    GOTO 1710
```

```
01700    PRINT" ** YOU DESTROYED THE ENEMY **"
01701    Z8 = Z8 + 1
01710    PRINT "DO YOU WANT TO PLAY AGAIN (TYPE
         Y OR N)";
01720    INPUT Y$
01730    IF Y$ = "Y" THEN 210
01731    PRINT "COMPUTER WON:"; Z9; " ", "THE
         HUMAN WON:";Z8
01732    PRINT "COMPUTER'S AVERAGE:";Z9/Z7;
         "THE HUMAN'S AVERAGE:";Z8/Z7
01733    PRINT
01740    PRINT" HOPE YOU DON'T FEEL FENCED IN"
01750    PRINT "TRY AGAIN SOMETIME."
01760    END
```

VIDEO GAMES

A personal computer with a memory-mapped video display and preferably dense graphics could emulate the popular video games. Although programs to duplicate such games as TV tennis do not execute as fast (and don't provide the same game controllers) when written in BASIC, assembly language versions do. Suggestions:

Maxwells Demon—Six floating molecules are trapped in one chamber of a two-chamber box. A gate connects the two compartments. The molecules are constantly bombarding each other and bouncing off walls; the object is to open and close the gate at the right time such that all molecules will be trapped in the other compartment.

Hockey/Tennis Type Games—Just as their video game counterpart, these computer games could be controlled with joysticks, simple potentiometers, or keyboard switches.

Tanks—A projectile-shooting battle between two tanks; the computer could act as the opponent. Similarily, a battle could be designed for jet fighters, biplanes, or ships instead of tanks.

Pinball—A moving set of paddles could replay a "ball" to hit targets and score points. A similar game could be designed around the Breakout ™ game seen at arcades.

Lunar Lander—The lunar lander program could be made more complex by requiring that one take-off from the moon, navigate over an obstacle of random size, and land again accurately.

Football, Baseball, Basketball—A graphic display of players, ball positions, and playing field could be used to display the action in these sports. Possibly, animation routines could be employed.

Racetrack—The object of this game is to finish the race in the least time. Hazards include: attaining too much speed to slow down before a curve, oil slicks, other cars. Hazards cause one to lose time.

Skydiver—The player in this game must control chute opening and jump time for a parachutist to land at a precise point. A wind of randomly selected direction and velocity presents a challenge to overcome.

Robot Bowl—The player controls a bowling robot in this game to try to knock down as many pins as possible. Release time, angle of approach, weight of ball, etc. are player selected.

Shooting Gallery—Several moving targets of different point values, and a directional "gun" could comprise a video version of the popular shooting gallery.

Golf—A golf game with a set of graphical holes (or design-your-own-hole provisions) would be interesting. Players choose the clubs they will use for each shot and the angle the ball will be hit. Hazards include sand traps, water, "dog-legs", and strong winds.

PROGRAM—PERSONALITY TEST

This program ought to be interesting to guests. A series of verses from literature is printed and one is asked to provide his interpretation. Although this program is based upon psychological research, don't take it too seriously. However, the day of the computer psychiatrist is near; computers have already been used to question patients and provide an overall psychological analysis.

```
10   REM  PERSONALITY  TEST—BASED  ON
     PSYCHOLOGICAL RESEARCH
20   PRINT "THE FOLLOWING PERSONALITY TEST IS
     NOT COMPREHENSIVE, BUT HAS"
30   PRINT "BEEN USED TO DETERMINE GENERAL
     CHARACTERISTICS."
40   PRINT
50   PRINT "INSTRUCTIONS: THREE VERSES WILL
     BE PRINTED. FOLLOWING"
```

```
60    PRINT "EACH VERSE WILL BE A LIST OF IN-
      TERPRETATIONS. INPUT"
70    PRINT "THE CORRESPONDING NUMBER FOR
      THE INTERPRETATION YOU"
80    INPUT "BELIEVE IS THE BEST. TYPE 'ENTER'
      WHEN READY."; A
90    CLS' CLEAR THE SCREEN
100   PRINT" A BOOK OF VERSES UNDERNEATH THE
      BOUGH,"
110   PRINT" A JUG OF WINE, A LOAF OF BREAD-AND
      THOU"
120   PRINT"  BESIDE ME SINGING IN THE
      WILDERNESS-"
130   PRINT " OH, WILDERNESS WERE PARADISE
      ENOW!"
140   PRINT
150   PRINT"1) HAPPINESS OR CONTENTMENT CAN
      BE FOUND WITHOUT MUCH PLANNING"
160   PRINT"2) HAPPINESS IS IN ACCEPTING & EN-
      JOYING SIMPLE THINGS"
170   PRINT"3) HAPPINESS IS ALWAYS PRESENT- IF
      WE TAKE THE TIME TO LOOK"
180   PRINT"4) IF YOU SET YOUR MIND TO IT, HAPPI-
      NESS CAN BE FOUND"
190   PRINT"5) HAPPINESS IS WHERE WE FIND IT"
200   INPUT X1
210   CLS 'CLEAR SCREEN
220   PRINT" THERE IS A TIDE IN THE AFFAIRS OF
      MEN,"
230   PRINT" WHICH, TAKEN AT THE FLOOD, LEADS
      ON TO FORTUNE;"
250   PRINT " OMITTED, ALL THE VOYAGE OF THEIR
      LIFE"
260   PRINT" IS BOUND IN SHALLOWS AND IN MIS-
      ERIES."
270    PRINT" "
280   PRINT "1) MAKE THE MOST OF YOUR CHANCE
      WHEN YOU GET IT"
290   PRINT"2) IN MANY CASES OF FAILURE, PEOPLE
      WERE AFFECTED BY CIRCUM-"
300   PRINT" STANCES OVER WHICH THEY HAD LIT-
      TLE CONTROL."
```

```
310    PRINT"3) ONE WHO PLANS WELL WILL SUR-
       VIVE WELL UNDER THE LAWS OF NATURE"
320    PRINT"4) LIFE IS SUCH THAT IT PAYS TO
       WATCH WHAT YOU DO BEFORE YOU"
330    PRINT "RUN INTO TROUBLE."
340    PRINT"5) ONE SHOULD BE ON THE WATCH FOR
       OPPORTUNITY TO KNOCK, OTHER-"
350    PRINT " WISE HE WILL MISS OUT ON GOING
       PLACES."
360    INPUT X2
370    CLS 'CLEAR SCREEN
380    PRINT" NO MAN IS AN ISLAND, ENTIRE OF IT-
       SELF."
390    PRINT
400    PRINT"1) EVERYONE SHOULD CONSIDER THE
       NEEDS & WANTS OF OTHERS"
410    PRINT"2) USE OTHER'S INFLUENCE TO HELP
       YOU PLAN YOUR LIFE."
420    PRINT"3) ONE WHO ACTS WITHOUT REGARD FOR
       OTHERS DOES NOT REALIZE"
430    PRINT" THAT HE IS A SOCIAL ANIMAL."
440    PRINT"4) TO GET WHERE YOU WANT TO BE IN
       LIFE YOU MUST REALIZE THE"
450    PRINT"NEED FOR HELP FROM OTHERS."
460    PRINT"5) ALTHOUGH I AM THE CAPTAIN OF MY
       SOUL, I MUST MAKE MY WAY"
470    PRINT"IN LIFE AMONG MANY OTHER CAP-
       TAINS."
480    INPUT X3
490    CLS 'CLEAR SCREEN
500    PRINT"THE TEST INDICATES THAT YOU POS-
       SESS THESE TRAITS:"
510    IF X1 = 1 PRINT "IRRESPONSIBLE" ELSE IF X1 =
       2 PRINT "CONVENTIONAL AND MORALISTIC
       "ELSE IF X1 = 3 PRINT "MORALISTIC" ELSE IF
       X1 = 4 PRINT "FORMAL" ELSE PRINT "PRAC-
       TICAL"
520    IF X2 = 1 PRINT "PRACTICAL AND LOGICAL
       "ELSE IF X2 = 2 PRINT "MORALISTIC" ELSE IF
       X2 = 3 PRINT "CONVENTIONAL" ELSE IF X2 = 4
       PRINT "HUMOROUS AND SENSIBLE" ELSE
       PRINT "EGO-CENTRIC"
```

530   IF X3 = 1 PRINT "CONVENTIONAL" ELSE IF X3 = 2 PRINT "PRACTICAL AND LOGICAL" ELSE IF X3 = 3 PRINT "OBJECTIVE" ELSE IF X3 = 4 PRINT "EGO-CENTRIC" ELSE PRINT "MORALISTIC"
540   PRINT "IF THE SAME TRAIT IS LISTED TWICE THEN IT IS ALL THE"
550   PRINT "MORE INDICATIVE OF YOU."
560   END

COMPUTERS AND CHESS

Perhaps, the most popular computer recreation is the game of chess. It has been said that once a computer can defeat any chess grandmaster, that task of emulating human thought will be achieved. Even the fastest computers of today, which analyze up to 500,000 possibilities before making each move, can be defeated by a chess grandmaster. Perhaps this fact is what makes computer chess so intriguing. A large scale computer chess program is described here to assist those willing to undertake the task of writing a chess program. Chess programs should preferably be written in assembly language (which is usually 10-20 times faster than a BASIC interpreter) as chess programs written in BASIC often require an intolerable five minutes or more per move.

The program described here is named OSTRICH, and competed in the First World Computer Chess Tournament. The OSTRICH program is composed of three modules: BOOK—which provides standard book opening moves for up to the first five moves, CHESS—the main program used during most of the game, and END GAME—which takes over in a rook/king or queen and king/king end games. CHESS, the main module, is comprised of approximately 9000 instructions which are divided into five subprograms:

1. A subroutine for control of input/output and for control of the size of the search tree. The search tree refers to the branching search for all move possibilities the computer considers for each move. The size of the tree indicates the depth or number of moves ahead that will be considered for each move.

2. A subprogram to generate all move possibilities or search the tree.

3. A subprogram to arrange each possible move on a hierarchy scale according to its plausibility (each move is

given a *plausibility score*). Following this initial ordering, another set of routines is called upon to improve the ordering.

4. A subprogram to calculate a *terminal score*, or an evaluation of the chess board at each terminal or branching point in the tree.

5. A subroutine to update all arrays, lists, and pointers used by the remainder of the program.

Reference arrays used by CHESS:

1. *List of the locations of each chess piece.* An 8 × 8 array holds an identification number for each of the pieces on the board in a corresponding memory location. The white pieces are identified as follows: king =6, queen =5, rook =4, bishop =3, knight =2, pawn =1 and the black pieces are identified as the negative of the corresponding white piece number. The board position array is updated after each move.

2. *Piece location array.* Two separate arrays are generated at the beginning of each tree search. One list contains the names and corresponding locations of the white pieces, the other is for the black pieces in like manner.

3. *Possible moves list.* A list of possible moves for ply 1 (ply refers to the depth searched), ply 2, ply 3, corresponding to each initial move is generated. Additionally, memory is reserved to indicate which moves will result in a capture.

4. *Control piece array.* This array stores the squares that each piece "controls" as well as the pieces that control a particular square. Thus, it is possible to determine the power of each piece along with what pieces are in control of a specific square in question.

5. *Change array.* All changes made at a node in the search tree are stored in this array when advancing to a new node. The purpose of the list is to expedite the restoring of positions.

6. *Pinned pieces.* A listing of all pinned pieces is maintained in this array.

7. *En prise pieces.* A separate list of en prise pieces at each search node is maintained.

8. *Alpha and Beta cut-offs.* Two lists, one of the last eight moves resulting in alpha refutations, the other beta refutations, are maintained.

9. *Ply 3 plausibility list.* A list of the best ply 3 move to each possible ply 2 opponent's move, for each ply 1 move investigated, is maintained.

10. *Principal variations*. Each principal variation originating in the tree search is stored in this list.

11. *Position records*. This listing of all moves since a recent capture or pawn move is used to determine whether a draw should be made due to repetition.

• Tree Size

Tree size is automatically controlled by the program such that decisions will not exceed a time limit. Conditions which warrant an extension of the tree size include potential checks, captures, Pawn promotions, Pawns on the seventh rank, and the presence of en prise pieces.

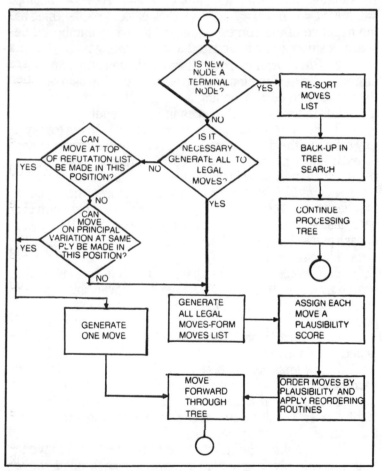

Fig. 7-1. Flowchart for node processing

The flow chart in Fig. 7-1 illustrates the processing that occurs each time a new node is reached. The node is determined to be either "terminal" or "non-terminal". A terminal node may be declared by a subroutine known as the gamma algorithm, by the fact that the node is past the tree length, or by the fact that the node is past the minimum ply, but the board has no special features. All other nodes are classified as non-terminal. Nonterminal node processing.

Non Terminal Node Processing

The One Move Generator subroutine is the first processing done at a non-terminal node. This subroutine determines whether one move is sufficient, or all legal moves must be generated; if the first move could cause a refutation, the program continues, and otherwise, the Move Generator determines all legal moves. Following move generation, a plausibility score is assigned to each move and moves are sorted according to decreasing plausibility. The list is then resorted by special routines.

• Plausibility Scoring

All possible moves are assigned a plausibility score which is based on the following parameters:

1. Captures—The score given to each capture is 2400 points plus the value of this computed formula:

additional points=(point value of captures—piece point value of capturing piece)/10

where the points for the chess pieces are: Pawn = 600, Knight = Bishop = 1800, Rook = 3000, Queen = 5400, King = 300,000.

2. Castling—The point value for castling is 10,000 points.

3. Randomizer—This routine adds a random number of points to each move such that no piece will have excessive moves on the moves list. Up to ten points may be added.

4. Advance—Any move which retreats a Queen, Knight,. or Bishop receives a penalty of twenty points.

5. Pawn Attack—Any move which places a Queen, Rook, Bishop, or Knight such that it can be captured on the next move by a pawn receives a penalty of 200 points.

6. Pawn scoring—A Pawn move past the fourth rank is awarded 300 additional points, and a move past the sixth rank is given 1000 additional points. A move of the King's or

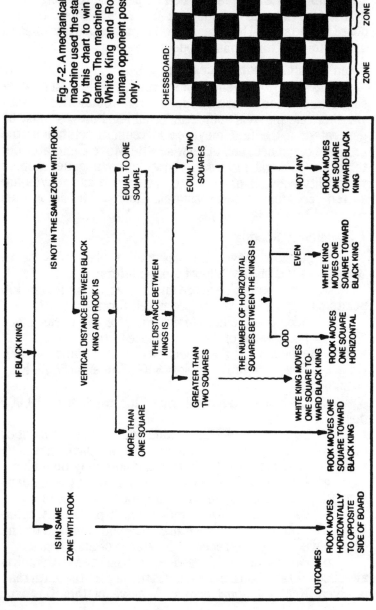

Fig. 7-2. A mechanical chess playing machine used the stategy indicated by this chart to win a chess end game. The machine possessed a White King and Rook while the human opponent possessed a King only.

CHESSBOARD:

ZONE · ZONE · ZONE

IF BLACK KING

IS IN SAME ZONE WITH ROOK

IS NOT IN THE SAME ZONE WITH ROOK

VERTICAL DISTANCE BETWEEN BLACK KING AND ROOK IS

EQUAL TO ONE SQUARE

MORE THAN ONE SQUARE

THE DISTANCE BETWEEN KINGS IS

EQUAL TO TWO SQUARES

GREATER THAN TWO SQUARES

THE NUMBER OF HORIZONTAL SQUARES BETWEEN THE KINGS IS

NOT ANY

EVEN

ODD

OUTCOMES:

ROOK MOVES HORIZONTALLY TO OPPOSITE SIDE OF BOARD

ROOK MOVES ONE SQUARE TOWARD BLACK KING

WHITE KING MOVES ONE SQUARE TOWARD BLACK KING

WHITE KING MOVES ONE SQUARE TOWARD BLACK KING

ROOK MOVES ONE SQUARE HORIZONTAL

ROOK MOVES ONE SQUARE TOWARD BLACK KING

242

Queen's Pawn is awarded 21 additional points, and a move of the Bishop's Pawn is given 15 additional points.

7. Rook scoring—Moves for Rooks past the sixth rank are given 200 additional points. Moves for Rooks on the first rank to another square on the first rank which has no Pawns on the second and third ranks is awarded 40 points.

8. Refutation moves—Any move on either the alpha or beta refutation list is given an additional 300 points.

9. En prise moves—Any move which defends an en prise piece is given a bonus of 300 points. Moves of en prise pieces are awarded 300 points if the move is to a safe square and are penalized 20 points if the move is to an unsafe square.

10. Attack moves—If a move will place a piece such that it can attack more pieces than before the move, additional points are awarded according to the pieces which may be attacked (and other factors).

• Reordering the Moves List

Following the plausibility score analysis, special reordering routines are used to generate a final listing of moves in the order of their advantages. The three reordering routines used by OSTRICH are as follows:

1. Capture reordering—The plausibility analysis arbitrarily places capturing moves at the top of the moves list, however, a capture is usually not the best move in most positions. This routine usually places captures by non-Pawns on the opponent's side behind the non-capturing moves next on the list. No capture is moved to a point on the list such that it will not be considered in the final analysis, however. Captures of pieces moved at the last ply are placed at the top of other captures, except at ply one where this is done only under the condition that the following move will be a recapture.

2. Special reordering—A move called "Second Best" is generated after each move; it is the second last move that the search evaluated as it search the first ply move list. This move is matched with the same move on the moves list, if it is there. Any such move is placed on the top of the moves list, if it is legal.

3. Midsearch reordering—A midsearch reorder is done to the ply one moves list when the third move at ply one is to be considered. A match is sought between the moves

remaining on the ply one list, and the move at the third ply is retrieved from the present principal continuation. If a match is found, that move is placed at the top of the moves list; if not, matches are sought between this move and the most recent refutations.

• Processing at Terminal Nodes

A scoring routine is applied to each terminal node, once it has been determined to be a terminal node. The seventeen scoring functions are as follows:

1. Board material—Credit is awarded for the number and types of pieces which will remain on the board. The values given to each piece are: Pawn=1, Bishop=Knight=3, Rook=5, Queen=9, King=300.

2. Material ratio—The material ratio routine scores favorably for trading pieces when ahead in material and penalizes for trading when behind: 100 points are awarded to the side ahead.

3. Castling—A King side castling is given 600 points while a Queen side castling is given 300 points.

4. Board control—Points are awarded in the following manner for control (ability to capture) of certain squares on the board: 12 points for each of the four center squares, 7 points for control of any square in the ring surrounding the four center squares, and 12 points for squares surrounding the opponents King.

5. Tempo—200 points are deducted from the score of either side for wasting time in one of the following ways: Moving one piece twice in the opening, moving King or Rook prior to castling, moving a piece to its last previous position, moving a piece in more than one move to a position it could move in one.

6. Opening Queen moves—Moves of the Queen before the eighth move are penalized 400 points.

7. Blocking unadvanced pawns—470 points are deducted for moves which block unadvanced King or Queen Pawns.

8. Minor piece development—A penalty of 140 points is given for each unmoved center Pawn, Bishop, or Knight.

9. Center Pawns—An additional 50 points are awarded for all Pawns on K4 or Q4; 70 points are awarded for a Pawn on K5 or Q5.

10. Pawn structure—Isolated Pawns are penalized 400 points; doubled Pawns are penalized 20 points; advancing Pawns are awarded 10 points.

11. Passed Pawns—Passed pawns on the seventh rank are worth 700 points, on the sixth 400 points, on the fifth 340 points, on the fourth 40 points, on the third 100 points, on the second 40 points. If Pawns and Kings are the only pieces left, the point values are doubled.

12. King defense—If there are more non-Pawn opposing pieces in the King's sector than defending pieces, a penalty of 75 points is assessed.

13. Doubled Rooks, Bishop Pairs—If the two rooks are on the same column, 150 points are awarded; if one side has two Bishops and the other side does not, 150 points are awarded.

14. Trades—If the piece that moved at the last ply is under attack, the score is adjusted as follows: The score is reduced by the value of the attacked piece if the number of defenders is zero. Otherwise, a sequence of trades is performed on the square and the score changed based on the pieces exchanged.

15. King vs Pawns—If, after move thirty, the King is within one square of an opposing Pawn, 200 points are awarded.

16. Knight position—Any Knight on column 0 or 7 is penalized 40 points.

17. Attacks—Ply one moves which place an opposing piece en prise are awarded 40 points.

• The Gamma Algorithm

The gamma algorithm was mentioned earlier in determining whether a node is terminal or non-terminal. Although the algorithm is complicated, the logic behind its decision-making is that "if the situation is becoming progressively worse and better moves are available, classify this node as terminal."

• Possibilities for Future Chess-Related Programs

1. Chess analysis program—A chess analysis program could compute numerical values for certain types of moves, strategies, etc. Games between chess grandmasters could be input for the analyses.

2. Chess end game program—Of course, computer analysis becomes much simpler at the end of a chess game, when only a few pieces are left. The beginning programmer may wish to write a chess program to play end games only, between a few selected pieces. The program would provide any initial set-up of pieces before the game.

3. Chess variations—Perhaps computers would be able to compete better in playing one of these chess variations:

- Marseille game—Each player moves two pieces in succession.
- Legal game—White uses eight extra pawns instead of a Queen.
- Marked Pawn—The first player to make a capture wins this chess variation.
- Chancellor—The Knight and Rook have the combined move capabilities as both individually.
- Grasshopper—Pieces may leap over others; captures are as usual.

4. Advisor—A computer updated with each move could advise you of situations you might miss. It would be interesting to compare the move you intend to make with the computer's suggestion.

ADDITIONAL GAME PROGRAMS

CARD SHUFFLER

```
00100   REM CARD SHUFFLING ROUTINE
00110   DIM M(52)
00120   N=52: FOR I=1 TO N
00130   M(I)=I: NEXT I
00140   FOR I=1 TO N-1
00150   R=(N + 1 - I)*RND (0)
00160   R=INT(R)+I
00170   T=M(R)
00180   M(R)=M(I)
00190   M(I)=T
00200   NEXT I
```

TENNIS

```
00010   DIM A (500)
00020   PRINT "     TO INITIALIZE OUR RANDOM
        NUMBERS PLEASE TYPE A"
00030   PRINT "POSITIVE INTEGER FROM 1 TO 150.";
00040   INPUT D
00050   IF D < 1 THEN 00080
00060   IF D > 150 THEN 00080
00070   GO TO 00100
00080   PRINT "THAT WAS NOT BETWEEN 1 AND 150,
        LETS TRY AGAIN"
00090   GO TO 00040

00100   PRINT "THANK YOU"
00110   PRINT
00120   FOR I = 1 TO 500
00130   A (I) = RND (0.0)
00140   NEXT I
00150   Y = 0
00160   I = D
00170   PRINT "DO YOU NEED INSTRUCTIONS ON
        THIS TENNIS GAME?"
00180   INPUT C$
00190   PRINT

00200   IF C$ = "NO" THEN 00360
00210   PRINT "THIS COMPUTER-TENNIS GAME IS
        DESIGNED SO THAT YOU MAY"

00220   PRINT "PLAY AGAINST THE COMPUTER OR
        AGAINST ANOTHER HUMAN."
00230   PRINT
00240   PRINT "IN THIS GAME, YOU WILL DECIDE
        YOUR STRATEGY BY SELECTING"
00250   PRINT "WHICH TYPE OF SHOT TO HIT;"
00260   PRINT " 1) A REGULAR BASE LINESHOT"
00270   PRINT "2) A HALF VOLLEY WHEN RUSHING
        NET"
00280   PRINT "3) A NET VOLLEY WHEN AT THE
        NET"
00290   PRINT "    4)    A LOB SHOT"
```

```
00300   PRINT "NOTE; TO USE A #3 SHOT, YOUR
        LAST SHOT MUST HAVE BEEN"
00310   PRINT "MADE EITHER AT THE NET OR AS
        RUSHING THE NET (IE. #2 OR #3)"
00320   PRINT"TO RETURN A LOB, ONLY A #1 OR #4
        SHOT MAY BE USED
00330   PRINT
00340   PRINT "CHOOSE A SERVER AND A RECEIVER
        FOR THE FIRST GAME."
00350   PRINT
00360   PRINT "WOULD YOU LIKE TO PLAY AGAINST
        THE COMPUTER";
00370   INPUT B$
00380   IF B$ = "NO" THEN 00440
00390   PRINT "WOULD YOU LIKE TO SERVE FIRST?
        TYPE 2 IF YES, 1 IF NO."

00400   INPUT Y
00410   PRINT
00420   GO TO 02630
00430   PRINT
00440   PRINT "GOOD LUCK ON COURT #2"
00450   PRINT
00460   T = N = M = S = 0
00470   PRINT
00480   PRINT " SCORE:"; N  ; T
00490   PRINT "HERE COMES THE SERVE"

00500   E = 5
00510   PRINT "RECEIVER MUST RETURN SERVICE
        WITH #1 SHOT"
00520   IF Y = 1 THEN 02260
00530   PRINT " RECEIVER'S TYPE SHOT";
00540   INPUT R
00550   IF R = 1 THEN 00630
00560   PRINT "RECEIVER MUST RETURN SERVICE
        WITH A #1 SHOT. -RETRY"
00570   GO TO 00540
00580   PRINT "RECEIVER  MAKES  A  NICE
        RECOVERY-RETURNS SHOT"
00590   E = R
```

```
00600   IF Y = 1 THEN 02260
00610   PRINT "RECEIVER'S TYPE SHOT";
00620   INPUT R
00630   I = I + 1
00640   IF I > 494 THEN 02150
00650   IF R = 1 THEN 00720
00660   IF R = 2 THEN 00760
00670   IF R = 4 THEN 00830
00680   IF E = 2 THEN 00800
00690   IF E = 3 THEN 00800

00700   PRINT "A #3 SHOT MAY NOT FOLLOW YOUR
        LAST #"; E; "SHOT"
00710   GO TO 00610
00720   IF P = 1 THEN 00920
00730   IF P = 2 THEN 00980
00740   IF P = 3 THEN 00960
00750   GO TO 00940
00760   IF P = 2 THEN 00960
00770   IF P = 4 THEN 01970
00780   IF P = 3 THEN 00960
00790   GO TO 00920

00800   IF P = 1 THEN 01000
00810   IF P = 4 THEN 01970
00820   GO TO 00900
00830   IF P = 2 THEN 00980
00840   IF P = 3 THEN 00860
00850   GO TO 00880
00860   IF A (I) < .5 THEN 01500
00870   GO TO 02110
00880   IF A (I) < .15 THEN 01500
00890   GO TO 01020

00900   IF A (I) < .55 THEN 01500
00910   GO TO 02110
00920   IF A (I) < .25 THEN 02130
00930   GO TO 01020
00940   IF A (I) < .3 THEN 01500
00950   GO TO 01020
00960   IF A (I) < .35 THEN 02030
00970   GO TO 01020
```

```
00980   IF A (I) < .4 THEN 01950
00990   GO TO 01020

01000   IF A (I) < .6 THEN 01500
01010   GO TO 02110
01020   PRINT "SERVER WAS READY FOR THAT - RE-
        TURNS SHOT"
01030   F = P

01040   IF Y = 2 THEN 02290
01050   PRINT "SERVER'S TYPE SHOT";
01060   INPUT P
01070   I = I + 1
01080   IF P = 1 THEN 01150
01090   IF P = 2 THEN 01190
01100   IF P = 4 THEN 01260
01110   IF F = 2 THEN 01230
01120   IF F = 3 THEN 01230
01130   PRINT "A #3 SHOT MAY NOT FOLLOW YOUR
        LAST #"; F; "SHOT"
01140   GO TO 01050
01150   IF R = 1 THEN 01350
01160   IF R = 2 THEN 01410
01170   IF R = 3 THEN 01390
01180   GO TO 01370
01190   IF R = 2 THEN 01390

01200   IF R = 4 THEN 01990
01210   IF R = 3 THEN 01390
01220   GO TO 01350
01230   IF R = 1 THEN 01430
01240   IF R = 4 THEN 01990
01250   GO TO 01330
01260   IF R = 2 THEN 01410
01270   IF R = 3 THEN 01390
01280   GO TO 01310
01290   IF A (I) < .5 THEN 01580

01300   GO TO 00580
01310   IF A (I) < .15 THEN 01580
01320   GO TO 00580
01330   IF A (I) < .55 THEN 01580
01340   GO TO 00580
```

```
01350    IF A (I) < .25 THEN 02070
01360    GO TO 02090
01370    IF A (I) < .3 THEN 01580
01380    GO TO 00580
01390    IF A (I) < .35 THEN 02010

01400    GO TO 00580
01410    IF A (I) < .4 THEN 02050
01420    GO TO 00580
01430    IF A (I) < .6 THEN 01580
01440    GO TO 00580
01450    PRINT "SERVER HITS AN ACE"
01460    IF A (I) > .96 THEN 02170
01470    GO TO 01590
01480    PRINT "RECEIVER RETURNS SERVE INTO
         NET - POINT SERVER"
01490    GO TO 01590

01500    PRINT "RECEIVER HITS A PUT AWAY SHOT -
         POINT RECEIVER"
01510    S = S + 1
01520    IF S > 3 THEN 01660
01530    T = S*15
01540    IF T = 45 THEN 01560
01550    GO TO 00470
01560    T = 40
01570    GO TO 00470
01580    PRINT "SERVER HIT A SUPER SHOT - POINT
         SERVER"
01590    M = M + 1

01600    IF M > 3 THEN 01660
01610    N = M*15
01620    IF N = 45 THEN 01640
01630    GO TO 00470
01640    N = 40
01650    GO TO 00470
01660    IF M - S > 1 THEN 01710
01670    IF S - M > 1 THEN 01750
01680    IF S = M THEN 01790
01690    IF S - M = 1 THEN 01810

01700    GO TO 01830
01710    PRINT
```

```
01720   PRINT "     GAME - SERVER"
01730   IF Y = 2 THEN 02610
01740   GO TO 01900
01750   PRINT
01760   PRINT "BROKEN SERVICE GAME - RECEIV-
        ER"
01770   IF Y = 1 THEN 02610
01780   GO TO 01900
01790   PRINT "THE SCORE IS TIED ----DEUCE----"

01800   GO TO 00490
10810   PRINT "          ADVANTAGE -OUT -BREAK-
        POINT"
01820   GO TO 00490
01830   PRINT "          ADVANTAGE-IN"
01840   GO TO 00490
01850   PRINT    "SERVER DOUBLE FAULTS ---
        POINT RECEIVER"
01860   GO TO 01510
01870   PRINT "THIS     WEATHER IS LOUSY ISN'T
        IT"
01880   PRINT " THANK YOU     HOPE YOU HAD
        FUN"
01890   GO TO 02230

01900   PRINT
01910   PRINT "ARE YOU FINISHED";
01920   INPUT F$
01930   IF F$ = "YES" THEN 01880
01940   GO TO 02630
01950   PRINT "SERVER SLIPS ON HIS - POINT RE-
        CEIVER"
01960   GO TO 01510
01970   PRINT "TO RETURN A LOB A #1 OR #4 MUST
        BE USED. TRY AGAIN"
01980   GO TO 00590
01990   PRINT "TO RETURN A LOB A #1 OR #4 MUST
        BE USED. TRY AGAIN"
02000   GO TO 01030

02010   PRINT "RECEIVER RETURNS SHOT OUT-OF-
        BOUNDS - POINT SERVER"
02020   GO TO 01590
```

```
02030   PRINT "RECEIVER CATCHES SERVER TOO
        CLOSE - POINT-RECEIVER"
02040   GO TO 01510
02050   PRINT "RECEIVER TRIPS ON HIS SHOELACE
        -POINT SERVER"
02060   GO TO 01590
02070   PRINT "RECEIVER IS CAUGHT IN NO MANS
        LAND - POINT SERVER"
02080   GO TO 01590
02090   PRINT "RECEIVER WAS IN POSITION FOR
        THAT - RETURNS SHOT"
02100   GO TO 00590
02110   PRINT "SERVER'S QUICK REFLEXES SAVES
        RALLY - RETURNS SHOT"
02120   GO TO 01030
02130   PRINT "SERVER MISJUDGES RETURN, LETS
        BALL FALL IN - POINT-RECEIVER"
02140   GO TO 01510
02150    PRINT "IT IS BEGINNING TO RAIN, WE ARE
        GOING TO HAVE TO QUIT"
02160   GO TO 01870
02170   PRINT "DID YOU HEAR ABOUT THE TENNIS
        TOURNAMENT IN EUROPE,"
02180   PRINT "WHERE IN THE FIRST ROUND - ENG-
        LAND MET FRANCE - AND"
02190   PRINT "POLAND DREW THE BYE. IN THE
        SECOND ROUND"
02200   PRINT "ENGLAND MET THE BYE"
02210   PRINT "          .....TENNIS HUMOR....."
02220   GO TO 01590
02230   PRINT
02240   PRINT ""; I
02250   GO TO 02710
02260   U = P
02270   W = E
02280   GO TO 02310
02290   U = R
02300   W = F
02310   I = I + 1
02320   IF E = 5 THEN 02470
02330   IF U = 4 THEN 02470
02340   IF W = 2 THEN 02400
```

```
02350   IF W = 3 THEN 02400
02360   IF U = 3 THEN 02440
02370   IF A (I) < .6 THEN 02490
02380   IF A (I) < .95 THEN 02470
02390   GO TO 02530
02400   IF U = 3 THEN 02420
02410   IF A (I) < .2 THEN 02530
02420   IF A (I) < .75 THEN 02510
02430   GO TO 02470
02440   IF A (I) < .15 THEN 02470
02450    IF A (I) < .25 THEN 02490
02460   GO TO 02530
02470   L = 1
02480   GO TO 02540
02490   L = 2
02500   GO TO 02540
02510   L = 3
02520   GO TO 02540
02530   L = 4
02540   IF Y = 1 THEN 02580
02550   PRINT "THE SERVING COMPUTER'S TYPE
        SHOT IS A #"; L
02560   P = L
02570   GOTO 01070
02580   PRINT" THE RECEIVING COMPUTER'S TYPE
        SHOT IS A"; L
02590   R = L
02600   GO TO 00630
02610   PRINT
02620   GO TO 01900
02630   IF Y = 1 THEN 02680
02640   IF Y = 0 THEN 00450
02650   Y = 1
02660   PRINT "IT IS NOW YOUR SERVE - THE COM-
        PUTER WILL BE THE RECEIVER.
02670   GO TO 00450
02680   Y = 2
02690   PRINT "IT IS NOW THE COMPUTER'S TIME TO
        SERVE."
02700   GO TO 00450
02710   END
BASEBALL
0008   REM ------------------ BASEBALL --------------------
0010   PRINT
```

```
0012  REM
0014  REM
0016  REM
0018  REM
0020  PRINT "YOU ARE ABOUT TO PLAY BASEBALL"
0030  PRINT
0040  PRINT "DO YOU NEED PLAYING INSTRUC-
      TIONS (YES OR NO)" ;
0050  INPUT A$
0060  IF A1 > = "Y" THEN 70
0065  GO TO 590
0070  PRINT
0080  PRINT "WHEN A QUESTION IS AS ASKED IN
      THE FORM OF A LETTER"
0090  PRINT "FOLLOWED BY A ?, TYPE IN THE DE-
      SIRED NUMERICAL CODE."
0100  PRINT
0110  PRINT "AT BAT, YOU HAVE THE FOLLOWING
      COMBINATIONS OF OPTIONS:"
0120  PRINT
0130  PRINT "VARIABLE", "OPTION", "CODE"
0140  PRINT
0150  PRINT "A:", "NO SWING", 0
0160  PRINT " ", "BUNT", 1
0170  PRINT " ", "BASE HIT", 2
0180  PRINT " ", "FULL SWING", 3
0190  PRINT
0200  PRINT " B: ", "HIGH", 1
0210  PRINT " ", "WAIST HIGH", 2
0220  PRINT " ", "LOW", 3
0230  PRINT " ", "(IN THE STRIKE ZONE)"
0240  PRINT
0250  PRINT " C:", "RIGHT FIELD", 1
0260  PRINT " ", "CENTER FIELD", 2
0270  PRINT " ", "LEFT FIELD", 3
0280  PRINT
0290  PRINT
0300  PRINT "IN THE FIELD, THESE ARE YOUR OP-
      TIONS :"
0310  PRINT
0320  PRINT "VARIABLE", "OPTION", "CODE",
      "COMMENT"
0330  PRINT
```

```
0340   PRINT "FIELD POSITION:"
0350   PRINT " D:",, "DENSE INFIELD", 1, "BUNTS,
       POP FLIES"
0360   PRINT " ", "NORMAL", 2, "BASE HITS, MED.
       FLIES"
0370   PRINT " ", "DEEP", 3, "LONG BASE HITS &
       FLIES"
0380   PRINT
0390   PRINT "PITCH:"
0400   PRINT " E:", "BALL", 0, "OUTSIDE STRIKE
       ZONE"
0410   PRINT " ", "SLOW BALL", 1
0420   PRINT " ", "NORMAL", 2
0430   PRINT " ", "FAST BALL", 3, ") MORE CHANCE OF
       BEING"
0440   PRINT " ", "CURVE BALL", 4 ") OUTSIDE STRIKE
       ZONE,"
0450   PRINT " ", " ", " ", ") OR HITTING BATTER."
0460   PRINT
0470   PRINT " F:", "HIGH", 1
0480   PRINT " ", "WAIST HIGH", 2
0490   PRINT " ", "LOW", 39
0500   PRINT
0510   PRINT " G:", "OUTSIDE", 1
0520   PRINT " ", "CENTER", 2
0530   PRINT " ", "INSIDE", 3
0540   PRINT
0550   PRINT " ", "(F AND G MEAN IN THE STRIKE
       ZONE FOR STRIKES. IT"
0560   PRINT " ", "IS ASSUMED THAT THE PITCHERS
       HAVE FAIR CONTROL OVER"
0570   PRINT " ", "EACH OF THESE VARIABLES, EX-
       CEPT ON FAST BALLS"
0580   PRINT " ", "AND CURVES.)"
0590   PRINT
0600   LET I = 1
0610   PRINT "A COIN IS TOSSED, PICK HEADS (1) OR
       TAILS (0) ";
0620   INPUT Z
0630   IF Z = 0 THEN 0650
0640   LET Z = 1
0650   IF Z <> INT (.5 + RND (-1)) THEN 0720
0660   PRINT
```

```
0670   PRINT "YOU WIN-CHOSE AT BAT (0) OR IN THE
       FIELD (1)";
0680   INPUT Y
0690   PRINT
0700   IF Y < > 1 THEN 0780
0710   GO TO 0790
0720   PRINT
0730   PRINT "YOU LOSE-MY CHOICE- ";
0740   IF RND(∅)>.6 THEN 780
0750   LET Y = 1
0760   GOSUB 1140
0770   GO TO 0800
0780   LET Y = 2
0790   GOSUB 1140
0800   LET E3 = 0
0810   DIM R(5,5)
0820   FOR A = 1 TO 5
0830   FOR B = 1 TO 5
0840   READ R(A,B)
0850   NEXT B
0860   NEXT A
0870   DIM S(9,9)
0880   FOR A = 1 TO 9
0890   FOR B = 1 TO 9
0900   READ S(A, B)
0910   NEXT B
0920   NEXT A
0930   DIM K (8)
0940   DIM L(4)
0950   LET L (2) = 0
0960   LET L (3) = 0
0970   DIM W(4,5)
0980   FOR A = 1 TO 4
0990   FOR B = 1 TO 5
1000   READ W(A,B)
1010   NEXT B
1020   NEXT A
1030   GO TO 1290
1040   LET E3 =1 – E3
1050   PRINT
1060   PRINT "THE SIDE RETIRES"
1070   PRINT H; "HITS ";J; "RUNS"; K(2) + (K(3) + (K(4);"
       LEFT ON BASE"
```

```
1080    LET L (Y + 1) = L (Y + 1) + J
1090    IF E3 < > 0 THEN 1130
1100    PRINT "END OF INNING"; I; "SCORE: ME"; L
        (2); "YOU"; L (3)
1110    IF I > = 9 THEN 1220
1120    LET I = I + 1
1130    GO TO 1250
1140    LET Y2 = Y
1150    LET N = 0
1160    LET O = 0
1170    IF Y = 2 THEN 1200
1180    PRINT "I'M AT BAT—YOU'RE IN THE FIELD"
1190    RETURN
1200    PRINT "I'M IN THE FIELD—YOU'RE AT BAT"
1210    RETURN
1220    IF L(2) = L(3) THEN 1120
1230    PRINT "THE GAME IS OVER"
1240    GO TO 5450
1250    IF I < > 9 THEN 1270
1260    IF L (Y + 1) < L (3 − Y + 1) THEN 1230
1270    LET Y = 3 − Y
1280    GOSUB 1140
1290    LET Q = 0
1300    LET H = 0
1310    LET J = 0
1320    FOR Z = 1 TO 8
1330    LET K(Z) = 0
1340    NEXT Z
1350    PRINT
1360    PRINT "FIRST BATTER—";
1370    GO TO 1410
1380    LET H = H − 1
1390    PRINT
1400    PRINT "NEXT BATTER—";
1410    LET Q2 = Q
1420    IF RND (∅) > .35 THEN 1460
1430    PRINT "LEFT";
1440    LET X = 1
1450    GO TO 1480
1460    PRINT "RIGHT";
1470    LET X = 0
1480    PRINT "—HANDED"
1490    LET H = H + 1
```

258

```
1500   PRINT "THE FIELD POSITION FOR THIS BAT-
       TER IS";
1510   LET K(1) = 1
1520   IF Y = 1 THEN 1550
1530   LET D = 1 + INT 3* RND (∅))
1540   GO TO 1590
1550   PRINT "D";
1560   INPUT D
1570   IF D < 1 THEN 1550
1580   IF D > 3 THEN 1550
1590   IF D <> 1 THEN 1610
1600   PRINT "DENSE INFIELD"
1610   IF D < > 2 THEN 1630
1620   PRINT "NORMAL
1630   IF D < > 3 THEN 1650
1640   PRINT "DEEP"
1650   LET S3 = 2
1660   LET S2 = 2
1670   IF Y = 1 THEN 1970
1680   PRINT "PITCH COMING —A";
1690   INPUT A
1700   IF A > 4 THEN 1690
1710   IF A < 0 THEN 1690
1720   IF A < > 0 THEN 1750
1730   LET S3 = 1
1740   GO TO 1830
1750   PRINT " ", "B" ;
1760   INPUT B
1770   IF B < 1 THEN 1750
1780   IF B > 3 THEN 1750
1790   PRINT " ", "C";
1800   INPUT C
1810   IF C < 1 THEN 1790
1820   IF C < 3 THEN 1790
1830   PRINT
1840   IF RND (∅) < .2 THEN 1880
1850   LET E = INT (4 * RND (∅)) + 1
1860   IF E > 4 THEN 1850
1870   GO TO 1890
1880   LET E = 0
1890   IF N*O < > 6 THEN 1920
1900   IF RND (∅) <.75 THEN 1920
1910   LET E = 0
```

259

```
1920   LET F = 1 + INT (3 * RND (Ø))
1930   LET G = 1 + INT (RND (Ø)* 3)
1940   IF E < > 0 THEN 2210
1950   LET S2 = 1
1960   GO TO 2210
1970   PRINT "BATTER READY —E";
1980   INPUT E
1990   IF E <0 THEN 1980
2000   IF E >4 THEN 1980
2010   IF E < > 0 THEN 2030
2020   LET S2 = 1
2030   PRINT " ", "F";
2040   INPUT F
2050   IF F < 1 THEN 2030
2060   IF F > 3 THEN 2030
2070   PRINT " ", "G";
2080   INPUT G
2090   PRINT
2100   IF G < 1 THEN 2070
2110   IF G > 3 THEN 2070
2120   IF RND (Ø)> .2 THEN 2150
2130   LET S3 = 1
2140   GO TO 2210
2150   LET A = ABS (INT (3*RND (−1)) + 2 − D)
2160   LET C = 1 + INT (3 * RND (−1))
2170   LET B = 1 + INT (3 * RND (−1))
2180   IF A = 0 THEN 2130
2190   IF A < = 4 THEN 2210
2200   LET A = 3
2210   LET C2 = 0
2220   IF E < 3 THEN 2250
2230   IF RND Ø > .5 THEN 2250
2240   LET C2 = 1
2250   LET B = B − 1
2260   LET C = C − 1
2270   LET A = A − 1
2280   LET E2 = E − 1
2290   IF RND (Ø)> .3 THEN 2360
2300   LET F = F + C2 * SGN (.5—RND (Ø))
2310   IF F > THEN 2340
2320   LET F = 0
2330   LET F = 0
2340   IF F < 5 THEN 2360
```

```
2350   LET F = 4
2360   IF RND (∅) > .3 THEN 2380
2370   LET G = G + C2 * SGN (.5 — RND (∅))
2380   IF G < > 2 THEN 2440
2390   IF F < > 2 THEN 2440
2400   LET S2 = 2
2410   IF E < > 0 THEN 2440
2420   LET E = 2
2430   LET E2 = 1
2440   IF G < 5 THEN 2480
2445   LET G = 4
2450   LET M = 1
2460   PRINT "THE PITCH HIT THE BATTER. ";
2470   GO TO 3440
2480   IF G = 0 THEN 2540
2490   IF S3 = 1 THEN 2550
2500   IF E < = 3 THEN 2520
2510   LET E2 = 2
2520   LET G2 = ABS (G — 4*X)
2530   IF R (F + 1, G + 1) < > 9 THEN 2550
2540   LET S2 = 1
2550   PRINT "THE PITCH IS";
2560   IF S2 < > 1 THEN 2590
2570   PRINT " A BALL -";
2580   GO TO 2690
2590   IF S2 < > 2 THEN 2610
2600   PRINT " IN THERE - A";
2610   IF E < > 1 THEN 2630
2620   PRINT " SLOW BALL";
2630   IF E < > 2 THEN 2650
2640   PRINT " STRAIGHT PITCH";
2650   IF E < > 3 THEN 2670
2660   PRINT " FAST BALL";
2670   IF E < > 4 THEN 2690
2680   PRINT " CURVE BALL";
2690   IF F < > 2 THEN 2710
2700   PRINT " WAIST";
2710   IF F > 2 THEN 2730
2720   PRINT "HIGH";
2730   IF F < 3 THEN 2750
2740   PRINT " LOW";
2750   PRINT " AND";
```

```
2760  IF G > 1 THEN 2780
2770  PRINT "OUTSIDE"
2780  IF G < > 2 THEN 2800
2790  PRINT " TO THE CENTER"
2800  IF G < 3 THEN 2820
2810  PRINT " INSIDE"
2820  IF Y = 2 THEN 3080
2830  PRINT "THE BATTER";
2840  IF S3 < > 1 THEN 2870
2850  PRINT " DOESN'T SWING.";
2860  GO TO 3080
2870  PRINT "SWINGS WITH A";
2880  IF A < > 0 THEN 2900
2890  PRINT " BUNT";
2900  IF A < > 1 THEN 2920
2910  PRINT " NORMAL SWING";
2920  IF A < > 2 THEN 2940
2930  PRINT " FULL SWING";
2940  IF B < > 1 THEN 2960
2950  PRINT " WAIST";
2960  IF B > 1 THEN 2980
2970  PRINT " HIGH";
2980  IF B < 2 THEN 3000
2990  PRINT " LOW";
3000  PRINT " AND AIMING TOWARDS";
3010  IF C < > 0 THEN 3030
3020  PRINT " RIGHT"
3030  IF C < > 1 THEN 3050
3040  PRINT " CENTER"
3050  IF C < > 2 THEN 3070
3060  PRINT " LEFT"
3070  PRINT "FIELD."
3080  IF S2*S3 = 4 THEN 3690
3090  IF S2*S3 < > 1 THEN 3120
3100  LET O = O + 1
3110  LET O2 = O
3120  PRINT "BALL"; O;
3130  IF O = 4 THEN 3260
3140  IF S2*S3 < > 2 THEN 3160
3150  LET N = N + 1
3160  PRINT " STRIKE"; N
3170  IF N = 3 THEN 3210
```

```
3180   IF N*O<>6 THEN 3200
3190   PRINT "FULL COUNT"
3200   GO TO 1650
3210   PRINT "HE'S";
3220   LET H=H−1
3230   PRINT "OUT.";
3240   LET Q=Q+1
3250   PRINT Q; "OUT"
3260   LET O2=O
3270   LET O=0
3280   LET N=0
3290   IF Q<>3 THEN 3430
3300   IF E3+I<>1 THEN 3400
3310   DIM T(3,16)
3320   FOR T1=1 TO 3
3330   FOR T2=1 TO 16
3340   LET T(T1,T2)=0
3350   NEXT T2
3360   NEXT T1
3370   DIM P(2)
3380   LET P(1)=0
3390   LET P(2) = 0
3400   LET T(Y+1, I+1)=J
3410   LET P(Y)=P(Y)+H
3420   GO TO 1040
3430   IF O2<>4 THEN 1390
3440   LET M=1
3450   PRINT
3460   PRINT "HE TAKES HIS BASE."
3470   LET H=H−1
3480   IF K(2)<1 THEN 3570
3490   IF K(3)<1 THEN 3550
3500   IF K(4)<1 THEN 3530
3510   LET K(4+M)=K(4)
3520   LET K(4)=0
3530   LET K(3+M)=K(3)
3540   LET K(3)=0
3550   LET K(2+M)=K(2)
3560   LET K(2)=0
3570   LET K(M+1)=K(1)
3580   LET K(1)=1
3590   IF K(5)+K(6)+K(7)+K(8)=0 THEN 3660
```

```
3600    FOR Z=5 TO 8
3610    LET H3=H3+K(Z)
3620    LET K(Z)=0
3630    NEXT Z
3640    LET J=J+H3
3650    PRINT "NUMBER OF RUNNERS SCORING=";H3
3660    GOSUB 5350
3670    LET H3=0
3680    GO TO 3260
3690    LET U=S(R(F+1,G2+1),B+1+C*3)
3700    IF U=9 THEN 3150
3710    IF U < 15 THEN 3930
3720    LET U2=INT(4*RND(Ø))
3730    PRINT "POP FLY-FOUL-TO THE";
3740    IF U <> 15 THEN 3790
3750    PRINT "RIGHT OF THE 1ST BASE LINE
3760    IF U2<>0 THEN 3840
3770    PRINT "CAUGHT BY THE 1ST BASEMAN";
3780    GO TO 3210
3790    IF U<>16 THEN 3930
3800    PRINT "LEFT OF THE 3RD BASE LINE"
3810    IF U2<>0 THEN 3840
3820    PRINT "CAUGHT BY THE 3RD BASEMAN.";
3830    GO TO 3210
3840    IF U2<>1 THEN 3870
3850    PRINT "CAUGHT BY THE CATCHER.";
3860    GO TO 3210
3870    PRINT "GOES INTO THE BLEACHERS.-";
3880    PRINT "FOUL BALL-";
3890    LET N=N+1
3900    IF N<3 THEN 3120
3910    LET N=2
3920    GO TO 3120
3930    IF U>4 THEN 3960
3940    LET V=0
3950    GO TO 4000
3960    IF U>9 THEN 3990
3970    LET V=1
3980    GO TO 4000
3900    LET V=2
4000    LET S=U-V*5
4010    PRINT "THE HIT IS A":
```

264

```
4020  IF S=4 THEN 3880
4030  LET W1=W(S+1, A+1+E2)
4040  IF W1<2 THEN 4080
4050  IF W1<3 THEN 4070
4060  PRINT "LONG";
4070  PRINT "DEEP";
4080  IF W1>1 THEN 4100
4090  PRINT "SHORT";
4100  IF S<>2 THEN 4130
4110  PRINT "GROUNDER";
4120  GO TO 4200
4130  IF S<>0 THEN 4150
4140  PRINT "HARD";
4150  IF S<>1 THEN 4170
4160  PRINT "LOW";
4170  IF S<>3 THEN 4190
4180  PRINT "HIGH";
4190  PRINT "FLY BALL";
4200  IF W1<>0 THEN 4220
4210  PRINT "BUNTED";
4220  PRINT "INTO THE";
4230  IF V<>0 THEN 4250
4240  PRINT "RIGHT"
4250  IF V <> 1 THEN 4270
4260  PRINT "CENTER";
4270  IF V<>2 THEN 4290
4280  PRINT "LEFT";
4290  IF W1>1 THEN 4310
4300  PRINT "IN";
4310  PRINT "FIELD AREA."
4320  LET M=W1
4330  IF (W1+1)*D>1 THEN 4440
4340  IF S*D<>3 THEN 4390
4350  IF W1*RND(-1)>.6 THEN 4380
4360  PRINT "CAUGHT BY THE PITCHER"
4370  GO TO 3210
4380  PRINT "OUT OF REACH OF THE PITCHER"
4390  IF .5<INT(ABS(S-2)*RND(Ø)) THEN 4430
4400  PRINT "SAFE AT 1ST"
4410  LET M=1
4420  GO TO 3510
4430  IF Q=2 THEN 4580
```

```
4440  IF (W1+1)*D>2 THEN 4690
4450  IF K(2)=0 THEN 4570
4460  IF Q=2 THEN 4570
4470  PRINT "** DOUBLE PLAY ??????????** - THE
      RUNNERS ARE:"
4480  LET Q2=Q+1
4490  IF RND(∅)<.35 THEN 4530
4500  PRINT "OUT";
4510  LET K(2)=0
4520  GO TO 4560
4530  PRINT "SAFE";
4540  LET H=H+1
4550  LET Q2=Q
4560  PRINT "AT 2ND AND";
4570  IF RND(∅)<.35 THEN 4650
4580  PRINT "OUT AT FIRST"
4590  LET H=H-1
4600  LET K(1)=0
4610  LET Q=Q2+1
4620  IF Q=3 THEN 3250
4630  PRINT " ";Q; "OUT"
4640  GO TO 4410
4650  IF Q2<=Q THEN 4400
4660  PRINT "(";Q2;"OUT)";
4670  LET Q=Q2
4680  GO TO 4400
4690  IF W1>1 THEN 4730
4700  IF S=2 THEN 4390
4710  IF RND(∅)>.5 THEN 4790
4720  GO TO 4350
4730  IF S<>2 THEN 4780
4740  IF RND(∅) + .25 * (3—D) > 1 THEN 4760
4750  LET M = M -1
4760  IF M = 1 THEN 4400
4770  GO TO 5310
4780  IF S* W1 < > 6 THEN 4880
4790  IF RND (∅) * (1 + ABS (D—2)) <.6 THEN 4820
4800  PRINT "OVER THE INFIELD PLAYERS' HEADS"
4810  GO TO 5310
4820  PRINT "CAUGHT BY THE";
4830  IF V>1 THEN 4860
4840  PRINT "2ND BASEMAN.";
```

```
4850    GO TO 3210
4860    PRINT "SHORTSTOP.";
4870    GO TO 3210
4880    IF W1*D>3 THEN 4930
4890    IF S=1 THEN 4930
4900    IF RND(∅)*D 2<.9 THEN 4820
4910    PRINT "PAST THE INFIELD PLAYERS"
4920    GO TO 5310
4930    LET X2=0
4940    IF W1<>D THEN 5090
4950    IF RND(∅)>.75 THEN 4990
4960    PRINT "CAUGHT BY THE";
4970    LET X2 = 1
4980    GO TO 5000
4990    PRINT "PAST THE";
5000    IF V<>0 THEN 5020
5010    PRINT "RIGHT FIELDER";
5020    IF V<>2 THEN 5040
5030    PRINT "CENTER FIELDER";
5040    IF V < > 2 THEN 5060
5050    PRINT "LEFT FIELDER";
5060    IF X2=1 THEN 3210
5070    IF X2=2 THEN 5130
5080    GO TO 5310
5090    IF W1>3 THEN 5180
5100    LET X2=2
5110    PRINT "THE";
5120    GO TO 5000
5130    IF RND (∅)>.6 THEN 5160
5140    PRINT "CATCHES IT-";
5150    GO TO 3210
5160    PRINT "CAN'T GET TO IT"
5170    GO TO 5310
5180    LET W7=INT(7*RND(∅))
5190    IF W7>1 THEN 5240
5200    PRINT "** OUT OF THE PARK **";
5210    PRINT "**HOMERUN**"
5220    LET H=H+1
5230    GO TO 3510
5240    IF W7*D>15 THEN 4960
5250    PRINT "BOUNCES OFF THE BACK FENCE."
5260    IF D=1 THEN 5210
```

```
5270    IF W7=2 THEN 5210
5280    LET M=3
5290    PRINT "–A TRIPLE"
5300    GO TO 3510
5310    IF M=3 THEN 5290
5320    IF M<2 THEN 4400
5330    PRINT "–A DOUBLE"
5340    GO TO 3510
5350    IF M=4 THEN 5430
5360    PRINT "RUNNERS AT:";
5370    IF K(2)<>1 THEN 5390
5380    PRINT "1ST";
5390    IF K(3)<>1 THEN 5410
5400    PRINT "2ND";
5410    IF K(4)<> 1 THEN 5430
5420    PRINT "3RD";
5430    PRINT
5440    RETURN
5450    PRINT
5460    PRINT " ", "HERE ARE THE STATISTICS:"
5470    PRINT
5480    FOR A=1 TO 3
5490    IF A<>1 THEN 5510
5500    PRINT "INNING–";
5510    IF A <>2 THEN 5530
5520    PRINT "      ME – ";
5530    IF A < > 3 THEN 5550
5540    PRINT "      YOU – ";
5550    FOR B = 1 TO I
5560    IF A < > 1 THEN 5580
5570    PRINT " ";B;
5580    IF A<>2 THEN 5600
5590    PRINT " ";T(2,B+1);
5600    IF A <>3THEN 5620
5610    PRINT " "; T (3, B + 1);
5620    NEXT B
5630    IF A < > 1 THEN 5650
5640    PRINT "SCORE/HITS"
5650    IF A<>2 THEN 5670
5660    PRINT " "; L(2);"/";P(1)
5670    IF A<>3 THEN 5690
5680    PRINT " ";L(3);"/";P(2)
```

```
5690   NEXT A
5700   DATA 9,9,9,9,9
5710   DATA 9,2,4,7,9
5720   DATA 9,1,5,8,9
5730   DATA 9,3,6,9,9
5740   DATA 9,9,9,9,9
5750   DATA 4,15,9,1,3,8,6,8,9
5760   DATA 4,4,5,2,1,3,7,6,8
5770   DATA 9,4,4,9,2,1,9,7,6
5780   DATA 1,3,9,6,8,9,11,13,9
5790   DATA 2,0,3,7,5,8,12,10,13
5800   DATA 9,2,0,9,7,5,9,12,10
5810   DATA 6,8,9,11,13,9,14,16,9
5820   DATA 7,6,8,12,11,13,14,14,16
5830   DATA 9,7,6,9,12,11,9,14,14
5840   DATA 0,1,2,4,4
5850   DATA 0,1,2,3,3
5860   DATA 0,1,1,2,3
5870   DATA 0,1,1,1,2
5880   END
```

Chapter 8
Control and Peripheral Applications

Control And Peripheral Applications

Ben Bagdikian in his book, *The Information Machines*, suggests these possibilities for the home computer:

1. As a household device, the computer can record all the utility meters, automatically instruct the householder's bank computer to "pay" the utility tax-deductable portions, and when income tax time comes, deliver all the other tax-related information the consumer needs.

2. It can be connected with thermostats so that an ominous pattern of high temperatures can automatically notify the fire-department. It can do the same with sensing devices on door locks and windows for burglaries. It can operate ovens in complicated patterns. It could even release fresh food and water to pets left at home for a long period, "know" when the animal has not eaten the food, and notify the veterinarian to check the home.

For the control applications discussed in the latter paragraph that time has come; a demonstration home has been built, incorporating these ideas and several others:

1. Climate control is just one of the many functions provided by the home computer system. The rate of temperature change and humidity is noted, and the air conditioner/heater is turned off before the house is at a preset level; the temperature will "coast" to the desired level. The hot water heater is also turned down during certain hours to conserve energy.

2. A vocal input interface to the home computer is continuously active, waiting for a command by one of the occupants. All appliances and lights controlled by the system may be switched on and off by voice command, or may be programmed to start and stop at selected times.

3. An intelligent alarm system will turn off all electricity/gas and call the fire department in case of fire. A burglar detection system calls the police if an intruder is detected ultrasonically.

4. The interfaces to stereo, television, and telephone are also interesting. The telephone controller acts as a phone message recorder, but with additional features. If a message is taken, the unit can be instructed to call someone at another number and deliver the message. A telephone call to the machine itself can allow one to change the recorded message, play back messages, or control any of the devices connected with the home computer. A telephone file of commonly referred-to numbers is computer retained. Additionally, one can dial numbers by simply calling them off vocally; if a busy signal is encountered the computer continually redials the number until the line is free.

5. The stereo interface transforms an ordinary stereo into a "jukebox" from which recordings may be selected and played at the touch of a button. A special device can monitor radio broadcasts and record all music; commercials and news are not recorded (voice patterns may be distinquished from music). Volume level, and type of music may be pre-programmed to provide musical interludes, background music for dinner, etc.

6. The television interface will turn on the set at selected times or record shows on video tape; a directional antenna is automatically turned for the best reception.

7. Even the bar is automated. Drinks of your choice are mixed automatically (bottles of ingredients are connected by hoses to the special machine).

Other applications now in practice by hobbyists include:

1. Voice/sound synthesizers incorporated with games to provide sound effects/dialogue.

2. Voice input computers for recording information called off by an operator (e.g. one hobbyist uses such a system to make simple calculations in his home workshop while his hands are full). Although such systems are usually

limited to a vocabulary of about thirty words, some hobbyists have managed to develop automatic "dictation-taking" typewriters for limited purposes (a word capacity of one-hundred is considered maximum).

3. A hobbyist has used his small computer to replace over 7000 mechanical relays necessary to control a pipe organ in his home. Similarly, computers could be used to light the keys on an organ to help one learn to play a song. Although a commercial piano player has been developed to digitally record music played and play it back later, the cost is high. If one was to implement such a system with his computer, additional features could be added: speed, sustain, attack, etc. could all be varied.

4. One hobbyist is using a microprocessor to create intelligent test equipment which can automatically perform a set of test routines on a given circuit (interesting application for amateur radio operators). A calculating oscilloscope is able to compute exact items for rises, perform integrals, differentials, compute peak areas, RMS values, peak to peak distances, n-point averaging; all data may be stored.

5. The program presented below was written by a hobbyist to convert alpha brain-wave signals to audible sound. Although it has not been tested, the program serves to demonstrate computer applications in transforming analog signals to practically any other form. If operational, this program could be used to transform your voice from very deep to "Mickey Mouse" level, for example. Such digital modulations obviously have application in future stereo music players for the general public; one would have the ability to change a given song any way he desires.

To use the program, a brainwave pickup, a DC amplifier, an active low-pass filter (with a corner frequency of 20Hz), and an 8-bit A/D converter must be connected to an 8080-based computer running at 2MHz. The computer should have 1K of full speed static RAM and an output port connected to an A/D converter which then drives another amp for the speaker. The program should raise all of the frequency components of the brainwave signal to the audible range while preserving the ratios between frequencies.

```
1000        0010  ;  MUSE    BRAINWAVE-TO-SOUND
                       CONVERSION
```

```
1000      0020 ; BY STEVE WITHAM 6/26/77
1000      0030;
1000      0040 OPI EQU 80; NUMBER OF OUTPUTS PER
               INPUT
1000      0050 OCIC EQU 80; NUMER OF OUTPUT CY-
               CLES PER INPUT CYCLE.
1000      0600 TABL EQU OF 800H; WAVEFORM STOR-
               AGE TABLE. SET AT BEGINNING.
1000      0070 ; OF POLY SCREEN RAM—THIS MUST
               BE A
1000      0080 ; MULTIPLE OF DIVD!!!
1000      0090 DIVD EQU 8; NUMBER OF INPUTS PER
               OUTPUT CYCLE. THIS MUST
1000      0100 ; BE A POWER OF TWO!!
1000      0110 DAC EQU 0; DIGITAL-TO-ANALOG OUT-
               PUT PORT.
1000      0120    ADC EQU 1; ANALOG-TO-DIGITAL
               INPUT PORT.
1000      0130 ;
1000      0140 THE FOLLOWING CONSTANTS SPECIFY
               LENGTHS OF TIME TO PAUSE
1000      0150 ; BETWEEN OUTPUTS. THEY ARE DIF-
               FERENT TO COMPENSATE FOR
1000      0160 ; TIME TAKEN UP BY DIFFERENT
               PARTS OF THE PROGRAM
1000      0170 TIME EQU 17; (312—54)/15
1000      0180 TIM1 EQU 14; (312—98)/15
1000      0190 TIM2 EQU 13; (312—123)/15
1000      0200 TIM3 EQU 12; (312—13)/15
1000      0210 ;
1000      0220 ; CYCLES
1000 21 00 F8 0230 MUSE LXI H, TABL; ——SET UP
               OUTPUT POINTET
1003 OE 50 0240 MVI C, OPI; — SET OUTPUTS-PER-
               INPUT COUNTER
1005      0250 RSTI EQU $; 106 CYCLES SO FAR.
1005 11 00 F8 0260 LXI D, TABL; +10 SET/RESET INPUT
               POINTER AND
1008 06 50 0270 MVI B, OCIC; +7 OUTPUT-CYCLE-
               PER-INPUT-CYCLE
100A      0280 ; COUNTER
100A 3E OC 0290 MVI A, TIM3; +7 PAUSE AFTER OUT-
               PUT + INPUT +
```

```
100C      0300 ; OUTPUT RESET + INPUT RESET
100C      0310;      = 130 CYCLES FOR 0 + I + OR + IR.
100C 3D 0320 LOOP DCRA 5 COUNT DOWN FOR DELAY
100D C2 0C 10 0330 JNZ LOOP; +10 = 15 CYCLES PER
                  DELAY LOOP.
1010      0340;
1010 7E 0350 MOV A,M; 7 GET VALUE FROM TABLE
1011 D3 00 0360 OUT DAC; +10
1013 23      0370 INX H; +5 MOVE OUTPUT POINTER
                  FOREWARD.
1014 OD   0380 DCR C; +5 ONE LESS OUTPUT TO DO
                  BEFORE
1015      0390 ; .INPUTTING
1015 CA 1K 10 0400 JZ INPT; +10 OH—NO MORE? THEN
                  INPUT NOW.
1018      0410; =37 CYCLES UP TO AN INCLUDING
                  THIS 'JZ'
1018 3E 11 0420 MVI A, TIMO; +7 PAUSE FOR AFTER
                  OUTPUT ONLY.
101A C3 OC 10 0430 JMP Loop; +10 = 54 CYCLES TO DO
OUTPUT ONLY.
101D      0440;
101D      0450 ; 37 CYCLES SO FAR.
101D OE 50 0460 INPT MVI C, OPI; +7 RESET # OF
                  OUTPUTS PER INPUT
101F DB 01 0470 IN ADC; +10
1021 13 0480 INDX D; + 5 ADVANCED INPUT POINTER.
1022 7B 0490 MOV A, E; +5 THE INPUT POINTER CON-
                  TAINS IMPORTANT
1023 E6 07 0500 ANI DIVD – 1; +7 INFORMATION IN ITS
                  BOTTOM BITS.
1025 CA 2D 10 0510 JZ RSTO; +10 HAVE DIVD INPUTS
(I.E. DIVD * OPI)
1028      0520 ; OUTPUTS) HAVE BEEN DONE SINCE
                  LAST
1028      0530 ; RESETTING OUTPUT POINTER?
1028      0540; = 81 CYCLES UP TO & INCLUDING THE
                  'JZ'.
1028 3E 0E 0550 MVIA, TIM1; +7 PAUSE AFTER OUT-
                  PUT + INPUT.
102A C3 0C 10 0560 JMP LOOP; +10 = 98 CYCLES TO DO
                  OUTPUT + INPUT.
```

```
102D      0570;
102D      0580 ; 81 CYCLES SO FAR.
102D 21 00 F8 0590 RSTO LXI H, TABL; +10 RESET
                        OUTPUT POINTER.
1030 05 0600 DCRB; +5 IF OCIC OUTPUT POINTER
                        RESETS
1031      0610 ; (OUTPUT CYCLES) HAVE BEEN DONE
                        THEN.
1031      0620 ; OCIC * DIVD INPUTS HAVE BEEN
                        DONE.
1031 CA 05 20 0630 JZ RSTI; +10 AND ONE INPUT
                        CYCLE IS COMPLETE
1034      0640; =106 CYCLES UP TO & INCLUDING
                        THIS 'JZ'.
1034 3E0D 0650 MVIA, TIM2; +7 OTHERWISE PAUSE
                        FOR OUTPUT + INPUT +
1036 C3 0C 10 0660 JMP LOOP; +10 RESETTING OUT-
                        PUT.
1039      0670 ; = 123 CYCLES FOR OUT + IN + OUT
                        RESET.
```

6.) A New Hampshire resident uses his home computer to control his wood stove; he reports a 10% to 30% improvement in efficiency.

MUSIC

A few music/voice synthesizers are now on the market as personal computer peripherals. Possible uses for these include:

1. Incorporation with games for special sound effects.

2. Incorporation with a music composing program to generate and play original music continuously.

3. Use as a programmable drummer to accompany other instruments. Various drum sounds, speeds, and patterns (Latin, swing, jazz, waltz, march, etc.) could be programmed. The metronome, cymbals, and other percussion devices could also be imitated.

4. Use a voice synthesizer to "sing" the vocals of a music piece, producing a unique composition.

If you have a plotter or graphic printer/terminal your musical compositions or those of the computer could be graphed as standard sheet music. Loops of proper speed and duration will generate a specific audible frequency on an AM radio placed next to a CPU. A machine language or BASIC program to make use of this effect could produce a resemblance to music. Theoretically, if music is digitized with the use of an A/D converter, it may be altered in practically any manner: 1. Selected voices/instruments could be removed/added 2. The music could be played at any selected rate without a change in pitch, or could be played backwards for special effect. Essentially, one can transform a given composition into another style.

Today's color organs, used to produce a pulsating lighted response to music, rely upon analog circuits and often do not produce good results. Perhaps a dedicated microprocessor could be used to control the lights instead, resulting in a favorable response.

An accoustical analysis of your stereo listening room (as described in stereo listening magazines) by computer could result in a better arrangement or assist in planning a new room (e.g. the distances between speakers and the listening position should form an equilateral triangle).

Perhaps you now have an idea of the control/peripheral applications possible with your home computer in household/business control for present and future. The cost of controlling external devices is dropping at a fast rate, and the above applications should be worthwhile and economical within the next few years. The project described below should serve to lower that cost even more.

AN EXTERNAL DEVICE CONTROLLER FOR YOUR COMPUTER

The controller described here will allow you to interface your computer with virtually any external electrical device, up to sixteen devices (channels) may be controlled simultaneously.

This interface switches on and off a small amount of current to control relays which in turn may control larger electrical loads (see Fig. 8-1). Practically all eight-bit computers can drive the interface, and a four-bit microprocessor could drive a modified interface for specialized control purposes.

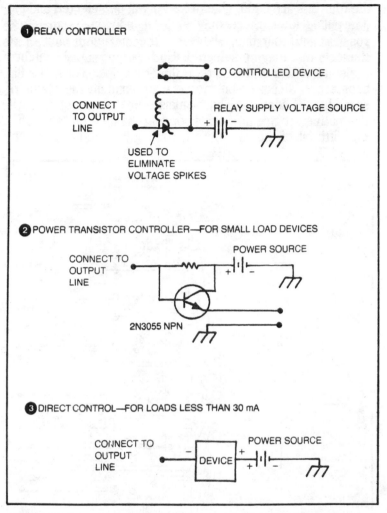

TO CONTROLLED DEVICE

CONNECT
TO OUTPUT
LINE

RELAY SUPPLY VOLTAGE SOURCE

+ ‖‖ −

USED TO
ELIMINATE
VOLTAGE SPIKES

❷ POWER TRANSISTOR CONTROLLER—FOR SMALL LOAD DEVICES

POWER SOURCE

CONNECT TO
OUTPUT
LINE

+ ‖ −

2N3055 NPN

❸ DIRECT CONTROL—FOR LOADS LESS THAN 30 mA

POWER SOURCE

CONNECT TO
OUTPUT
LINE

− DEVICE +
+

+ ‖ −

Fig. 8-1. Diagram of output devices which can be selected to match the controlled load.

The interface consists of three modules: a sixteen-channel demultiplexer, a sixteen-bit "memory", and sixteen single transistor driver amplifiers (see Fig. 8-2); the construction cost should not exceed $30. It is designed to be connected directly with a parallel output port.

The four low-order bits of data coming from the parallel output port are inputted to the demultiplexer. The demultiplexer selects the appropriate output pin and pulls it low (e.g. if the four bits are 0000, channel zero will be selected and pin one pulled low). Since only sixteen individual signals are possible with four bits, sixteen is the maximum number of channels that may be selected. Each output signal switches the state of one of the sixteen flip flop chips. Thus, the flip flops act as a sixteen-bit memory to maintain the status of each channel continuously. Signals sent to one flip flop will alternatively toggle the corresponding channel "on" and "off". The fifth bit of the data byte is first buffered and then con-

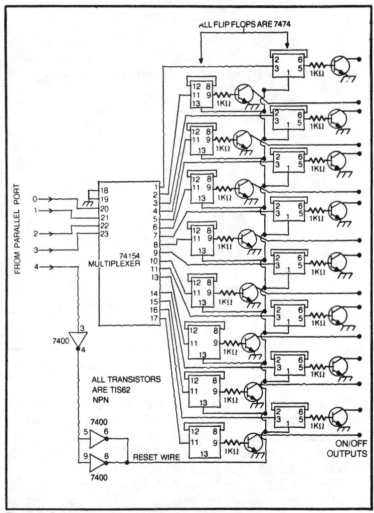

Fig. 8-2. Schematic diagram of the control latch system.

nected to the reset pin of each flip flop. Thus, all channels may be reset (turned off) simultaneously with the fifth bit.

The software must output the signal corresponding to the correct channel to control devices connected to the interface. However, a channel may not be switched on and off continuously by selecting that channel over and over again. This is due to the fact that the flip flops only switch on rising edges from the demultiplexer, which occur only if the multiplexer has changed to select a different channel. Therefore, to switch a given flip flop on and then off follow these steps: 1) select that channel with the proper data byte, 2) select any other channel (e.g. an unused channel), 3) wait for the first channel to toggle on 4) reselect the first channel to turn it off.

AN A/D CONVERTER FOR YOUR COMPUTER

The A/D converter has many applications for use with personal computers. It will alow one to interface joysticks/ potentiometers for use with editing, video drawing, or games. With proper software, music, sound effects, and synthetic speech may be produced. Automation of test equipment and control over robots/machines are among many other applications.

The eight-channel interface described here is designed for use in converting signals in the range of about 0.1 Hz to 100Hz, which is sufficient for the above listed applications (see Fig. 8-3). The "sample-and-hold" principle is used in the design to store an analog signal as a capacitor charge until it is processed. The two power supplies necessary should respectively fall between: 4.5 to 6.5V and 12 to 15V.

An assembly language software description is provided below; you supply the op codes for your particular microprocessor:

1. Initialize the pointer
2. Load the next byte for output
3. Output the byte
4. Set accumulator equal to the pointer
5. Select the next channel and enable the sample and hold process
6. Turn off the sample and hold strobe
7. Turn off the selected sample and hold
8. Decrement the value of the pointer

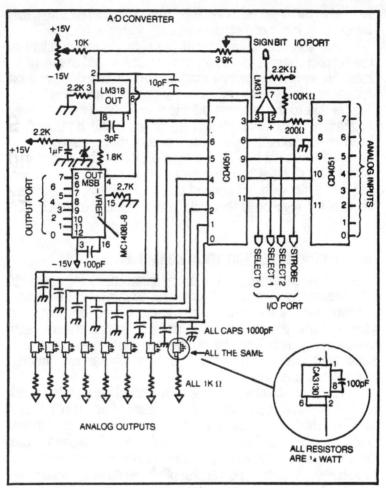

Fig. 8-3. Schematic diagram of the A/D converter.

9. If the pointer is greater than or equal to zero loop back to step #2, otherwise return to the main program.

As can be seen, the program sequentially addresses a channel, outputs the voltage which is to be held, disables that channel, repeats the process for the other channels, and then returns to the main program. One could arrange the program to act as an interrupt handler signaled by a clock strobe on an interrupt line.

282

Chapter 9
Artificial Intelligence and
the Future Personal Computer

Artificial Intelligence And
The Future Personal Computer

In his book, *Future Shock*, Alvin Toffler describes a future home computer system named OLIVER, the primary purpose of which is to help one deal with decision overload.

"In its simplest form, OLIVER would merely be a personal computer programmed to provide the individual with information and to make minor decisions for him. At this level, it could store information about his friends' preferences for Manhattans or martinis, data about traffic routes, the weather, stock prices, etc. The device could be set to remind him of his wife's birthday or to order flowers automatically. It could renew his magazine subscriptions, pay the rent on time, order razor blades and the like. As computerized information systems expand, they would tap into a worldwide pool of data stored in libraries, corporate files, hospitals, retail stores, banks, government agencies, and universities. OLIVER would thus become a kind of universal question-answerer for him. However, some computer scientists see much beyond this. It is theoretically possible to construct an OLIVER that would analyze the content of an owner's words, scrutinize his choices, deduce his value system, update its own program to reflect changes in his values, and ultimately handle larger and larger decisions for him."

Perhaps these predictions are a bit too optimistic, but home computer applications likely to be feasible and economic within the next decade include:

Medical monitoring—A specially designed microcomputer could be programmed to make checks of your bodily functions. Information such as nutritional and caloric intake, pulse rate, blood pressure, and weight loss/gain could be entered into a program especially tailored for your metabolism. Specific conditions which warrant a visit to the doctor could be computed and outputted.

With a telephone modem, the computer could transmit such information to a larger data bank for processing. Additionally, answers to common medical questions could be provided by the data bank.

Information research—The facilities to tap computerized information banks (e.g. New York Times and World Trade Center information banks) are already available via telephone modems connected to such service companies as The Source™. Such services are especially useful to businessmen, authors, and educators in the location of specialized information. In addition, a home computer interfaced to a standard modem could tap the Library of Congress computerized card catalog as well as numerous other data banks (although, of course, there is a charge for the use of such services).

Personalized news service—A home computer on-line with a news service could select news items by category and store them for review later by the home owner. United Press International wire service provides all major national and world news; news items are coded by category, and thus, computer on-line could select items of interest.

Travel information—A travel service data bank, filled with information regarding flights, schedules, prices, availability, reservations, etc. could supply all information necessary to plan a vacation, outing, etc. via a telephone modem.

Stock market quotes—A continual Dow Jones listing service could supply stock market quotes to the home computer via a telephone modem. Such a service would be a boon to those attempting stock market analyses with their computer.

Educational programs—Quality, comprehensive educational programs are needed for the growing home computer market. Perhaps a home video tape player could be used in conjunction with the computer to provide the graphics that cannot be provided on a video screen.

Business extentions—Computer programmers, professional investors, and other professionals who do most of their work with a computer system will begin to install home terminals; traveling to an office will be unnecessary.

Amateur computer networks—The formation of an amateur computer network is in progress, but much has yet to be done (e.g. standardization of data transmission). Professional "conferencing" networks have already been demonstrated, although no permanent network exists.

Intelligent devices—A home computer interfaced with household devices could create a complete home management system. Climate control, solar energy system control, television set timing, cooking device control, etc. could all be done simultaneously by a home computer properly equipped. With falling costs for microcomputers, such control applications are becoming economical.

Other possibilities include a complete, computer-controlled diagnostic system for your automobile.

A few examples of home computer applications suggested in the media, but without proper base, are included here. The problems associated with implementing these ideas are great at the present time and will continue to be so for several years.

Personal security system—By determining heights, weights, and diameters of all who come to your doorstep, your computer will be able to recognize whether that person is an acquaintance (based on previously stored information) or not.

The problems associated with this application are obvious; the equipment to determine heights and diameters of a person in motion would be difficult to interface, and no purpose is given for spending hundreds of dollars to accomplish such a feat.

Robot maid—Some authors have irresponsibly claimed that domestic androids will be available within a few years to do such chores as vacuuming a home, walking the dog, washing dishes, preparing food, etc. and will the capability of carrying on a natural conversation with the owner.

Several major problems must be overcome before such robots can be mass-produced for homeowners. The mechanical problems are minor compared to the problem of computers in recognizing "universals." Dennis Gabor described this problem in his book *Innovations:*

"One can say that it is incomparably easier to design a computer for solving a wave equation beyond the reach of the best analyst than to design one which will pick up and empty ashtrays, because ashtrays come in so many shapes."

Presumably, the use of the television camera is the only way to give a robot "sight." Computer analysis of the thousands of dots in a television picture to determine what objects are in the picture has not reached a level near satisfactory.

The problems of speech input are also numerous. Very large memory capacity and high processing speed are necessary to understand anything even approaching normal conversation. However, there is a considerable hobbyist interest in "robotics," and over the new few years increasingly sophisticated "toy" robots will be produced by hobbyists.

Controlling an automobile—The problems associated with computerized control (driving) of an automobile are much the same as those for domestic androids.

Supermarket ordering—A few authors have predicted elaborate computer systems at supermarkets which will respond to your computerized shopping list sent over the telephone; your order would be automatically processed and delivered to your home. Of course, the shopping list would be generated by the computer since it would also be controlling your pantry inventory. There are doubly as many disadvantages with such a system as advantages.

A LOOK AT THE FUTURE

Each of the following specifications may be true of personal computers before 1985.

1. CPU
   a. Eight-or sixteen-bit MOS single-chip processor, four megahertz minimum clock speed. A limited market will also make use of thirty-two bit machines for number crunching.
   b. Memory will be 32K-64K average MOS RAM or nonvolatile RAM
   c. Real time clock, possibly more than one, readable and settable under program control.
   d. Front panel not provided.

e. Customized chips for handling graphics, music, and speech in conjunction with the CPU.

2. Mass Storage
    a. Cassettes used only in limited applications, or in conjunction with specialized computers.
    b. Floppy disk, at least one. Storage capacity will be ½-1 Megabyte per disk.
    c. Video disks containing computer software, encyclopedic reference information, perhaps integrated with video pictures for use in educational applications. The estimated storage capacity of a two-hour video disk is 1×10^{11} bits or the approximate contents of a 60,000 volume library.
    d. Economical rigid disks available for limited applications.
    e. Magnetic card storage, each card capable of storing hundreds of program steps.
    f. ROM packages, plug in extra memory.
    g. Mark-sense cards for special applications.

3. Display
    a. High-bandwidth video monitors, video projectors, or very high density plasma terminals (the average resolution of a plasma terminal is 300,000 individually definable dots. Slides and movies may also be projected through the back of a plasma screen).
    b. Light-pen, joystick/potentiometer, bit pad, touch sensitive controllers widespread.
    c. Vector graphics hardware.
    d. Color video.
    e. Animation hardware/software.
    f. User-defined characters/graphic symbols.

4. Printer
    a. Dot matrix impact printer available capable of printing a variety of typefaces with typewriter quality. Typewriter quality may be achieved by making more than one printing pass on each line, advancing the paper slightly each time. Graphical characters could also be printed.
    b. DIABLO™-type daisy-wheel printers, price

economical
5. Software
   a. Super extended BASIC. BASIC compilers running in at least 25K memory could offer the desirable features of other current high-level languages. BASIC will be used in general application.
   b. FORTRAN
   c. COBOL, for business applications and limited hobby applications.
   d. PASCAL
   e. APL
   f. PILOT, TUTOR, other languages for educational use.
   g. Specialized graphic display control languages especially designed for video/plasma screens or printers/plotters.
   h. Specialized video/plasma screen game design languages, animation routines included.
   i. Cross-assembler languages. Write assembly language for another processor.
   j. Household management. Specialized languages for specialized microprocessors for use in the kitchen, for tax preparation, scientific and statistical processing, preparation, etc.

You can expect to find complete, quality software packages (in the form of ROM packages cassettes, or floppy disks) for all of the applications discussed in this book. Programs will be available from large, reputable corporations merchandising local stores.

6. Additional Peripherals
   a. "Hobby" robots will be available for entertainment and limited practical applications.
   b. Pocket programmable calculators will offer compatible BASIC or other high-level languages.
   c. Electrostatic plotters.
   d. Modem with a "hobbyist standard" method of data transmission.
   e. Specialized keyboards. Inexpensive membrane "keyboards" will be used in conjunction with games and other special programs. Special plug-in game controllers may also be available.

f. Simple one-chip circuits will be available with pre-programmed vocal output vocabularies. Improved vocal recognition systems will also be available.

g. Audio synthesizers—Complete sound synthesizing units will be used in creating electronic music, sound effects, etc.

h. Inexpensive controller interfaces will be available to allow computer control of appliances, climate control, etc.

i. Computer controlled stereo systems, which may play a specified sequence of tunes from a variety of sources. New digital music systems will allow unlimited alteration of a tune to suit your personal taste (e.g. remove certain instrumental elements, change tempo without changing pitch, etc.)

j. Multi-user systems (time-sharing) will be in widespread use.

Chapter 10
Utility Programs

Utility Programs

With the advent of the many different home computers, it is often times difficult to choose the right computer for your own use. There are many features, but seldom are they all incorporated in one machine. To help overcome this problem, small utility programs can be written and run as subroutines of a larger program. In this way many of the features can be obtained through software.

MULTI-PURPOSE PROGRAMS

Although some computer systems provide the features found below, others don't. The person who develops programs to perform these and other utility functions will most often have a readily saleable product.

1. Diagnostic programs—Programs to test all of the statements and commands found in given BASIC are useful in determining whether BASIC has loaded properly for execution. Programs to test memory by filling and reading all locations are also helpful.

2. Memory-map program—A machine language program to output a memory map.

3. Menu selection program—A machine language routine to automatically find and execute any programs online.

4. Binary coded decimal with parity to decimal conversion.

5. Improved data file handling for floppy disks or cassettes.

6. Machine language programs to automatically convert one cassette/floppy disk standard to another.

7. Variable list program—A program to output the current value and location for all variables used in a program, useful in large program debugging.

8. Renumber or resequence program—A program to renumber the statements in an assembly language program or BASIC program.

9. Base conversion program, useful in assembly language programming.

10. BASIC patches to allow such commands as "INKEY$" or "ENTER" which permit program inputs without hitting the "ENTER" key and can be limited to a certain amount of time.

11. Vector graphic assembly language routines.

12. Cross-assemblers or conversion programs between BASIC, FORTRAN, APL, etc.

13. Routines for handling fractions instead of decimals for greater precision in certain applications.

14. Specialized compilers for BASIC. Although writing a complete BASIC compiler would be difficult, specialized compilers could be written to handle string, mathematical, or sorting functions. The advantage, of course, is the ten-or-more fold increase in execution speed.

15. BASIC patches to provide increased debugging power. Suggested additions include: error simulation routines to test a program (ERROR(code) and ON ERROR GOTO commands), TRACE commands to output a listing of each line number as it is executed and powerful editing functions.

16. Memory routines—Relocating memory loaders (which may be written in extended BASIC) to add two programs together, add machine language calls, etc. A memory dump program could be provided to output programs in a variety of formats (decimal, hexadecimal, octal, etc.). A memory search program could be used to identify all occurances of a specific byte value between any starting and ending addresses; such a program would be useful in disassembling and debugging.

17. AUTO command—The AUTO command automatically provides line numbers for typing in a program.

18. PLOT command—The PLOT command is useful in automatically displaying the values of a user-defined instruction in graphical form.

19. Multiple-precision routines—The scientific user of small computers (and some business users) needs multiple-precision capability to handle large numbers.

Additionally, a useful reference manual could be developed to list commonly used assembly language routines to simplify programming for the beginner in that area.

PROGRAM—CHECK DIGIT GENERATOR AND VERIFIER

Checks digits are often used in commercial computing to increase computer accuracy. A check digit is a number from 1-9 which is assigned to any other number by a series of calculations. This digit is then added to the number at the end or beginning and is disregarded when doing calculations. After being stored or processed, the same set of calculations are performed to insure that the check digit is correct. If it is not the same, a computer error has been indicated and appropriate measures may be taken. Those intending to use a personal computer in business or other important applications may wish to make use of check digits to insure accuracy.

```
10   REM CHECKSUM GENERATOR AND VERIFIER
20   INPUT"ENTER THE NUMBER"; A$
30   PRINT"TO GENERATE CHECKSUM TYPE'1' "
40   INPUT"TO VERIFY CHECKSUM TYPE '2' ";Z
50   IF Z=2 THEN 200
60   GOSUB 100
70   PRINT"THE CHECK DIGIT IS";C;"MAKING THE
     NUMBER =";A$+RIGHT$(STR$(C),1)
80   END
100  REM CHECKSUM GENERATOR
110  FOR X=1 TO LEN(A$)
120  S=S+ASC(MID$(A$,X,1))
130  NEXT X
140  S$=STR$(S)
150  C=VAL(RIGHT$(S$,1))
160  RETURN
200  REM VERIFY CHECKSUM
210  REM FOR CHECKSUMS ADDED TO END OF NO.
220  B$=RIGHT$(A$,1)
230  A$=LEFT$(A$,LEN(A$)-1)
```

```
240   GOSUB 100
250   IF  VAL(B$)=C  THEN  PRINT"CORRECT
      CHECKSUM"  ELSE  PRINT"INCORRECT
      CHECKSUM"
260   END
```

ADDITIONAL UTILITY PROGRAMS

```
00100   REM MATRIX ADDITION 3-D
00110   FOR I=1 TO N1
00120   FOR J=1 TO N2
00130   FOR K=1 TO N3
00140   C(K,J,I)=A(K,J,I)+B(K,J,I)
00150   NEXT K
00160   NEXT J
00170   NEXT I
00180   RETURN
```

```
00100   REM MATRIX TRANSPOSTION 2-D
00110   FOR I=1 TO N1
00120   FOR J=1 TO N2
00130   B(J,I)=A(I,J)
00140   NEXT J
00150   NEXT I
00160   RETURN
```

```
00100   REM MATRIX MULTIPLICATION BY ONE VAR-
        IABLE 3-D
00110   FOR I=1 TO N3
00120   FOR J=1 TO N2
00130   FOR K=1 TO N1
00140   B(K,J,I)=A(K,J,I)*X
00150   NEXT K
00160   NEXT J
00170   NEXT I
00180   RETURN
```

```
1000    REM INSTRING SUBROUTINE
1010    FOR I=1 TO LEN(X$)-LEN(Y$)+1
1020    IF Y$=MID$(X$,I,LEN(Y$)) THEN RETURN
1030    NEXT I
1040    RETURN
```

```
00100   REM MATRIX INPUT ROUTINE 3-D
00110   FOR I=1 TO N1
00120   PRINT "PAGE";I
00130   FOR J=1 TO N2
00140   PRINT "INPUT ROW";J
00150   FOR K=1 TO N3
00160   INPUT X(J,K,I)
00170   NEXT K
00180   NEXT J
00190   PRINT
00200   NEXT I
00210   RETURN
```

```
00100   REM MATRIX INPUT SUBROUTINE (TWO DI-
        MENTION)
00110   FOR H=1 TO N
00120   PRINT "ENTER ROW";H
00130   FOR I=1 TO N1
00140   INPUT X(H,I)
00150   NEXT I,H
00160   RETURN
```

```
00100   REM MATRIX PRINT SUBROUTINE 3-D
00110   FOR I=1 TO N1
00120   FOR J=1 TO N2
00130   FOR K=1 TO N3
00140   PRINT X(J,K,I),
00150   NEXT K
00160   PRINT
00170   NEXT J
00180   PRINT
00190   NEXT I
00200   PRINT
00210   RETURN
```

```
00200   REM MATRIX READ FROM DATA STATE-
        MENTS IN 3-D
00210   FOR I=1 TO N1
00220   FOR J=1 TO N2
00230   FOR K=1 TO N2
00240   READ X(J,K,I)
```

```
00250    NEXT K,J,I
00260    RETURN
00270    DATA 'DATA INSERTED HERE
                  _____

00100    REM MAT=ZER MATRIX SET TO ZERO SUB-
         ROUTINE 3-D
00110    FOR I=1 TO N1
00120    FOR J=1 TO N2
00130    FOR K=1 TO N3
00140    X(K,J,I)=0
00150    NEXT K,J,I
00160    RETURN        _____

00100    REM MAT=ZER MATRIX SET TO ZERO SUB-
         ROUTINE 3-D
00110    FOR I=1 TO N1
00120    FOR J=1 TO N2
00130    FOR K=1 TO N3
00140    X(K,J,I)=0
00150    NEXT K,J,I
00160    RETURN
                  _____

00100    REM IMPROVED RIPPLE SORT ROUTINE
00110    C=0: N=N-1
00120    IF N=0 GOTO 200
00130    FOR I=1 TO N
00140    IF A(I)<=A(I+1) THEN 00180
00150    T=A(I)
00160    A(I)=A(I+1)
00170    A(I+1)=T
00179    C=1
00180    NEXT I
00195    IF C=1 THEN 00110
                  _____

00100    REM BUBBLE SORTING ROUTINE
00110    FOR I=1 TO N-1
00120    FOR J=I+1 TO N
00130    IF A(I)<=A(J) THEN 00170
00140    T=A(I)
00150    A(I)=A(J)
00160    A(J)=T
```

```
00170   NEXT J
00180   NEXT I
```

```
  50    REM ALPHABATIZING PROGRAM
  60    REM OUTPUTS LISTING ONLY (DOESN'T
        REARRANGE MEMORY)
 100    CLEAR 5000
 110    DIM A$(100), N$(100)
 120    FOR N=1 TO 1000
 130    INPUT "WORD";N$(N)
 140    IF N$(N)="STOP"THEN 160
 150    NEXT N
 160    '
 170    FOR I=1 TO N
 180    A$(I)=N$(I)
 190    NEXT I
 200    I=1: K=0
 210    FOR J=2 TO N
 220    IF A$(I)<A$(J) GOTO 230 ELSE I=J
 230    NEXT J
 240    IF N$(I)="STOP" THEN 250 ELSE PRINT N$(I)
 250    A$(I)="ZZZ"
 260    K=K+1
 270    IF K=N THEN 280 ELSE 200
 280    PRINT:PRINT
 290    END
```

Chapter 11
Miscellaneous Applications

Miscellaneous Applications

Calculating the difference in time between two time zones is essential for those making overseas telephone calls or flying into another zone. A microcomputer could accomplish the task easily.

TIME CALCULATIONS

Calculation of the difference in hours or days between two given times is another business application (e.g. for use in determining hours worked for payroll, accumulated interest, etc.).

```
00010   REM TIME DIFFERENCE CALCULATION
00020   REM COMPUTES DIFFERENCE IN HOURS,
        MINUTES, AND SECONDS
00030   PRINT "INPUT THE FIRST TIME IN 24. HR.
        CLOCK FORMAT-"
00040   PRINT "HOURS,MINUTES,SECONDS."
00050   INPUT H1,M1,S1
00060   PRINT "INPUT FINAL TIME IN 24. HR. FOR-
        MAT."
00070   INPUT H2,M2,S2
00080   NH=H2-H1
00090   NM=M2-M1:IFNM<0  THEN  NH=NH-
        1:NM=60+ NM
```

```
00100    NS=S2—S1:IF    NS<0THEN    NM=NM—
         1:NS=60+NS
00110    PRINT "THE DIFFERENCE IN H,M,S IS:";NH;
         NM; NS
00140    PRINT
00150    END
```

AID TO THE HANDICAPPED

The use of microcomputers to aid the handicapped has suddenly become an important application now that the potential is realized.

The computer can act as a "robot" for the handicapped. One system was used by a paraplegic to communicate with others; the computer scanned the alphabet and once a particular letter was reached, the patient would make a certain movement to signal that that letter was to be typed out. In this manner, words and sentences were produced.

Voice synthesizers and decoders are especially helpful for those who cannot interact with a computer through a video terminal. Once the patient can communicate with the computer, it may be used as a general calculator or be programmed.

An economical system for translating inputted text into braille could be developed.

The computer could be used to monitor patients who are chronically ill, likely to suffer heart attacks, etc.; twice a day the patient would be required to input something otherwise medical personnel would be alerted with telephone dialing and vocal output peripherals.

TEST YOUR TYPING SPEED

Those learning to type will appreciate a measurement of their progress in speed. A program to test typing speed would have to be written in assembly language if your BASIC doesn't provide INKEY$, ENTER or WAIT type commands.

SPEED READING

A program to help you learn to speed read could be easily implemented by using a timing loop. Lines from a piece of literature could be stored in data statements and flashed momentarily on the screen; only one line at one time should be displayed. The timing loop is simply a BASIC FOR-NEXT loop which will require a specified amount of time to be executed (e.g. for X=1 TO 500: NEXT X requires approximately 1 second to execute with several BASICS.) The amount of time allowed to read each line should be gradually decreased until a speed of several hundred words (e.g. 500) per minute is obtained.

```
00010   REM SPEED READING PRACTICE PROGRAM
00020   N=500 'SET INITIAL TIMING PER LINE
00030   CLS 'CLEAR SCREEN
00040   PRINT "THE HOME COMPUTER REVOLU-
        TION HAS ARRIVED...OVER 50,000 HOB-
        BYISTS NOW"
00050   GOSUB 300
00060   PRINT "OWN A MICRO-COMPUTER SYSTEM
        FOR PERSONAL COMPUTING APPLICATIONS.
        EXPERTS"
00070   GOSUB 300
00080   PRINT "PREDICT THAT THE MARKET WILL
        GROW RAPIDLY UNTIL 'EVERYONE HAS A
        COMPUTER."
00090   GOSUB 300
00100   PRINT "RECENTLY, A BOOK TITLED THE
        PERSONAL COMPUTER APPLICATIONS
        HANDBOOK WAS"
00110   GOSUB 300
00120   PRINT "PUBLISHED; THE BOOK IS FILLED
        WITH POTENTIALS RANGING FROM GAMES
        TO BUSINESS."
00130   GOSUB 300
00140   N=N—50
00150   GOTO 00010
00300   FOR X=1 TO N
00310   NEXT X 'TIMING LOOP
00320   RETURN
```

CO-OP SCHEDULING AND FINANCES

A computer analysis of costs and duties could equally divide costs and duties between members of residence/

student co-operational organizations by the week, month, etc.

TAILOR'S CALCULATIONS

Alterations to dress, suit, and other patterns for "tailor-made" clothing could be mathematically determined by your computer. If you have a printer with a line length large enough, the altered pattern could be printed in actual size.

PHONE CODE

A relatively simple program could be written to produce a listing of all the possible letter combinations on the phone dial for a given phone number. Businessmen may use this listing to find an appropriate, easy-to-remember word representing their phone number (e.g. a computer store number was 266-7883 and COMPUTE was the telephone word). An interesting word may appear for you to use with your home phone.

BRAINSTORMER

A few years ago a large sphere containing thousands of plastic squares with a different word printed on each was sold as a "brainstormer". The idea behind the device was to rotate the sphere, mix up the words, and then peek through a window at whatever words appeared. From this combination of adjectives and nouns, the user was to come up with a new invention or idea. Amazingly enough, the "brainstormer" often worked (e.g. if the words "tape recorder," "office," and "dictation" appeared, one might brainstorm the idea for an office dictation machine). Obviously, with a computer, all one has to do is create a large array of nouns and adjectives and use a random number generator to call them up on the video screen.

A similar program could be called an "idea stimulator." Instead of words randomly appearing, a set of adjectives would be displayed for use in brainstorming in addition to an idea already in mind (e.g. if one was attempting to invent a new food cooking device, and the word "slower" appeared, the brainstormed idea could be a slow "crock pot" cooker).

Brainstorm Chart: Product, Process, or Service

In what other way can it be made more effective?

Is there a surer way to do it?
Is there a cleaner, neater way to do it?
Is there a more comfortable way to do it?
Is there a more healthful way to do it?
Is there a safer way to do it?
Is there a more durable form?
Is there a more pleasant way to do it?
Is there a quicker way to do it?
Is there an easier way to do it?
In what other way can it be improved?
Can the package be improved?
Can the distribution methods be improved?
Can it be made disposable or portable?
Can a combination with other devices be evolved?
Can something be added to enhance its value?
Can it be adapted to some other use?
Is there a way to increase its usefulness; become multipurposed?
Can it be made more attractive?
Is there a cheaper way to do it?
Can a similar result be obtained in any other way?

PROGRAM—INVENTOR'S IDEA STIMULATOR

This program can be very useful to those who have a creative and intuitive mind. A large list of "idea words" are shuffled and outputted three at one time. The object is to apply your thinking to these words in relation to another idea. For example, if you had to design a new product, such as a cigarette lighter, and the word "disposable" appeared, the idea of a disposable lighter would come to you.

```
50   REM INVENTOR'S IDEA STIMULATOR
51   DIM A$(98), M(98)
60   PRINT "THE PURPOSE OF THIS PROGRAM IS TO
     STIMULATE YOUR CREATIVE"
70   PRINT "THINKING WHEN WORKING ON AN IN-
     VENTION OR PRODUCT. A SERIES"
80   PRINT "OF THREE WORDS WILL BE PRINTED.
     THINK ABOUT EACH CAREFULLY"
90   PRINT "AND TRY TO APPLY THEM TO YOUR IN-
     VENTIVE PROCESS. FOR EXAMPLE"
```

```
 91   PRINT "IF YOU WERE TRYING TO DEVELOP A
      PRODUCT TO IMPROVE OFFICE"
 92   PRINT "COMMUNICATION AND THE WORD 'EF-
      FICIENT' APPEARED, YOU MIGHT"
 93   PRINT "THINK OF A DICTATING MACHINE,
      ETC."
 94   PRINT "TYPE 'ENTER' WHEN READY"
 95   FOR X=1 TO98: READ A$(X):NEXT X
100   RANDOM
120   N=98: FORI=1 TO N
130   M(I)=I: NEXT I
140   FOR I=1 TO N−1
150   R=(N+1−I)*RND(0)
170   R=INT(R)+I
180   T=M(R)
190   M(R)=M(I)
200   M(I)=T
210   NEXT I
220   PRINT "TYPE 'ENTER' WHEN FINISHED WITH
      EACH WORD SET"
230   FOR X=1 TO 33STEP3
240   PRINT A$(M(X))
250   PRINT A$(M(X+1))
260   PRINT A$(M(X+2))
270   INPUT B$
280   NEXT X
290   END
300   DATA LARGER, SMALLER, LONGER, SHORTER,
      THICKER, THINNER, DEEPER, SHALLOWER,
      STAND VERTICALLY/HORIZONTALLY, MAKE
      SLANTED OR PARALLEL
310   DATA STRATIFY, INVERT, CONVERGE, ENCIR-
      CLE, INTERVENE, DELINEATE, BORDER,
      MORE, LESS, CHANGE PROPORTIONS, FRAC-
      TIONATE, JOIN SOMETHING
320   DATA ADD SOMETHING, COMBINE, COM-
      PLETE, CHANGE ARRANGEMENT, FASTER,
      SLOWER, LAST LONGER, CHRONOLOGIZE,
      MAKE PERPETUAL, SYNCHRONIZE
330   DATA RENEWABLE, ALTERNATING, STIMU-
      LATED, ENERGIZED, STRENGTHENED,
      LOUDER, LESS NOISE, COUNTERACTING,
```

STRONGER, WEAKER, ALTERED
340 DATA CONVERTABLE, SUBSTITUTED, INTER-
CHANGED, STABILIZED, REVERSED, RESI-
LIENT, UNIFORM, CHEAPER, ADD/CHANGE
COLOR, IRREGULAR DESIGN
350 DATA CURVED DESIGN, MODERN DESIGN,
HARDER, SOFTER, SYMMETRICAL, NOTCHED,
ROUGHER, SMOOTHER, DAMAGE AVOIDED,
DELAYS AVOIDED
360 DATA THEFT AVOIDED, ACCIDENTS PRE-
VENTED, CONFORMABILITY, ANIMATED,
STILLED, DIRECTED, MOTION, ATTRACTED/
REPELLED MOTION, LOWERED
370 DATA BARRED, OCILLATED, AGITATED, HOT-
TER, COLDER, OPENABLE, PREFORMED, DIS-
POSEABLE, INCORPORATED, SOLIDIFIED,
LIQUEFIED, VAPORIZED
380 DATA PULVERIZED, ABRADED, LUBRICATED,
WETTER, DRYER, INSULATED, EFFERVESCED,
COAGULATED, ELASTICIZED, RESISTANT,
LIGHTER, HEAVIER
390 DATA FOR MEN/WOMEN/CHILDREN, FOR
ELDERLY/HANDICAPPED, FOREIGN MARKET-
ING

SOURCE INDEX

Addresses for manufacturers, institutions, organizations, etc. may be stored in computer form and indexed for
future reference. Any source for information or materials
which you don't have use for at present, yet know you may
need in the future, should be stored (e.g. manufacturers and
suppliers of peripherals for your system). These sources
should be indexed under the material they can provide.

UTILITY COST CALCULATION

A simple program could calculate the amount of gas,
electricity, or water billed for based upon the latest meter
reading entered and the stored meter reading for the end of
the last billing period. Your utility should be able to supply the

information on how to read the meter and the rate charged. Compare your result with your bill to detect mistakes.

PEOPLE MATCHING

At a party or other social gathering it is often best to arrange so that those who are most similar will meet each other. Recently, at a convention, a microcomputer was used to create special name cards for each guest. Everyone who attended had previously filled out a questionaire indicating his/her occupation, hobbies, age, sex, likes and dislikes, etc. This data was inputted to the computer which subsequently produced a special name card with differently colored dots on it, one for each individual. Each color indicated a specific characteristic of that person, and thus, the guests could instantly find others who had the same color dots and characteristics themselves.

Computers have prepared seating charts for dinners, arranged blind dates, and paired athletes according to individual characteristics (partner or opponent matching).

An interesting people matching game would involve participants in ranking the most important things to themselves in life. A list of possible goals could be as follows:

1. Active and self-satisfying life
2. Active and satisfying athletic life
3. Power over things (e.g. automobiles, boat building, computers)
4. Socially significant activity
5. Good health
6. Opportunities for risk and adventure
7. Resilience (ability to "bounce-back")
8. Prestige family life
9. Artistic ability
10. Ability to initiate and maintain friendships
11. Intellectual ability
12. Ability to draw love from others
13. Ability to influence others with your ideas
14. Ability to be a caring person
15. Ability to give love
16. Close and supportive relationships
17. Intellectual stimulation
18. Approval by opposite sex

19. Wealth
20. Ability to be self-sufficient
21. Physical attractiveness

Each participant could rank each item in terms of its importance to him. Next, everyone would be allotted a certain amount of "money" to use in bidding for the items of the most importance to themselves. Participants will realize what is of the most significance in their life and that of others.

GREETING CARD PRODUCER

Some clever hobbyists have written programs to produce assorted types of greeting cards/announcements/ invitations on their printers. The cards are usually personalized and make use of computer art.

SUNDIAL DESIGN PROGRAM

```
00100   REM SUNDIAL DESIGN PROGRAM
00110   REM COMPUTES NECESSARY ANGLES FOR
        YOUR LATITUDE
00120   PRINT "ENTER YOUR LATITUDE";
00130   INPUT A
00140   PRINT "CUT OUT A STYLE SUCH THAT THE
        UPPER EDGE MAKES AN ANGLE"
00150   PRINT "OF ";A; "DEGREES WITH THE BASE."
00160   S=SIN(A)
00170   X=1
00180   FOR B=15 TO 90 STEP 15
00190   T=TAN(B)
00200   C=S*T
00210   X=X+1
00220   PRINT "AT" ;X; " O'CLOCK, THE ANGLE
        SHOULD BE"; ATN(C)*57.29578
00230   REM IN STATEMENT 220 THE CONSTANT
        57.29578 IS USED TO CONVERT
00240   REM FROM RADIANS TO DEGREES.
00250   NEXT B
00260   END
READY.
```

Use this program to compute the correct angles used in constructing a sundial for your latitude.

Chapter 12
A Compendium of
Additional Applications

A Compendium Of Additional Applications

Additional business applications include a *supermarket comparison service* which could collect price data for various foods at various markets and analyze the data with a computer. A report showing comparative prices for foods could be outputted and sold, or the most economical market to shop may be determined. *Financial computations* well suited to a small computer include *price, yield, or accumulated yield* on bills, notes, bonds, certificates, debentures, warrants, or certificates of deposit. The economics of a *bond-note switch* could also be calculated, taking account of the time. The *compound growth theory*, or other theories, could be analyzed for various input values. An additional function of an investment feasibility program would be to compute factors for an investment in which the majority of the purchase price must be financed. *Dollar averaging* determination could be done as well. Using the *rule of 78s*, your computer may calculate interest rebate, as well as other financial factors. For *direct reduction loans*, amortization schedules, accumulated interest, and remaining balance may be determined; balloon payments could also be considered. Persons involved in real estate would find an *appraisal tabulator program* helpful in objectively rating a house. Such a program would assign values to various house features and use appraisal estimates in reaching a conclusion; a formatted report could also be outputted. Also related to real estate are *own vs rent* and *lease vs rent* analysis programs. Any salesman could find a *bid prep-aration* program useful in calculating variable sales prices, keeping running totals, and figuring mark-up or mark-down. A simple investment program could determine the profit made on an investment relative to the bank interest that would have been earned. The calculation of factors involved in the *periodic withdrawal* from an investment would be a useful application as would computation of the true *annual percen-tage rate* from other rates. Businessmen involved in optimiza-tion will find the small computer helpful. An example of an equation to be optimized is:

$$TPL = FC + VC\ (Q) + E$$

where TPL = total product cost
       FC = fixed costs
      VC = variable cost per unit of production
        Q = quantity produced
        E = variance (error) factor

One final investment factor which could be determined is the *book value of a stock*.

Additional mathematic recreation applications include *The Two Move Game*. In the first half of this game, the two players secretly enter four non-negative numbers totaling the same number into the cells of a 2x2 matrix:

x1	x2		y1	y2
x3	x4		y3	y4

The entries are then exposed and a third 2x2 matrix is developed in which the entries are $x_i - y_i$. This final matrix is then analyzed by the first player who chooses a column and tries to maximize. The second player then chooses a row and tries to maximize. The player with the greatest variation wins. A mathematical strategy exists to win this game; can you find it? The game of *Sim* involves a gameboard like this:

```
    x     x
  x         x
    x     x
```

The players take alternate turns drawing lines between two points. The first player to draw an equilateral triangle or square loses. Likewise, a mathematical strategy exists to win this game as well. With a poker or bridge hand the hobbyist could compute the *probability* that m*n cards held by a defen-der in a bridge hand will be split m and n, or the probabilities for obtaining a certain hand in poker after certain cards have been played. One difficult problem would be to write a program to prove simple *geometrical theorems*.

Among additional control applications is a *digital/audio file* in which a standard cassette interface is used to record digital information in between songs (audio) on a standard cassette. The digital information could be used to index songs, prompt a vocal announcement by a voice synthesizer, or control volume, speakers, times, etc. Additionally, a computerized *sound mixer* could be designed for the serious audiophile. One hobbyist has suggested connecting a computer to his *exercise equipment* to keep track of the energy expended and time. For instance, a pressure sensitive pad could be used by the jogger to record speed and number of "jogs". One idea ahead of its time consists of a watch/radio, voice synthesizer, radio broadcaster, and computer. Using this equipment one could store an *itinerary* in the computer and have it vocally remind him remotely of all appointments. One additional device would be a *portable power supply* to allow one to take a computer anywhere.

Additional recreational and game applications include *two-terminal games* in which opposing players cannot see each others playfields; this would be a hardware and software challenge to implement. *Maze running "rats"* (mechanical devices) have become a popular artificial intelligence application (one contest drew over 400 entries). If you lack the technical knowledge of hardware, you could attempt to write a video graphics program which could *draw a maze* and *animate a mouse* attempting to find the end of the maze. An interesting device to interface would be a *wired chessboard* to be used in computer/human matches; movement of pieces would be sensed by the board. Another application in artificial intelligence would be a *"mind reading"* program based upon mathematics. The human would have a choice of thinking of one of two words after which the computer will output the word it "believes" corresponds. After a number of trials the computer should be able to formulate a strategy for which word will be choosen next, as humans never can be random; theoretically, the computer should be able to achieve better than 50% correct responses. Among games to be computerized (the computer acting as scorekeeper, bookkeeper, or opponent) is the *marked square game*. The gameboard is 9×9 and players alternatively mark one square with their initials. At the end of the game (all squares filled), players receive 1, 2, or 3 points for 3, 6, or 9 squares with their initial in a row respectively; the player with the most points wins. A game based on *Watergate* could involve role playing; the question is "What are the rules?" Other role playing games include *detective* in which a crime is to be solved on the basis of the fewest clues; *criminal* in which one must attempt an escape or crime with the obvious hazards; and *spy mission*, in which an intelligence agent must locate information. Among little-known games of the world (reference a game encyclopedia) suited to be computerized are *Teeko, Hasami Shogi, Dreidel, Bell & Hammer, Asalto, Yofe, Ur*, and *Alquerque*. Card games, such as *Kalah, Qubic, Tripoli* and *solitaire* are also interesting in computer form. Among commercial games, *Diplomacy, Decline and Fall, The Sigma File, Tritactics, Speculate, Ploy, Stay Alive, Osero* and *Confrontation* are best suited to be computerized (some playfields are too complex to be displayed on a video screen). A program called *War* could involve the player (or players) in control of the Russian forces or Nazis in the Battle of Leningrad. Artillery may be deployed along with soldiers and tanks to capture the city, or return in defeat. The game of *Minefield* would involve a video-graphic mindfield through which the player must maneuver without being destroyed. *Word games* include a game in which the computer selects letters randomly and output them in matrix form. Players race against the clock in an attempt to find the most words hidden in the matrix. Another program could produce *ciphers* for one to decode. The popular word search puzzles could also be produced or let the computer find words you can't. One interesting graphics program is called the *"random walk"*; the computer randomly sketches lines on a video screen to produce unusual art work. Additional game/simulation programs include an *atomic fission* demonstration to illustrate exponential expansion; *stock* simulates the action of wall street.

Additional scientific applications include *astronomy calculations*, in which kilometers, astronomical units, light years, and parsecs may be converted and *biology* simulations of life chains, etc.

Additional miscellaneous applications include *coin price evaluation* for numismatists. Bullion value, numismatic premium, value on basis of cost, bid price and asking price computations could be performed. One hobbyist uses his computer to compute amounts of chemicals necessary to maintain a *seawater aquarium* environment. Complex calculations are necessary to obtain exact values over a range of temperatures and conditions. The computer could also be used in *planning a vacation;* factors such as mileage, cost, time, and itinerary could be planned. A program to store information used in selecting and mixing *drinks* could be stored for instant retrieval; one such program even stored pictures of the size and shape glasses to use with each drink. The computer could even suggest an appropriate cheese to accompany the selected wine. Your local organization, or business, could use a computer *car-pool matching* program if there are many people involved. A *telegram* of information could be sent over the phone in a computer format in a fraction of the time necessary to vocalize it; save on phone calls. One hobbyist, who is often obligated to make speeches, intends to use his computer to *store anecdote material* for easy reference while writing.

Glossary

Glossary

audio cassette interface (ACR)—A circuit which allows computer data to be audibly stored on a standard cassette tape with a standard recorder. Several different speeds and types of cassette interfaces are available.

access—The ability to use a computer.

address—The location in memory where a given binary bit or word of information is stored.

alphanumeric—The set of punctuation, letters of the alphabet, and numerical characters often used for computer input.

analog/digital (A/D) conversion—An A/D converter measures incoming voltages and outputs a corresponding digital number for each voltage, or vice-versa.

ASCII—The American Standard Code for Information Interchange.

assembly language—A low level symbolic programming language which comes closest to programming a computer in its internal machine language. Instead, machine language code is represented by mneumonics.

binary—The number system of base two which has two symbols: 1 and 0, representing the on and off states of a circuit.

bit—One binary digit.

byte—An assembly of a group of bits (usually eight for microcomputers). The memory capacity of a computer is usually measured in terms of bytes.

chip—An integrated circuit.

compiler—A program which converts the program statements of a high-level language into machine codes for execution.

CPU (Central Processing Unit)—The major operations center of the computer where decisions and calculations are made.

data—Computer-coded information.

data rate—The amount of information (data) transmitted through a communication line per unit time.

debug—Remove program errors (bugs) from a program.

digital—A circuit which has only two states: on and off, and is usually represented by the binary number system.

disk—A memory storage device which makes use of a magnetic disk.

DOS—Disc operating system; allows the use of general commands to manipulate data stored on a disk.

firmware—Software permanently stored in a computer using a read-only-memory (ROM) device.

floppy disk—See disc.

flowchart—A diagram of the various steps to be taken by the computer in running a program.

hexadecimal—A base sixteen number system often used in programming in machine language.

hardware—The manufactured equipment of a computer system, as opposed to the programs for a computer.

input—Information (data) fed into the computer.

input/output (I/O) devices—Peripheral hardware devices which communicate to or receive communications from the computer.

interface—A device which converts electronic signals such that two devices may communicate with each other. Also called a "port".

interpreter—A program which accepts one statement at one time of a high-level language, converts that statement to machine language, and proceeds to the next statement. BASIC is usually an interpreter high-level language.

keyboard—A series of switches, usually in the form of a typewriter keyboard, which a computer operator uses to communicate with the computer.

languages—The sets of words/commands which are understood by the computer used in writing a program.

loop—A portion of a program which is to be repeated (looped) several times.

machine language—The internal low-level language of the computer.

mainframe—Referring to the hardware of the central processing unit (CPU).

memory—Data (information) stored for future reference by the computer in a series of bytes.

microcomputer—A miniaturized small computer containing all the circuitry of a "minicomputer" on a single integrated circuit chip.

microprocessor—The single integrated circuit chip which forms the basis of a computer (the CPU).

mnemonic—An abbreviation or word which stands for another word or phrase.

modem—A peripheral device which converts digital signals to audio and vice-versa.

MPU—See CPU.

octal—A base eight number system often used in machine language programming.

opcode—An operation code signifying a particular task to be done by the computer.

parallel port—A data communication channel which uses one wire for each bit in a single byte.

peripherals—Input/output devices such as printers, mass storage devices, terminals, etc.

program—A set of instructions for accomplishing a task which the computer understands.

RAM (random access memory)—Memory devices from which data may be procured or stored by the computer.

ROM (read only memory)—Memory devices from which data may be procured only; the memory contents may not be changed.

RS232—A standard form for serial computer interfaces.

serial port—A method of data communication in which bits of information are sent consecutively through one wire.

software—Computer programs, instructions, and languages.

statement—A single computer instruction.

subroutine—A smaller program (routine) within a larger program.

terminal—An input/output device using a keyboard and video or printer display.

TVT—A television typewriter, or computer terminal.

word—A basic unit of computer memory usually expressed in terms of a byte.

Appendix

Financial Formulas

INPUTED VARIABLES	OUTPUTTED VARIABLE	USES	FORMULA
n, PV, FV	i	investments	$i = \sqrt[n]{\dfrac{FV}{PV}} - 1$
n, PV, PMT	i	yields	$i = \dfrac{PMT}{PV}(1 - (1 + i)^n)$
n, FV, PMT	i	comparisons	$i = \dfrac{PMT}{FV}((1 + i)^n - 1)$
i, PF, FV	n	investments	$n = \dfrac{\log FV/PV}{\log (1 + i)}$
i, PMT, PV	n	horizons	$n = \dfrac{1}{\dfrac{\log \frac{1}{1 + i\, PV/PMT}}{\log (1 + i)}}$
i, PMT, FV	n	comparisons	$n = \dfrac{\log \left\{1 + \dfrac{iFV}{PMT}\right\}}{\log (1 + i)}$
n, i, FV	PV	net percentages	$PV = FV/(1 + i)^n$
n, i, PMT	PV	analysis	$PV = PMT\, \dfrac{1 + (1 + i)^n}{i}$
n, i, PV	FV	growth computations	$FV = PV (1 + i)^n$
n, i, PMT	FV	analysis	$FV = PMT\, \dfrac{(1 + i)^n - 1}{i}$
n, i, FV	PMT	affordability	$PMT = FV\, \dfrac{i}{(1 + i)^n - 1}$
n, i, PV	PMT	analysis	$PMT = PV\, \dfrac{i}{1 + (1 + i)^n}$

where FV = Future Value
PV = Present Value
PMT = Payment to be Made
n = the no. of periods
i = the interest rate per year as %

Microcomputer Manufacturers

Allied Computers
B-58
Ashok Nagar
Madras 600 083 India

Altos Computer Systems
2378 B Walsh Av
Santa Clara CA 95050

Andromeda Systems
17875-N Sky Pk
North Irvine CA 92714

APF Electronics Inc
444 Madison Av
New York NY 10022

Apple Computer Co
12060 Bandley Dr
Cupertino CA 95014

Atari Inc
1272 Borregas Av
Sunnyvale CA 94086

Central Data
POB 2484 Station A
Champaign IL 61820

CGRS Microtech
POB 368
Southampton PA 18966

CMC Marketing Corp
5601 Bintliff Suite 515
Houston TX 77036

Commodore Business Machines Inc
901 California Av
Palo Alto CA 94304

Comptronics
19824 Ventura Blvd
Woodland Hills CA 91364

Compucolor Corp
POB 569
Norcross GA 30071

Computer Data Systems
5460 Fairmount Dr
Wilmington DE 19808

Computer Power and Light
12321 Ventura Blvd
Studio City CA 91604
Computer Products of America
633 W Katella Av
Orange CA 92667

Cromemco Incorp
280 Bernado AV
Mountain View CA 94040

Digi-Key Corp
POB 677
Thief River Falls MN 56701

Digital Micro Systmes
BOX 1212
Orem UT 84057

Digital Sport Systems
Seventh and Elm St
West Liberty IA 52776

E & L Instruments Inc
61 First St
Derby CT 06418

Electro-Atomic Products
25 Old State Rd
New Milford CT 06776

Electronic Control Technology
763 Ramsey Av
Hillside NJ 07205

Electronic Product Associates (EPA) Inc
1157 Vega St
San Diego CA 92110

Electronic Tool Co
4736 W El Segundo Blvd
Hawthorne CA 90250

Environmental Technology
2821 W Sample
South Bend IN 46619

Exidy Inc
969 W Maude Av
Sunnyvale CA 94086

Fire Bird Sales
POB 116 03 Oak St
Woodland IL 60974

Gimix
1337 W 37th Pl
Chicago Il 60609

Harris Corp
Computer Systems Division
Dept EM POB 23550
Fort Lauderdale FL 33307
Heath Co
Benton Harbor MI 49022

Iasis Inc
275 Humboldt Ct
Sunnyvale CA 94086

IMSAI Mfg
14860 Wicks Blvd
San Leandro CA 94577

Industrial Micro Systems
633 W Katella Av-L
Orange CA 92667

Infinite Inc
1924 Waverly Pl
Melbourne FL 32901

Intel Corp
3065 Bowers AV
Santa Clara CA 95051

Intelligent Systems
5965 Peachtree Corners E
Norcross GA 30071

Interact Electronics Inc
POB 8140
Ann Arbor MI 48107

Intersil
10900 N Tantau Av
Cupertino CA 95014

Mattel Electronics Inc
5150 Rosecrans Av
Hawthorne CA 90250

Micro Data Systems
POB 36051
Los Angeles CA 90036

Micro Products Unlimited
POB 1525
Arlington TX 76010

Midwest Scientific Instruments Inc
220 West Cedar
Olathe KS 66061

Miniterm Associates Inc
Dundee Pk
Andover MA 01910

Modern Microcomputers
290 Linden Av
Westbury NY 11590

Motorola Inc
POB 27065
Tempe AZ 85282

NEC Microcomputers Inc
Five Militia Dr
Lexington MA 02173

Netronics R & D Ltd
333 Litchfield Rd
New Milford CT 06776

North Star Computers
2547 Ninth St
Berkeley CA 94710

Northwest Microcomputer Systems
121 E 11th
Eugene OR 97401

Ohio Scientific Instruments
1333 S Chillicothe Rd
Aurora OH 44202

Olson Electronics
21850 Center Ridge Rd
Rocky River OH 44116

Parasitic Engineering
POB 6314
Albany CA 94706

Pertec Computer Corp
Pertec Division
9600 Irondale Av
Chatsworth CA 91311

PolyMorphic Systems
460 Ward Dr
Santa Barbara CA 93111

Processor Technology
7100 Johnson Inductrial Dr
Pleasanton CA 94566

Quay Corp
POB 386
Freehold NJ 07728

Quest Electronics
POB 4430
Santa ClaraCA 95054

Radio Shack
1400 One Tandy Ctr
Fort Worth TX 76102
Rank Penpherals

Rank Peripherals
POB 7
Victoria Station
Montreal PO H2X 2V4
Canada

RCA Corp
Solid State Division
Route 202
Somerville NJ 08876

RDA Inc
5012 Herzel Pl
Beltsville MD 20705

Realistic Controls Corp
404 W 35th St
Davenport IA 52806

Rockwell International
Electronic Devices Division
3310 Miraloma Av
POB 3669
Anaheim CA 92803

SD Systems
POB 288 10B
Dallas TX 75228

Signetics Corp
811 E Orques
Sunnyvale CA 94086

Smoke Signal Broadcasting
POB 2017
Hollywood CA 90028

Space Byte Corp
1720 Pontius Av No 201
Los Angeles CA 90025

Southwest Technical Products Corp
219 W Rhapsody
San Antonio TX 78216

Synertek
POB 552
Santa Clara CA 95052

Tano Corp
4521 W Napoleon Av
Metane LA 7001

Technico
9130 Red Branch Rd
Columbia MD 21045

Texas Instruments
POB 1444
Houston TX 77001

Vector Graphic
31364 Via Colinas
Westlake Village CA 91361

Videobrain Computer Co
2950 Patrick Henry Dr
Santa Clara CA 95050

Western Data Systems
3650 Charles St
Dept H
Santa Clara CA 95050

Wintek Corp
902 N 9th St
Lafayette IN 47904

Xitan Inc
POB 3087
1101-H State Rd
Princeton NJ 08540

Metric Conversions

Linear Measure

metric to anglo	anglo to metric
1 meter = 39.37 inches = 3.281 feet = 1.0936 yards	1 inch = 2.540 cm 1 ft. = 30.48 cm = .3048 m 1 yard = .9144 m 1 mile = 1609 m = 1.609 km

Square Measure

1 sq. cm = .155 sq. inches 1 sq. meter = 10.764 sq. feet	1 sq. inch = 6.4516 sq. cm 1 sq. ft. = .0929 sq. m

Volume Measure

1 liter = 2.1134 pints = 1.0567 qts. = .2642 gallons	1 fl. oz = 29.573 ml 1 pint = .4732 l 1 liquid qt. = .9463 l 1 gallon = 3.7853 l

Weight

1 gram = .0353 oz. 1 kilogram = 2.2046 lbs.	1 oz. = 28.35 gram 1 lb = 453.6 gram = .4536 kg

l = Liters kg = Kilograms m = Meter	km = Kilometer mi = Milliliters cm = Centimeters

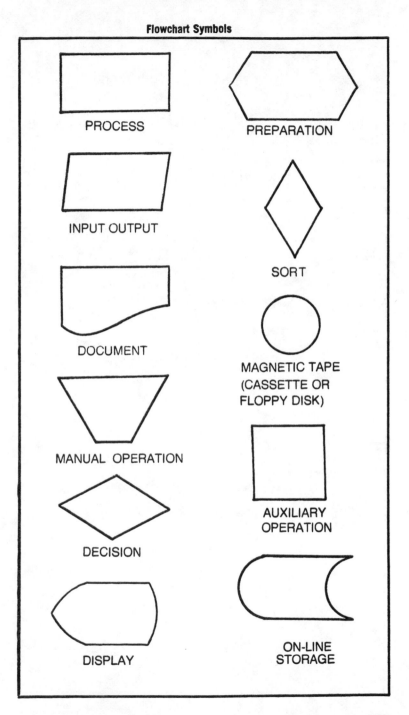

PROCESS

PREPARATION

INPUT OUTPUT

SORT

DOCUMENT

MAGNETIC TAPE
(CASSETTE OR
FLOPPY DISK)

MANUAL OPERATION

AUXILIARY
OPERATION

DECISION

DISPLAY

ON-LINE
STORAGE

Index

Index